UNITY

TO KILL A KING

MATT KINDT | DOUG BRAITHWAITE | BRIAN REBER

CONTENTS

Collection Cover Art: Doug Braithwaite

VALIANT.

UNITY®: To Kill a King. Published by Valiant Entertainment, LLC. Office of
Publication: 424 West 33rd Street, New York, NY 10001. Compilation copyright
©2014 Valiant Entertainment, Inc. All rights reserved. Contains materials
originally published in single magazine form as UNITY #1-2 Copyright ©2013,
and UNITY #3-4 Copyright ©2014 Valiant Entertainment, Inc. All rights reserved.
All characters, their distinctive likeness and related indicia featured in this
publication are trademarks of Valiant Entertainment, Inc. The stories, characters,
and incidents featured in this publication are entirely fictional. Valiant
Entertainment does not read or accept unsolicited submissions of ideas, stories,
or artwork. Printed in the U.S.A. First Printing.
ISBN: 9781939346261.

MATT KINDT | DOUG BRAITHWAITE | BRIAN REBER

UNITY®

VALIANT®

#1

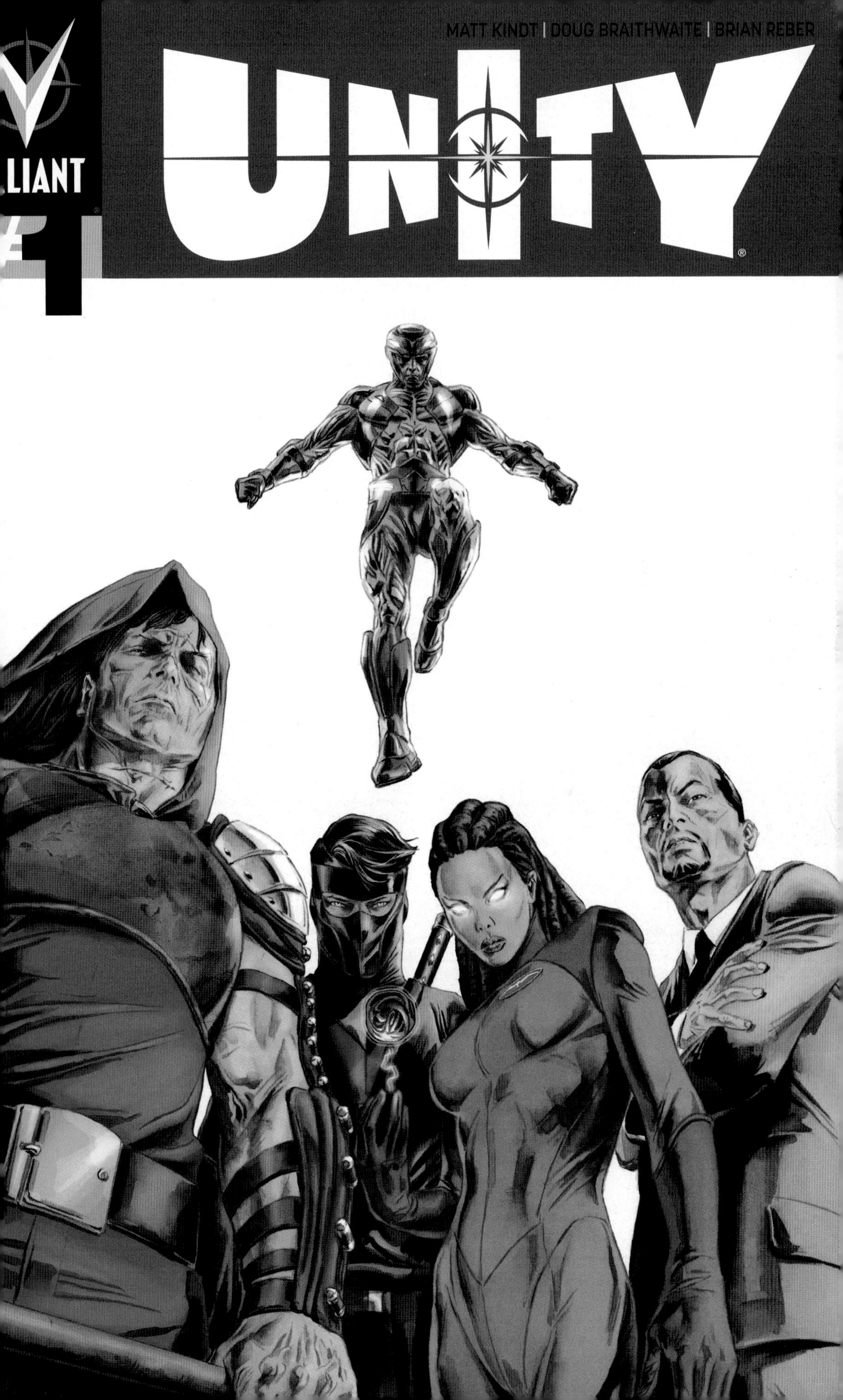

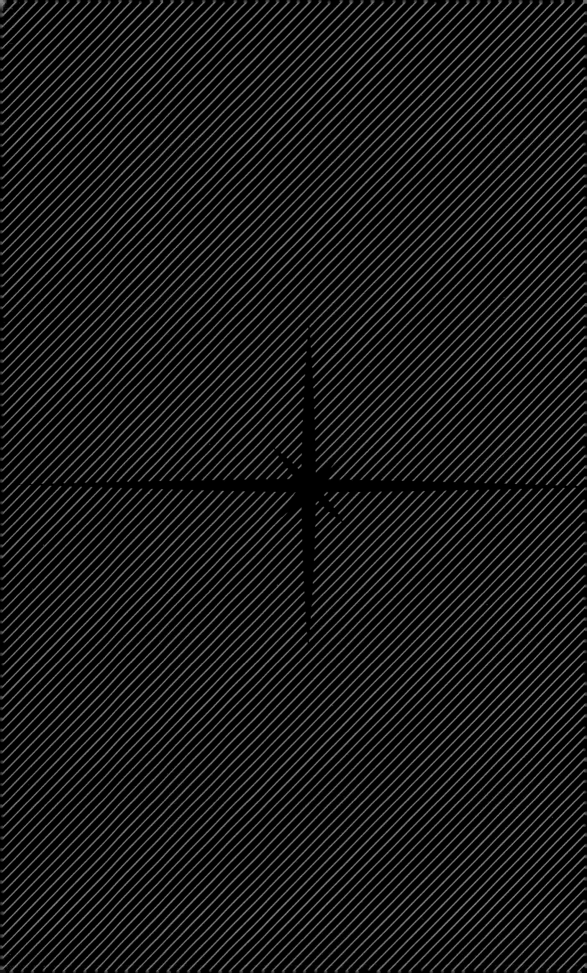

ROMANIA

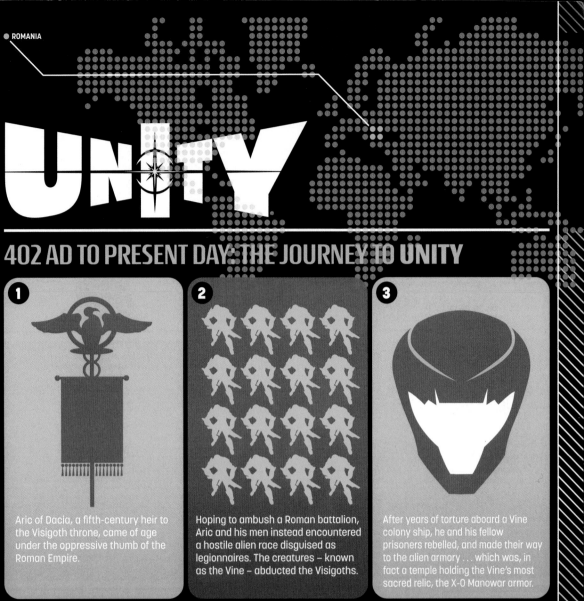

UNITY

402 AD TO PRESENT DAY: THE JOURNEY TO UNITY

1

Aric of Dacia, a fifth-century heir to the Visigoth throne, came of age under the oppressive thumb of the Roman Empire.

2

Hoping to ambush a Roman battalion, Aric and his men instead encountered a hostile alien race disguised as legionnaires. The creatures – known as the Vine – abducted the Visigoths.

3

After years of torture aboard a Vine colony ship, he and his fellow prisoners rebelled, and made their way to the alien armory . . . which was, in fact a temple holding the Vine's most sacred relic, the X-O Manowar armor.

4

Bonding with it, Aric escaped the ship and returned to Earth, only to find that 1,600 years had passed. Furious, Aric left Earth and traveled to the alien homeworld . . .

5

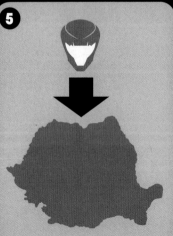

. . . and discovered that the Vine's slaves were descendants of the Visigoths. Aric freed his people and brought them to Earth, where he declared their ancestral homeland of Dacia – now Romania – his kingdom.

6

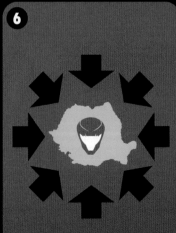

The world, however, will not take the invasion of Romania lying down . . .

Design: Rian Hughes

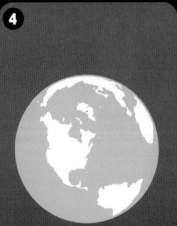

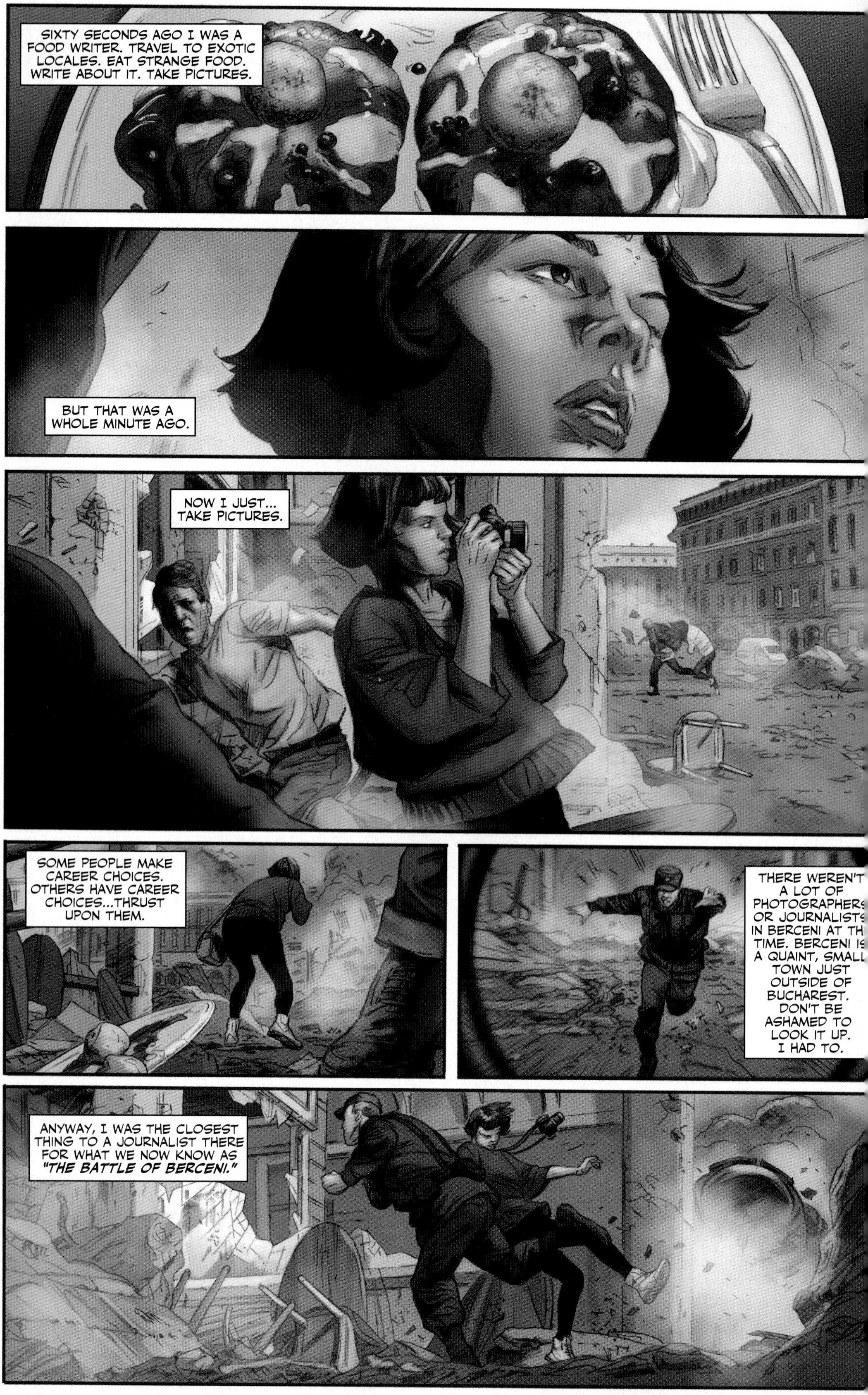

SIXTY SECONDS AGO I WAS A FOOD WRITER. TRAVEL TO EXOTIC LOCALES. EAT STRANGE FOOD. WRITE ABOUT IT. TAKE PICTURES.
BUT THAT WAS A WHOLE MINUTE AGO.
NOW I JUST... TAKE PICTURES.
SOME PEOPLE MAKE CAREER CHOICES. OTHERS HAVE CAREER CHOICES...THRUST UPON THEM.
THERE WEREN'T A LOT OF PHOTOGRAPHERS OR JOURNALISTS IN BERCENI AT TH TIME. BERCENI IS A QUAINT, SMALL TOWN JUST OUTSIDE OF BUCHAREST. DON'T BE ASHAMED TO LOOK IT UP. I HAD TO.
ANYWAY, I WAS THE CLOSEST THING TO A JOURNALIST THERE FOR WHAT WE NOW KNOW AS *"THE BATTLE OF BERCENI."*

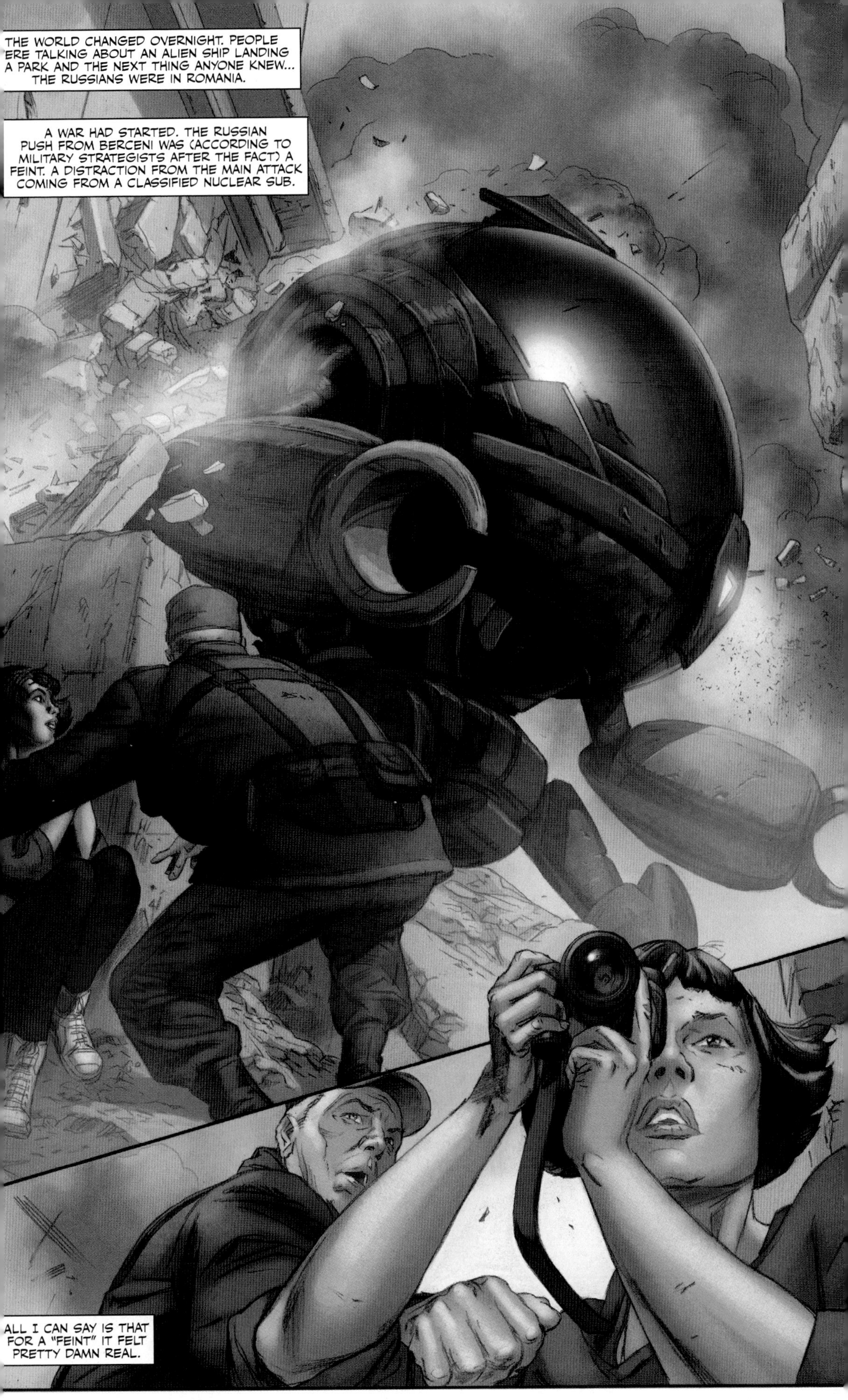
THE WORLD CHANGED OVERNIGHT. PEOPLE
ERE TALKING ABOUT AN ALIEN SHIP LANDING
A PARK AND THE NEXT THING ANYONE KNEW...
THE RUSSIANS WERE IN ROMANIA.
A WAR HAD STARTED. THE RUSSIAN PUSH FROM BERCENI WAS (ACCORDING TO MILITARY STRATEGISTS AFTER THE FACT) A FEINT. A DISTRACTION FROM THE MAIN ATTACK COMING FROM A CLASSIFIED NUCLEAR SUB.
ALL I CAN SAY IS THAT FOR A "FEINT" IT FELT PRETTY DAMN REAL.

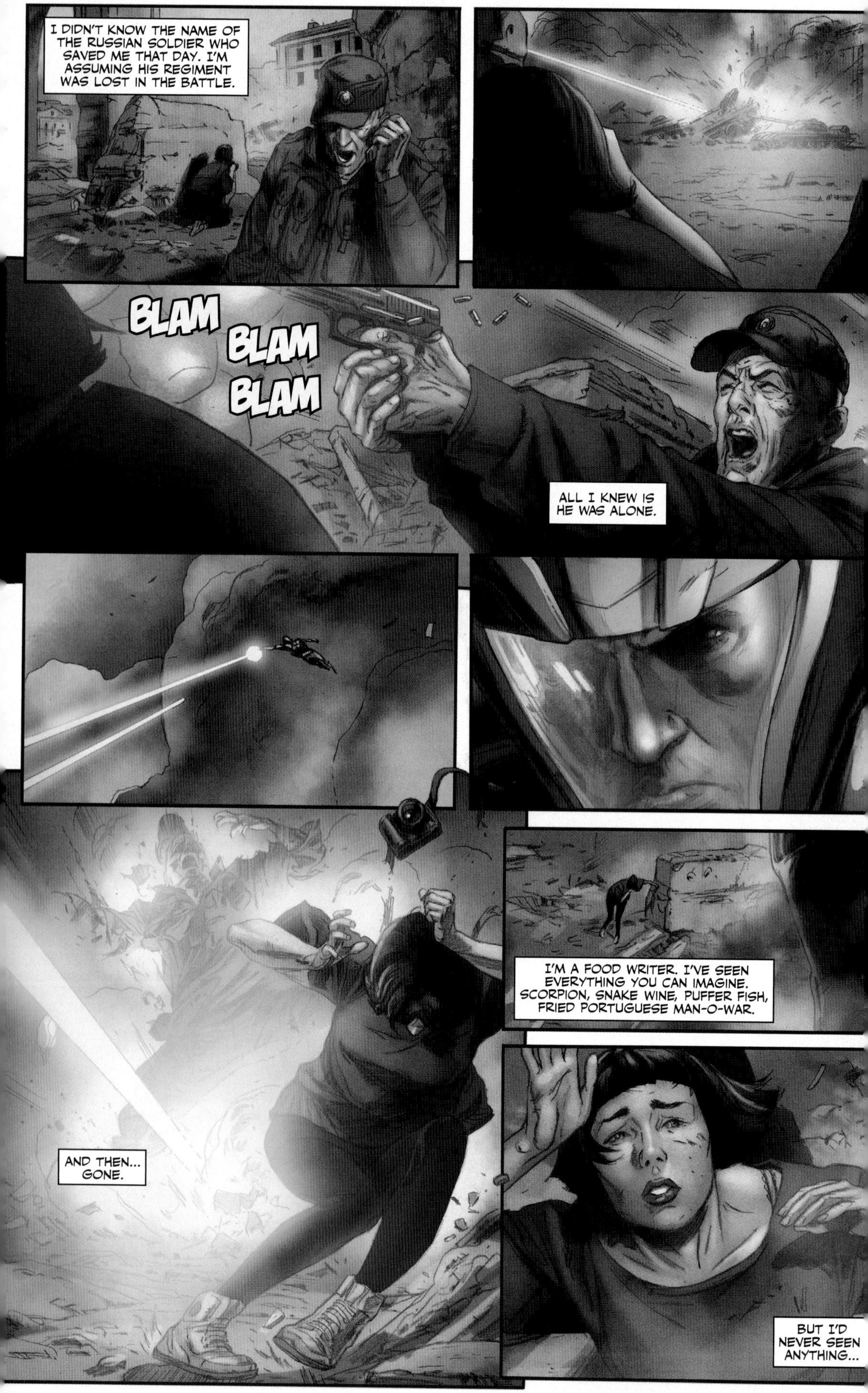
I DIDN'T KNOW THE NAME OF THE RUSSIAN SOLDIER WHO SAVED ME THAT DAY. I'M ASSUMING HIS REGIMENT WAS LOST IN THE BATTLE.
BLAM
BLAM
BLAM
ALL I KNEW IS HE WAS ALONE.
I'M A FOOD WRITER. I'VE SEEN EVERYTHING YOU CAN IMAGINE. SCORPION, SNAKE WINE, PUFFER FISH, FRIED PORTUGUESE MAN-O-WAR.
AND THEN... GONE.
BUT I'D NEVER SEEN ANYTHING...

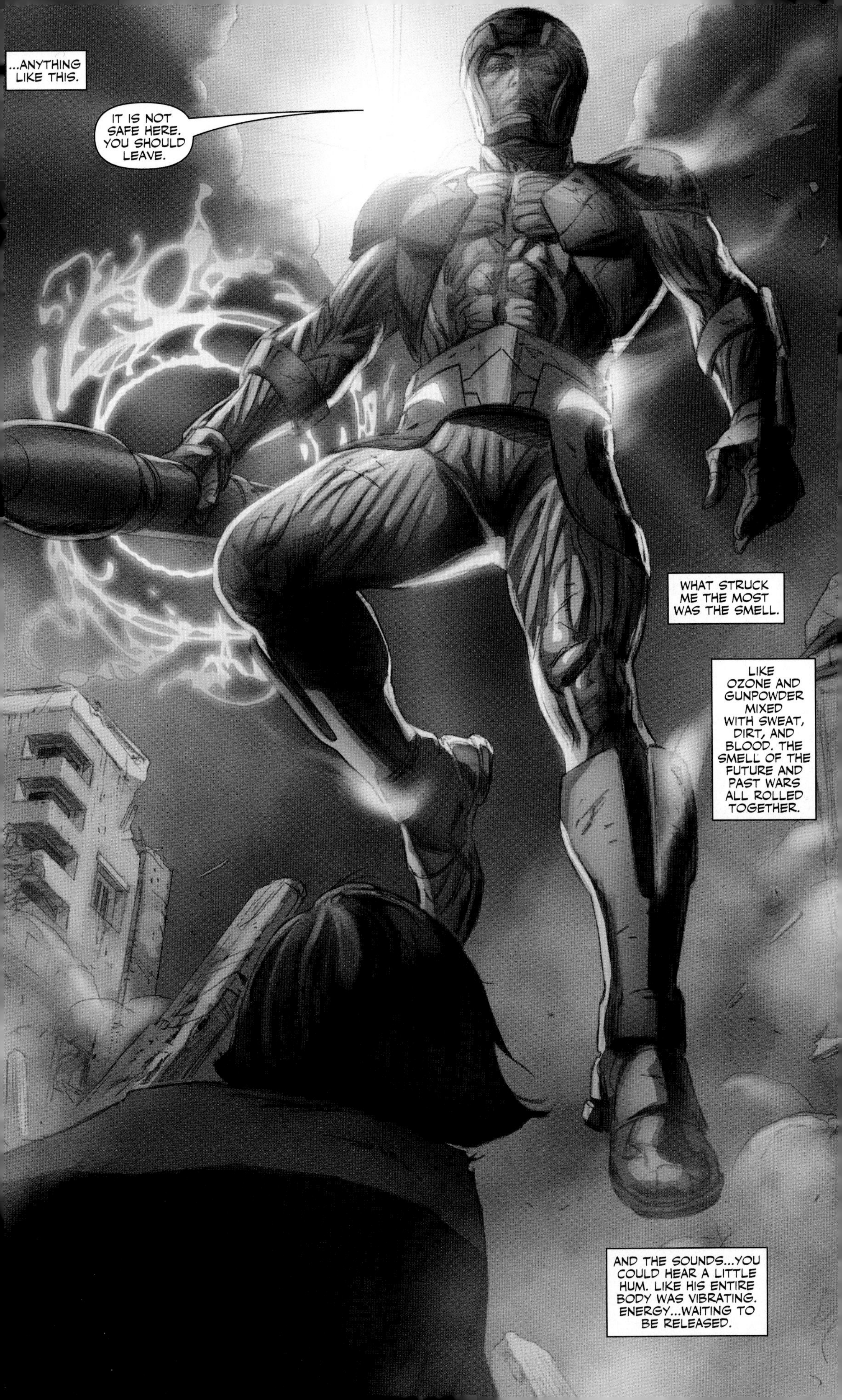
...ANYTHING LIKE THIS.
IT IS NOT SAFE HERE. YOU SHOULD LEAVE.
WHAT STRUCK ME THE MOST WAS THE SMELL.
LIKE OZONE AND GUNPOWDER MIXED WITH SWEAT, DIRT, AND BLOOD. THE SMELL OF THE FUTURE AND PAST WARS ALL ROLLED TOGETHER.
AND THE SOUNDS...YOU COULD HEAR A LITTLE HUM. LIKE HIS ENTIRE BODY WAS VIBRATING. ENERGY...WAITING TO BE RELEASED.

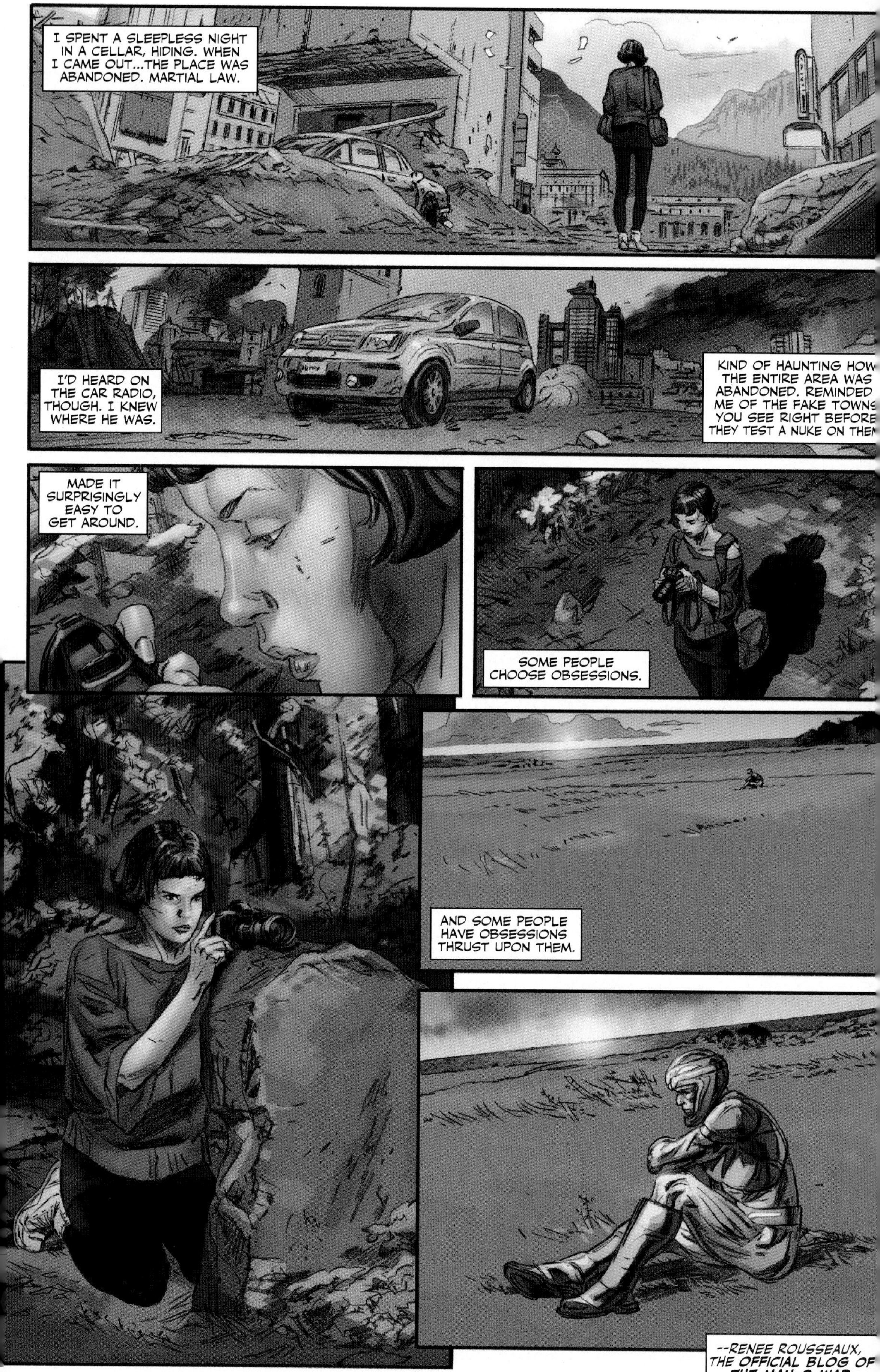
I SPENT A SLEEPLESS NIGHT IN A CELLAR, HIDING. WHEN I CAME OUT...THE PLACE WAS ABANDONED. MARTIAL LAW.
I'D HEARD ON THE CAR RADIO, THOUGH. I KNEW WHERE HE WAS.
KIND OF HAUNTING HOW THE ENTIRE AREA WAS ABANDONED. REMINDED ME OF THE FAKE TOWNS YOU SEE RIGHT BEFORE THEY TEST A NUKE ON THEM
MADE IT SURPRISINGLY EASY TO GET AROUND.
SOME PEOPLE CHOOSE OBSESSIONS.
AND SOME PEOPLE HAVE OBSESSIONS THRUST UPON THEM.
--RENEE ROUSSEAUX, THE OFFICIAL BLOG OF THE MAN-O-WAR.

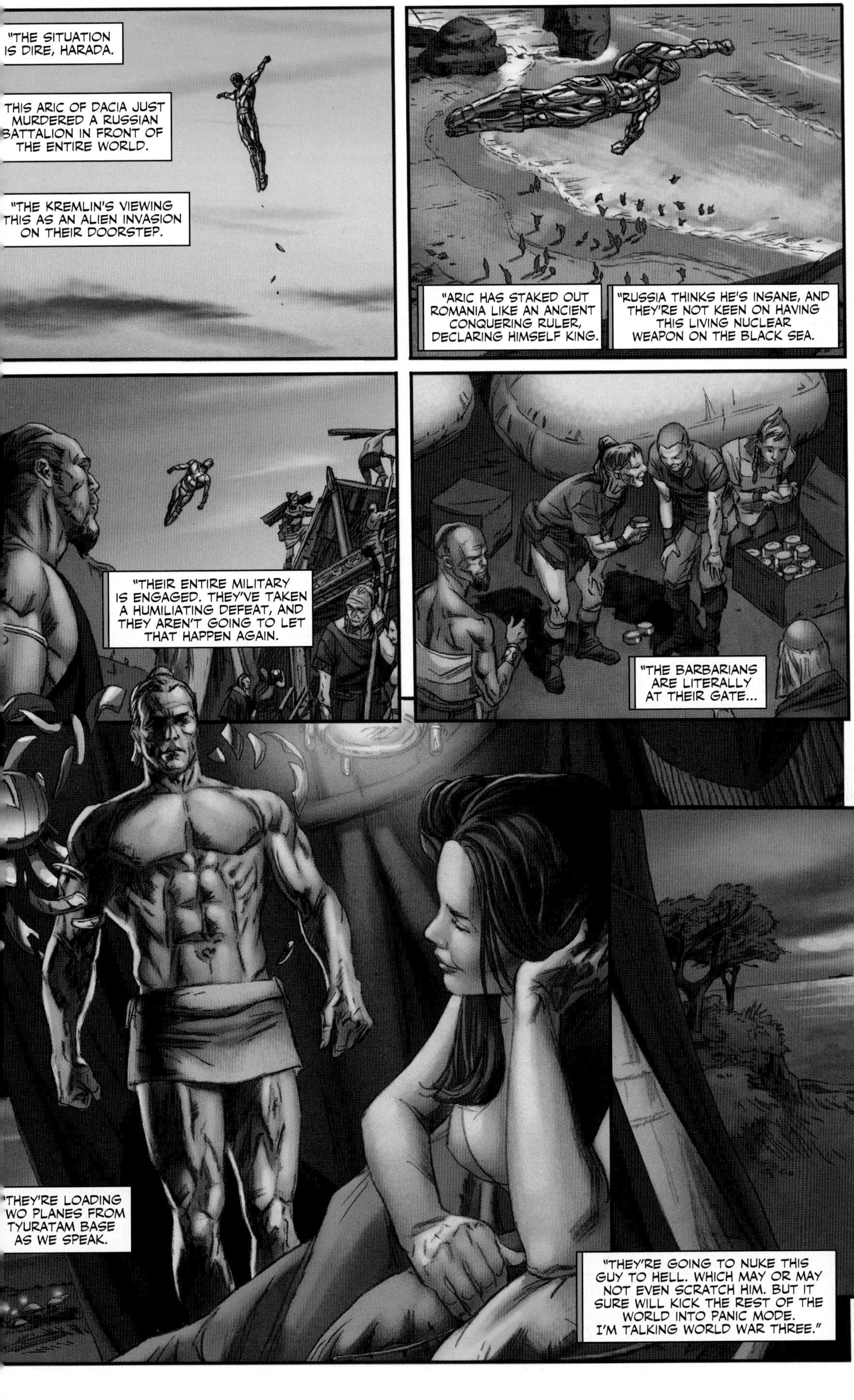

"THE SITUATION IS DIRE, HARADA.
THIS ARIC OF DACIA JUST MURDERED A RUSSIAN BATTALION IN FRONT OF THE ENTIRE WORLD.
"THE KREMLIN'S VIEWING THIS AS AN ALIEN INVASION ON THEIR DOORSTEP.
"ARIC HAS STAKED OUT ROMANIA LIKE AN ANCIENT CONQUERING RULER, DECLARING HIMSELF KING.
"RUSSIA THINKS HE'S INSANE, AND THEY'RE NOT KEEN ON HAVING THIS LIVING NUCLEAR WEAPON ON THE BLACK SEA.
"THEIR ENTIRE MILITARY IS ENGAGED. THEY'VE TAKEN A HUMILIATING DEFEAT, AND THEY AREN'T GOING TO LET THAT HAPPEN AGAIN.
"THE BARBARIANS ARE LITERALLY AT THEIR GATE...
"THEY'RE LOADING WO PLANES FROM TYURATAM BASE AS WE SPEAK.
"THEY'RE GOING TO NUKE THIS GUY TO HELL. WHICH MAY OR MAY NOT EVEN SCRATCH HIM. BUT IT SURE WILL KICK THE REST OF THE WORLD INTO PANIC MODE. I'M TALKING WORLD WAR THREE."

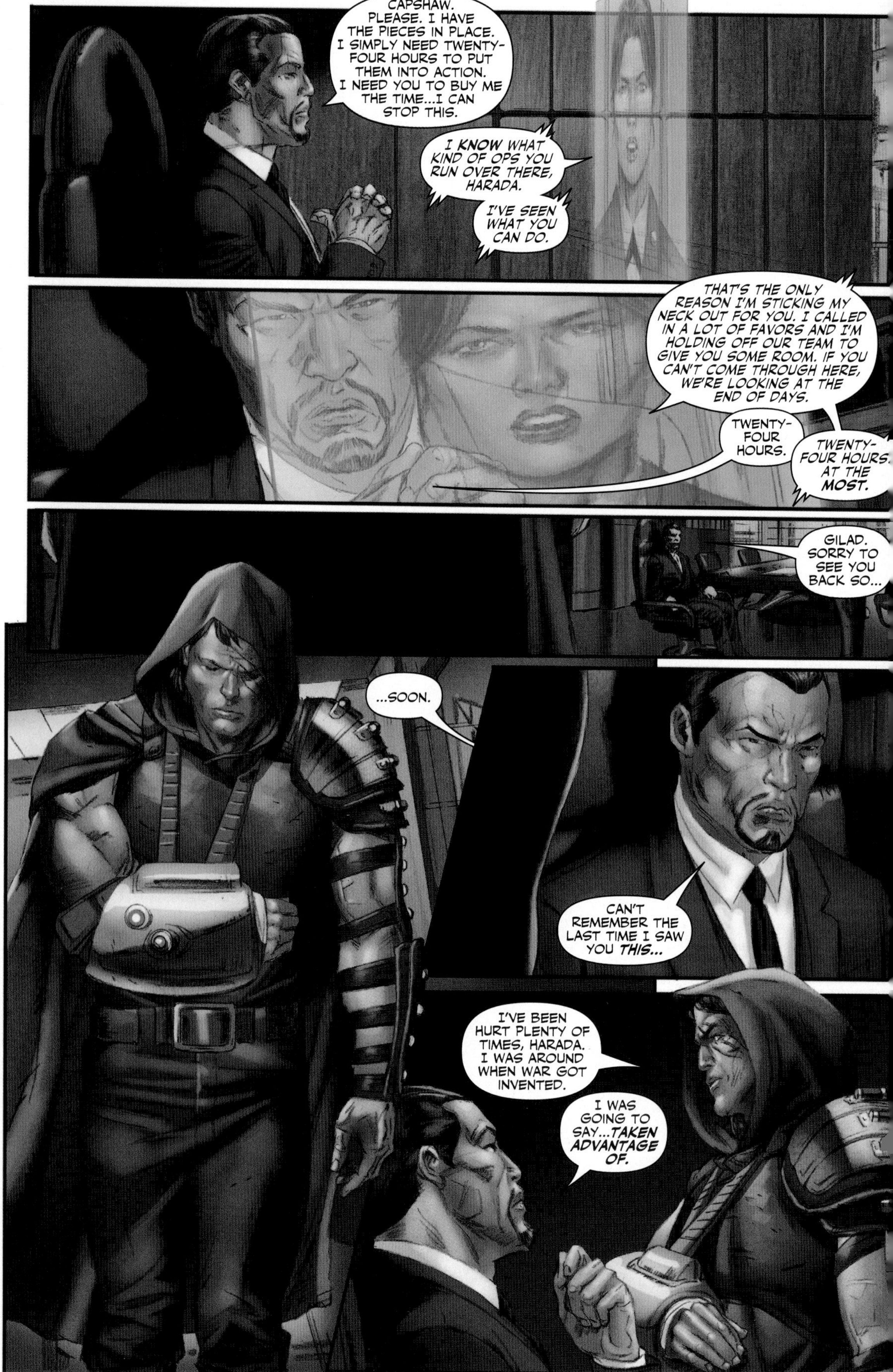

CAPSHAW. PLEASE. I HAVE THE PIECES IN PLACE. I SIMPLY NEED TWENTY-FOUR HOURS TO PUT THEM INTO ACTION. I NEED YOU TO BUY ME THE TIME...I CAN STOP THIS.
I KNOW WHAT KIND OF OPS YOU RUN OVER THERE, HARADA.
I'VE SEEN WHAT YOU CAN DO.
THAT'S THE ONLY REASON I'M STICKING MY NECK OUT FOR YOU. I CALLED IN A LOT OF FAVORS AND I'M HOLDING OFF OUR TEAM TO GIVE YOU SOME ROOM. IF YOU CAN'T COME THROUGH HERE, WE'RE LOOKING AT THE END OF DAYS.
TWENTY-FOUR HOURS.
TWENTY-FOUR HOURS. AT THE MOST.
GILAD. SORRY TO SEE YOU BACK SO...
...SOON.
CAN'T REMEMBER THE LAST TIME I SAW YOU THIS...
I'VE BEEN HURT PLENTY OF TIMES, HARADA. I WAS AROUND WHEN WAR GOT INVENTED.
I WAS GOING TO SAY...TAKEN ADVANTAGE OF.

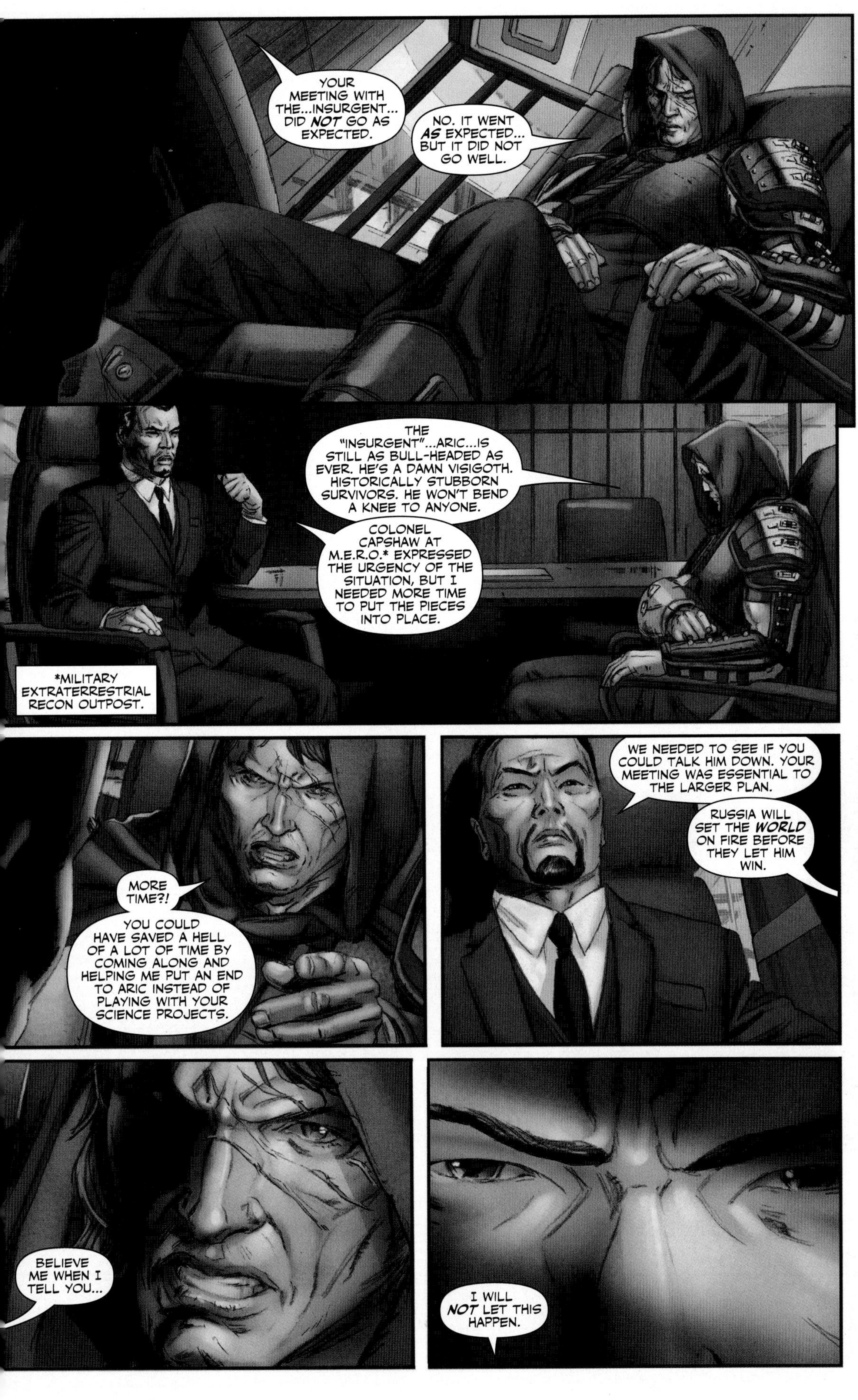
YOUR MEETING WITH THE...INSURGENT... DID NOT GO AS EXPECTED.
NO. IT WENT AS EXPECTED... BUT IT DID NOT GO WELL.
THE "INSURGENT"...ARIC...IS STILL AS BULL-HEADED AS EVER. HE'S A DAMN VISIGOTH. HISTORICALLY STUBBORN SURVIVORS. HE WON'T BEND A KNEE TO ANYONE.
COLONEL CAPSHAW AT M.E.R.O.* EXPRESSED THE URGENCY OF THE SITUATION, BUT I NEEDED MORE TIME TO PUT THE PIECES INTO PLACE.
*MILITARY EXTRATERRESTRIAL RECON OUTPOST.
MORE TIME?!
YOU COULD HAVE SAVED A HELL OF A LOT OF TIME BY COMING ALONG AND HELPING ME PUT AN END TO ARIC INSTEAD OF PLAYING WITH YOUR SCIENCE PROJECTS.
WE NEEDED TO SEE IF YOU COULD TALK HIM DOWN. YOUR MEETING WAS ESSENTIAL TO THE LARGER PLAN.
RUSSIA WILL SET THE WORLD ON FIRE BEFORE THEY LET HIM WIN.
BELIEVE ME WHEN I TELL YOU...
I WILL NOT LET THIS HAPPEN.

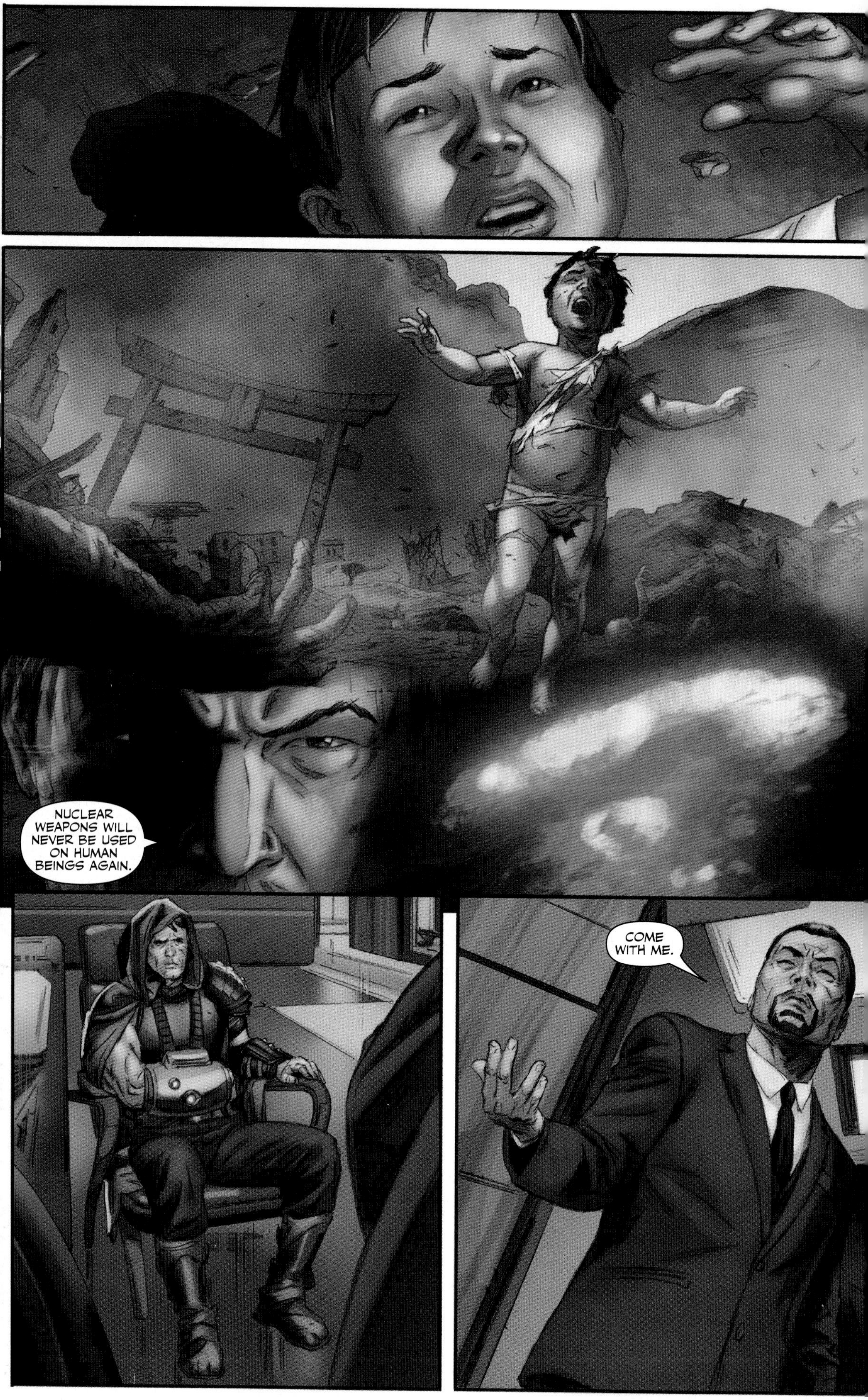
NUCLEAR WEAPONS WILL NEVER BE USED ON HUMAN BEINGS AGAIN.
COME WITH ME.

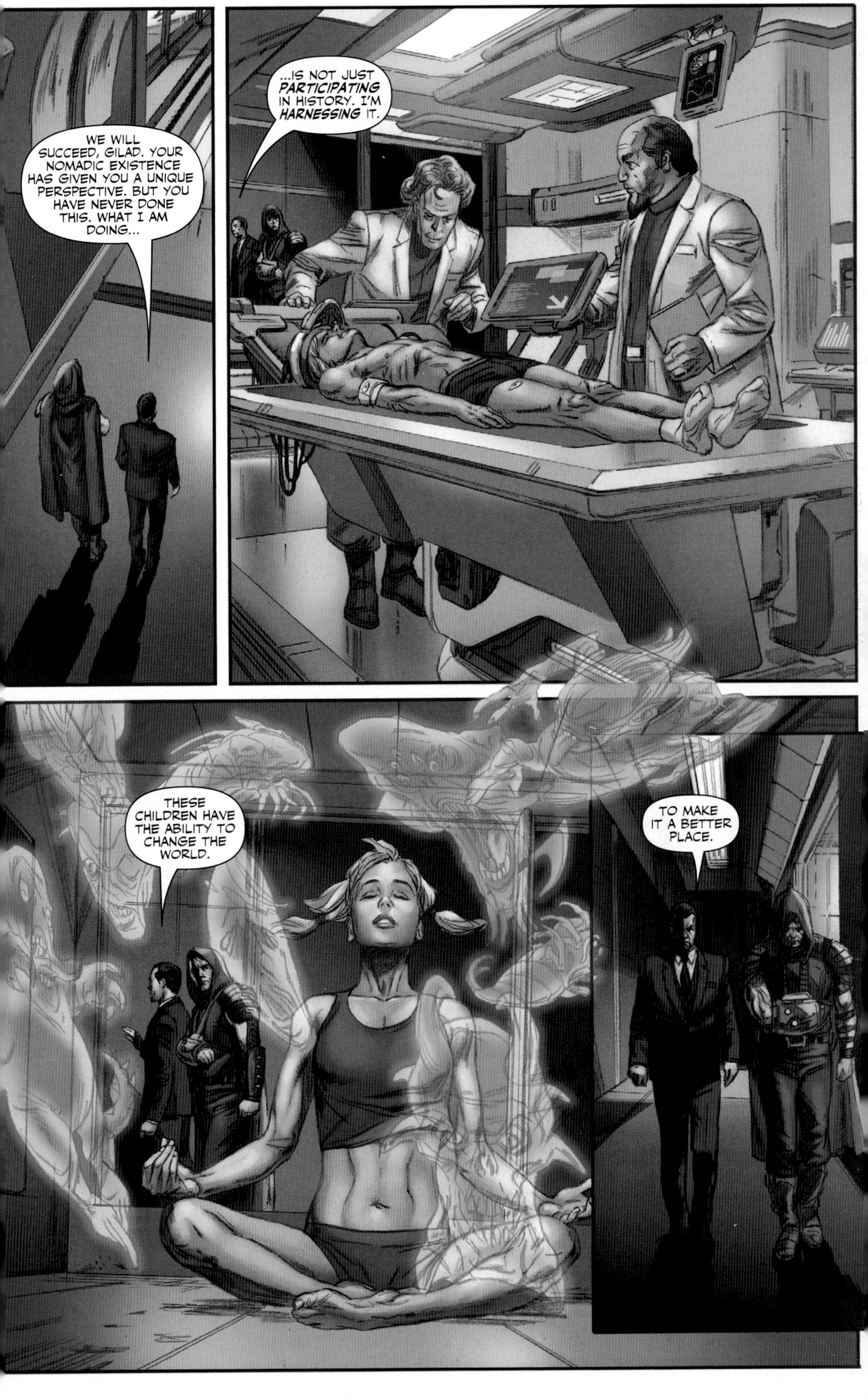
WE WILL SUCCEED, GILAD. YOUR NOMADIC EXISTENCE HAS GIVEN YOU A UNIQUE PERSPECTIVE. BUT YOU HAVE NEVER DONE THIS. WHAT I AM DOING...
...IS NOT JUST PARTICIPATING IN HISTORY. I'M HARNESSING IT.
THESE CHILDREN HAVE THE ABILITY TO CHANGE THE WORLD.
TO MAKE IT A BETTER PLACE.

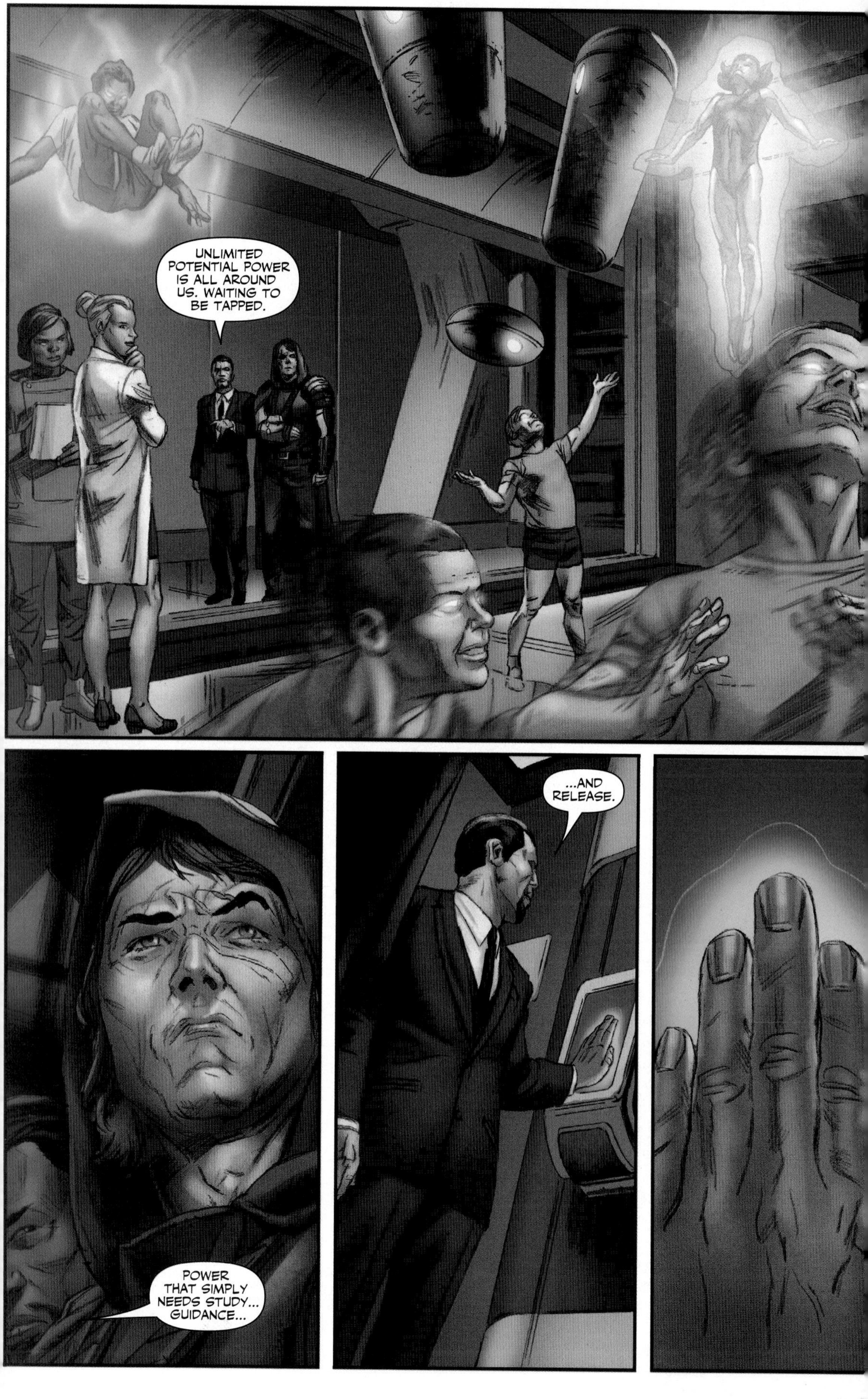
UNLIMITED POTENTIAL POWER IS ALL AROUND US. WAITING TO BE TAPPED.
POWER THAT SIMPLY NEEDS STUDY... GUIDANCE...
...AND RELEASE.

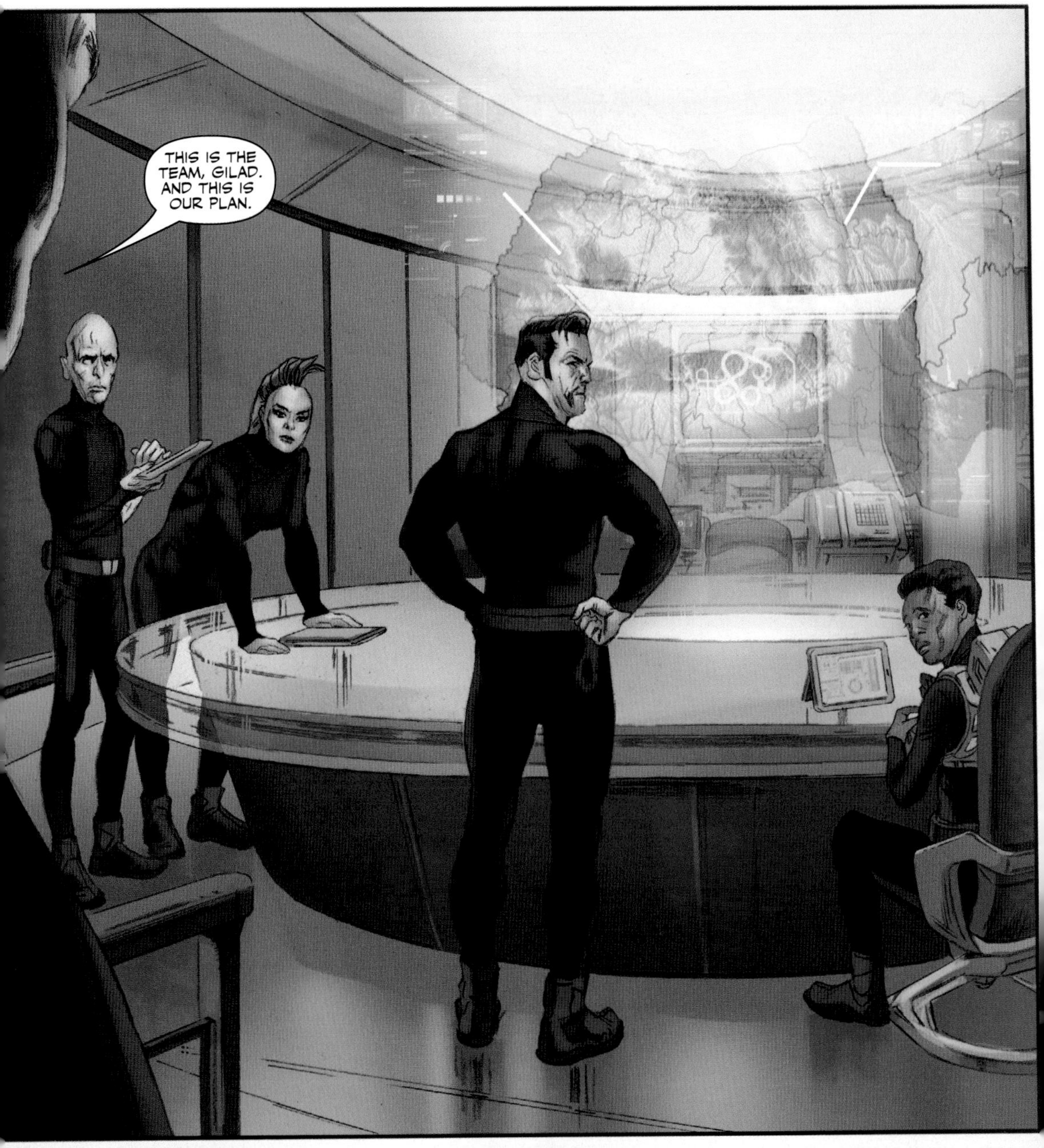
THIS IS THE TEAM, GILAD. AND THIS IS OUR PLAN.

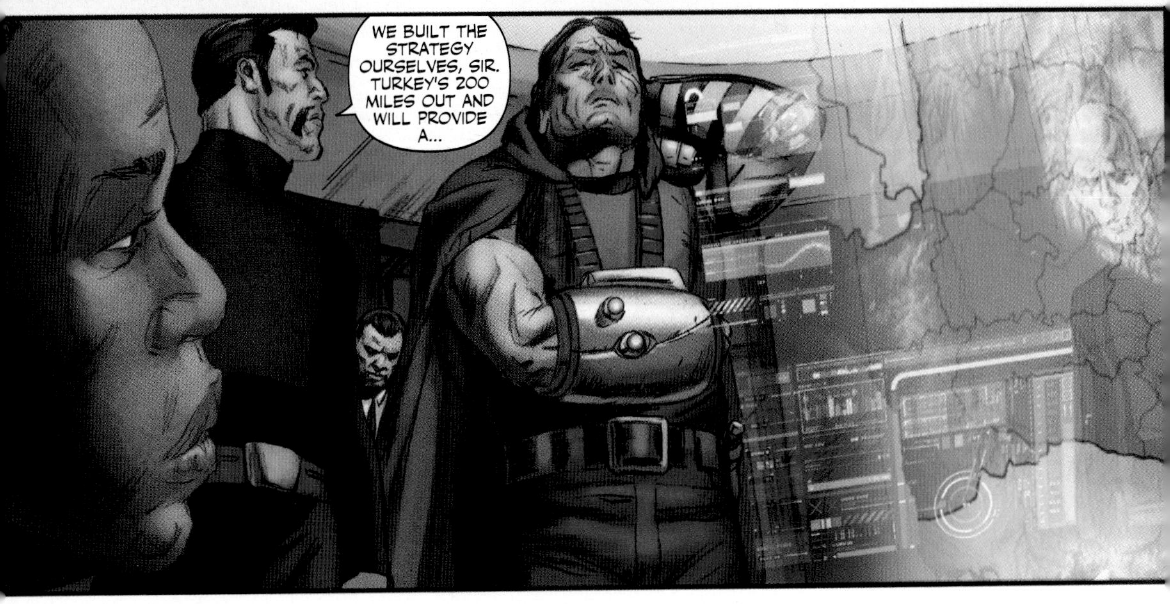
WE BUILT THE STRATEGY OURSELVES, SIR. TURKEY'S 200 MILES OUT AND WILL PROVIDE A...

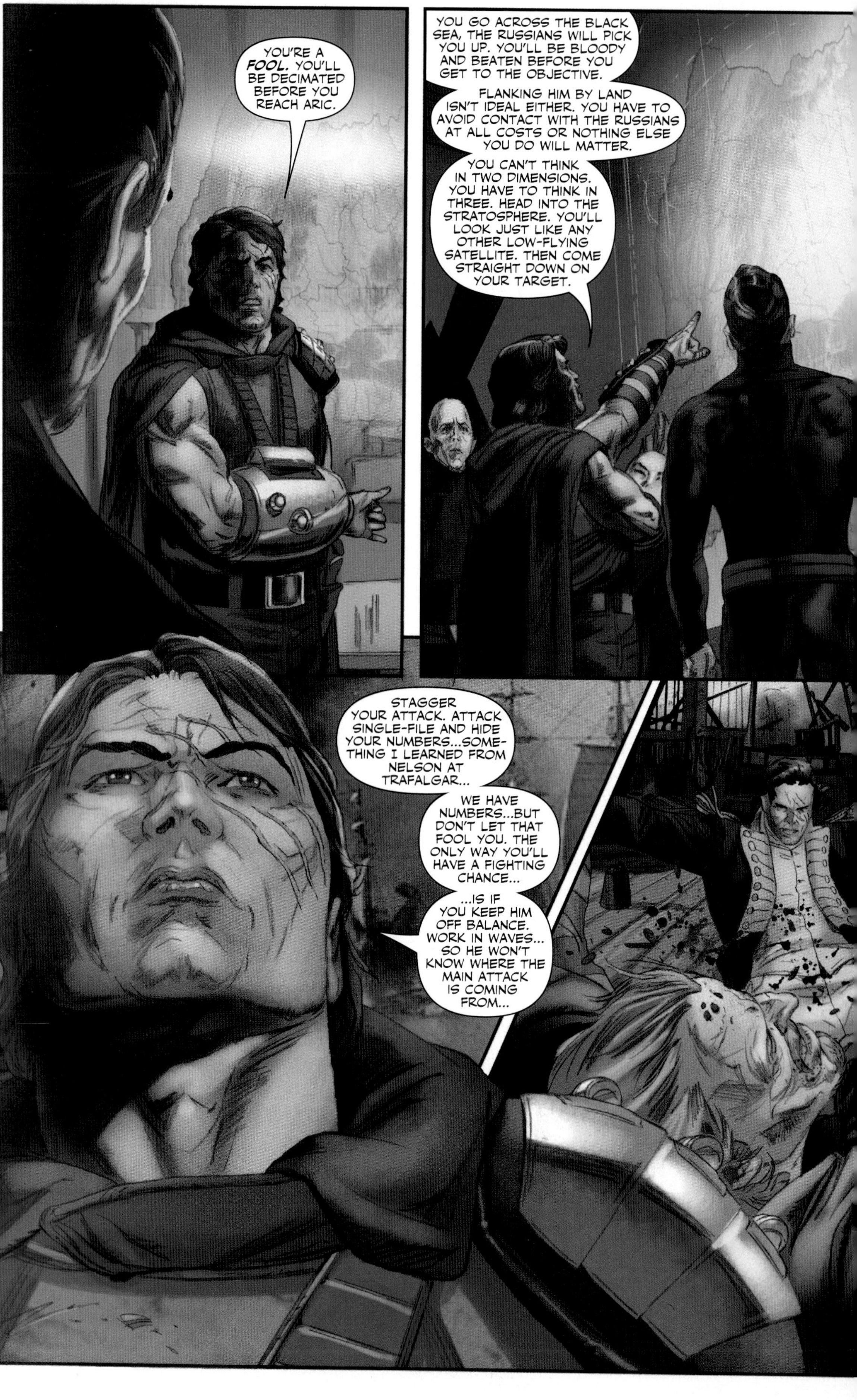
YOU'RE A *FOOL.* YOU'LL BE DECIMATED BEFORE YOU REACH ARIC.
YOU GO ACROSS THE BLACK SEA, THE RUSSIANS WILL PICK YOU UP. YOU'LL BE BLOODY AND BEATEN BEFORE YOU GET TO THE OBJECTIVE.
FLANKING HIM BY LAND ISN'T IDEAL EITHER. YOU HAVE TO AVOID CONTACT WITH THE RUSSIANS AT ALL COSTS OR NOTHING ELSE YOU DO WILL MATTER.
YOU CAN'T THINK IN TWO DIMENSIONS. YOU HAVE TO THINK IN THREE. HEAD INTO THE STRATOSPHERE. YOU'LL LOOK JUST LIKE ANY OTHER LOW-FLYING SATELLITE. THEN COME STRAIGHT DOWN ON YOUR TARGET.
STAGGER YOUR ATTACK. ATTACK SINGLE-FILE AND HIDE YOUR NUMBERS...SOMETHING I LEARNED FROM NELSON AT TRAFALGAR...
WE HAVE NUMBERS...BUT DON'T LET THAT FOOL YOU. THE ONLY WAY YOU'LL HAVE A FIGHTING CHANCE...
...IS IF YOU KEEP HIM OFF BALANCE. WORK IN WAVES... SO HE WON'T KNOW WHERE THE MAIN ATTACK IS COMING FROM...

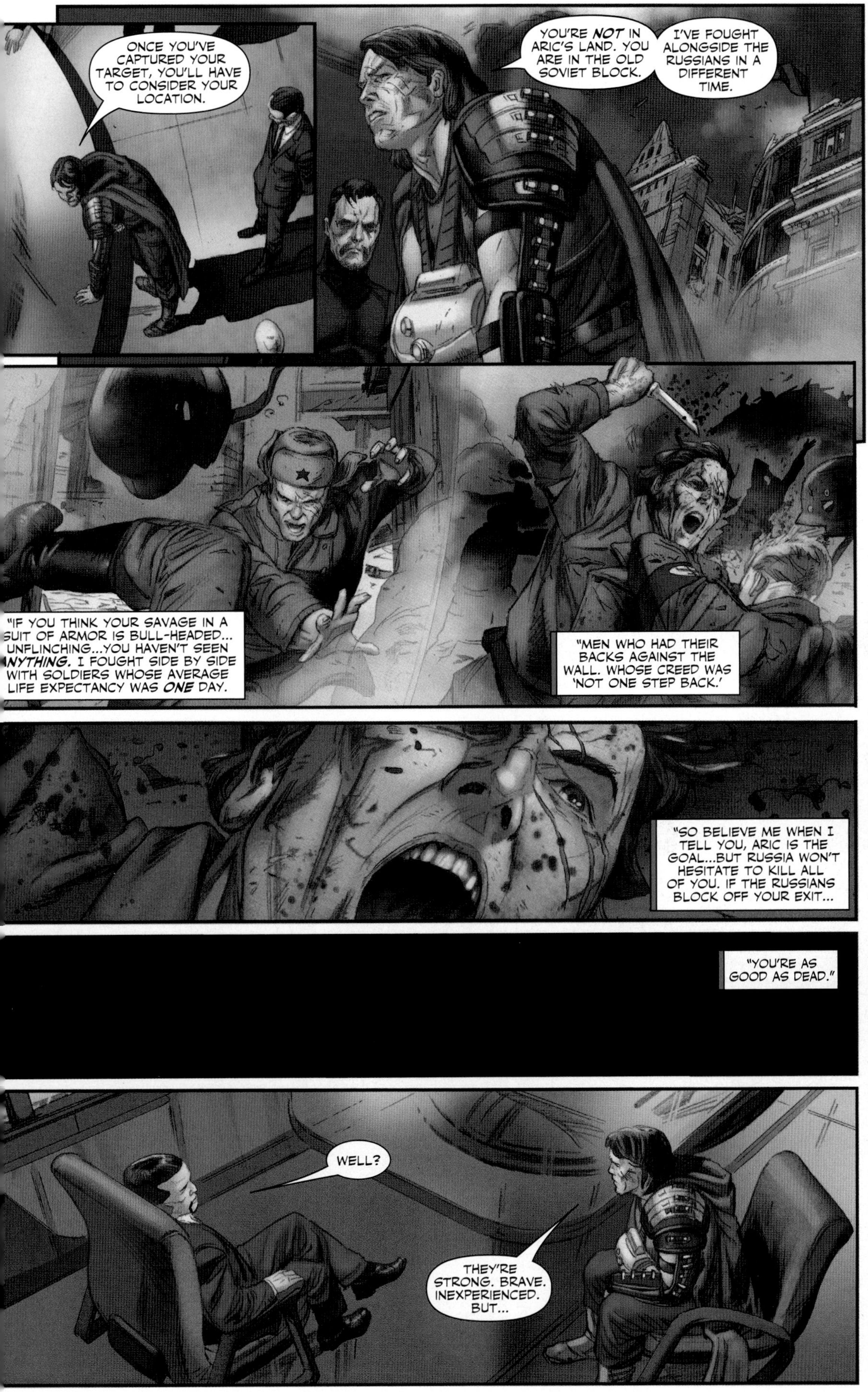
ONCE YOU'VE CAPTURED YOUR TARGET, YOU'LL HAVE TO CONSIDER YOUR LOCATION.
YOU'RE NOT IN ARIC'S LAND. YOU ARE IN THE OLD SOVIET BLOCK.
I'VE FOUGHT ALONGSIDE THE RUSSIANS IN A DIFFERENT TIME.
"IF YOU THINK YOUR SAVAGE IN A SUIT OF ARMOR IS BULL-HEADED... UNFLINCHING...YOU HAVEN'T SEEN ANYTHING. I FOUGHT SIDE BY SIDE WITH SOLDIERS WHOSE AVERAGE LIFE EXPECTANCY WAS ONE DAY.
"MEN WHO HAD THEIR BACKS AGAINST THE WALL. WHOSE CREED WAS 'NOT ONE STEP BACK.'
"SO BELIEVE ME WHEN I TELL YOU, ARIC IS THE GOAL...BUT RUSSIA WON'T HESITATE TO KILL ALL OF YOU. IF THE RUSSIANS BLOCK OFF YOUR EXIT...
"YOU'RE AS GOOD AS DEAD."
WELL?
THEY'RE STRONG. BRAVE. INEXPERIENCED. BUT...

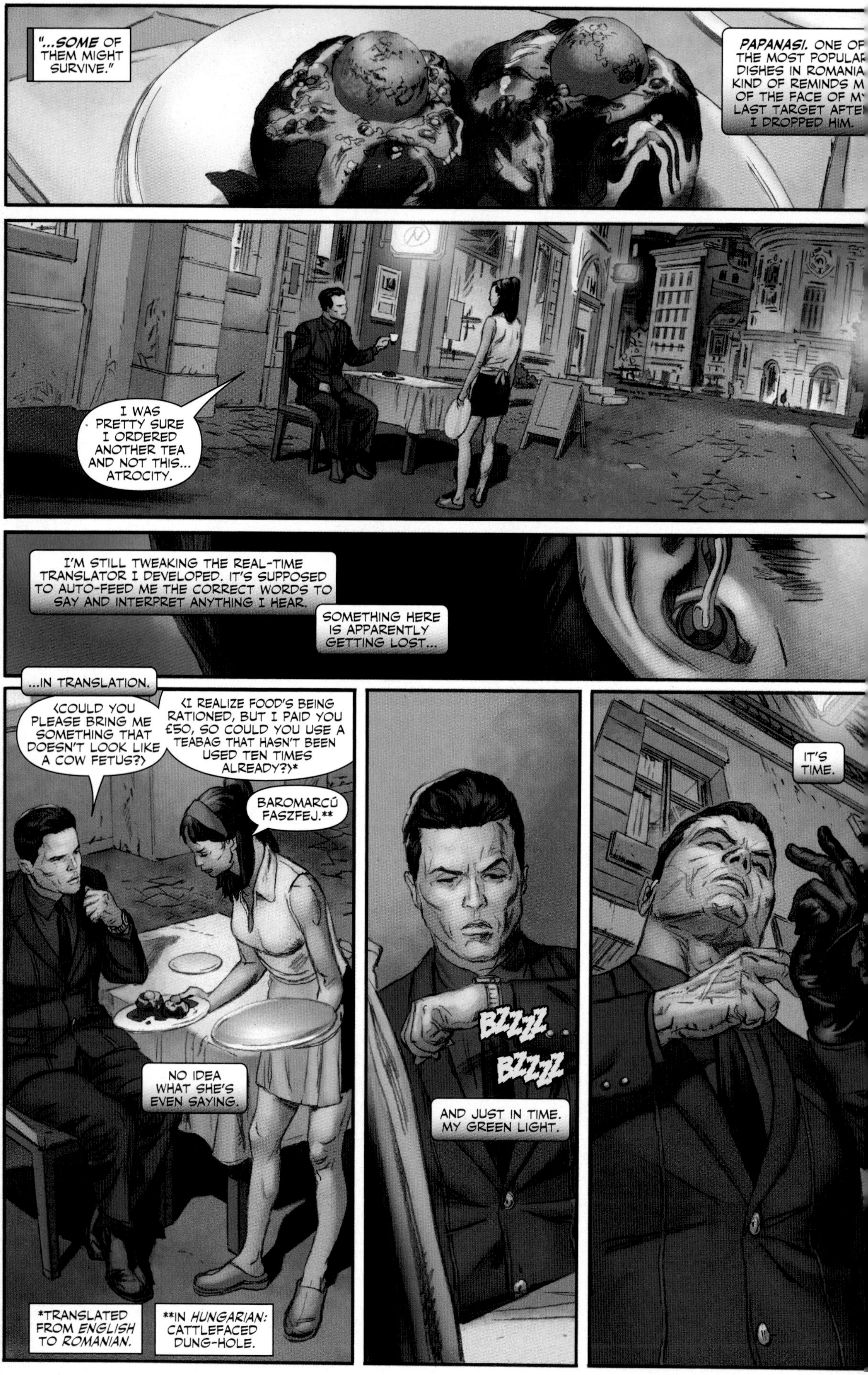
"...SOME OF THEM MIGHT SURVIVE."
PAPANASI. ONE OF THE MOST POPULAR DISHES IN ROMANIA. KIND OF REMINDS M OF THE FACE OF M LAST TARGET AFTE I DROPPED HIM.
I WAS PRETTY SURE I ORDERED ANOTHER TEA AND NOT THIS... ATROCITY.
I'M STILL TWEAKING THE REAL-TIME TRANSLATOR I DEVELOPED. IT'S SUPPOSED TO AUTO-FEED ME THE CORRECT WORDS TO SAY AND INTERPRET ANYTHING I HEAR.
SOMETHING HERE IS APPARENTLY GETTING LOST...
...IN TRANSLATION.
‹COULD YOU PLEASE BRING ME SOMETHING THAT DOESN'T LOOK LIKE A COW FETUS?›
‹I REALIZE FOOD'S BEING RATIONED, BUT I PAID YOU £50, SO COULD YOU USE A TEABAG THAT HASN'T BEEN USED TEN TIMES ALREADY?›*
BAROMARCÚ FASZFEJ.**
NO IDEA WHAT SHE'S EVEN SAYING.
*TRANSLATED FROM ENGLISH TO ROMANIAN.
**IN HUNGARIAN: CATTLEFACED DUNG-HOLE.
BZZZZ
BZZZZ
AND JUST IN TIME. MY GREEN LIGHT.
IT'S TIME.

'T SURE I LIKE HAVING HARADA AS MY FIELD HANDLER, BUT 'PARENTLY HE'S GOT SOME *INSIGHT* INTO THE *PROBLEM.*

HE OFFERED ME $10 MILLION FOR THIS JOB, SO I KNEW HE 'AS DESPERATE EVEN BEFORE I INTERCEPTED NATO AND RUSSIAN DISPATCHES TALKING 'BOUT NUCLEAR OPTIONS. AS THEY SAY...

"I'D 'A DONE THIS JOB FOR FREE."

ALL I NEED TO DO IS SET UP A PERIMETER AROUND THE SECOND MOST DANGEROUS MAN ON EARTH. NO PROBLEM. SAVING THE WORLD $10 MILLION AT A TIME.

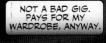

NOT A BAD GIG. PAYS FOR MY WARDROBE, ANYWAY.

SMART BOOTS AND GLOVES USE ELECTRIFIED HAIR-POLYMER TO GRIP AND RELEASE ON THE MICROSCOPIC LEVEL.

BULLETPROOF HEX-WEAVE FABRIC IS FIREPROOF...

...AND DESIGNED FOR MULTI-PURPOSE WEAR.

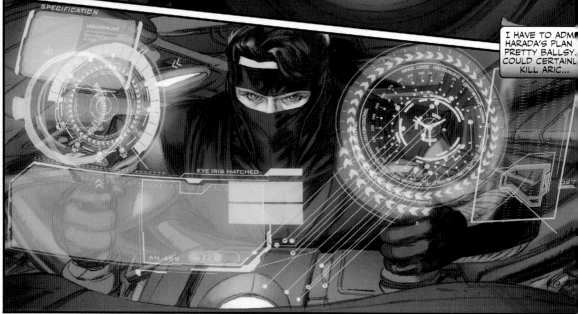

I HAVE TO ADM[...] HARADA'S PLAN [...] PRETTY BALLSY. [...] COULD CERTAINL[...] KILL ARIC...

SPECIFICATION

EYE IRIS MATCHED

AN 459

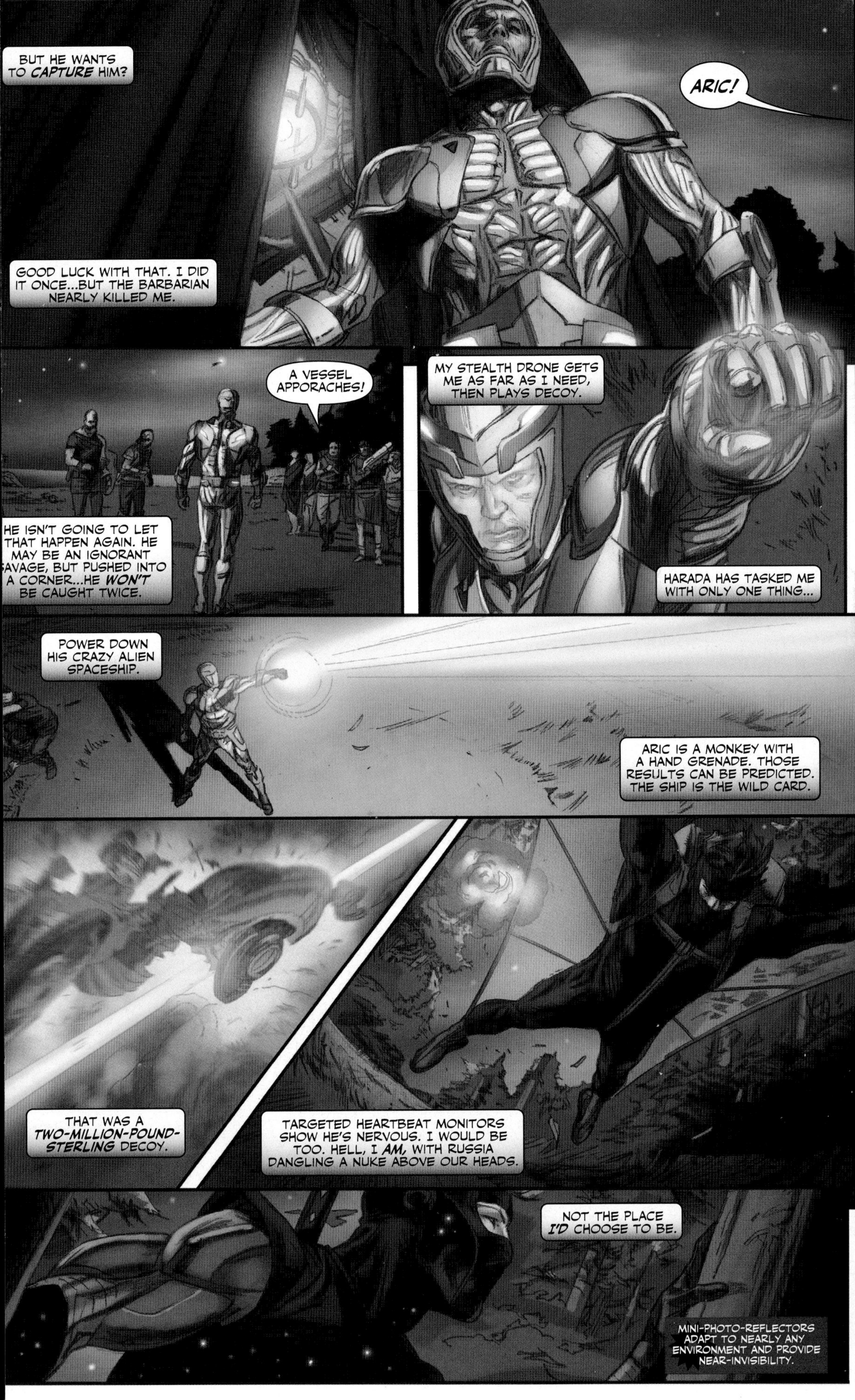

BUT HE WANTS TO CAPTURE HIM?
ARIC!
GOOD LUCK WITH THAT. I DID IT ONCE...BUT THE BARBARIAN NEARLY KILLED ME.
A VESSEL APPORACHES!
HE ISN'T GOING TO LET THAT HAPPEN AGAIN. HE MAY BE AN IGNORANT SAVAGE, BUT PUSHED INTO A CORNER...HE WON'T BE CAUGHT TWICE.
MY STEALTH DRONE GETS ME AS FAR AS I NEED, THEN PLAYS DECOY.
HARADA HAS TASKED ME WITH ONLY ONE THING...
POWER DOWN HIS CRAZY ALIEN SPACESHIP.
ARIC IS A MONKEY WITH A HAND GRENADE. THOSE RESULTS CAN BE PREDICTED. THE SHIP IS THE WILD CARD.
THAT WAS A TWO-MILLION-POUND-STERLING DECOY.
TARGETED HEARTBEAT MONITORS SHOW HE'S NERVOUS. I WOULD BE TOO. HELL, I AM, WITH RUSSIA DANGLING A NUKE ABOVE OUR HEADS.
NOT THE PLACE I'D CHOOSE TO BE.
MINI-PHOTO-REFLECTORS ADAPT TO NEARLY ANY ENVIRONMENT AND PROVIDE NEAR-INVISIBILITY.

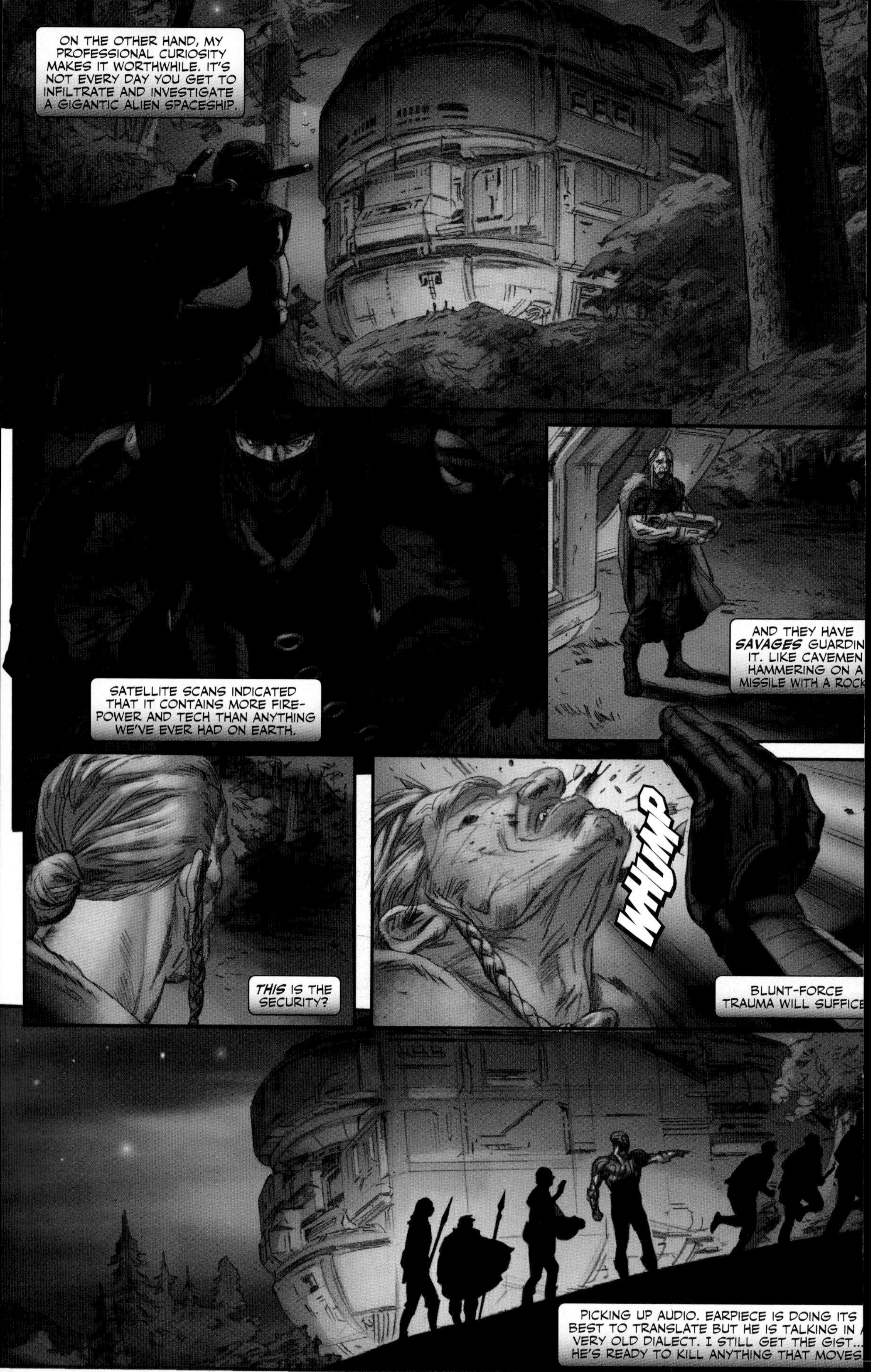

ON THE OTHER HAND, MY PROFESSIONAL CURIOSITY MAKES IT WORTHWHILE. IT'S NOT EVERY DAY YOU GET TO INFILTRATE AND INVESTIGATE A GIGANTIC ALIEN SPACESHIP.
SATELLITE SCANS INDICATED THAT IT CONTAINS MORE FIRE-POWER AND TECH THAN ANYTHING WE'VE EVER HAD ON EARTH.
AND THEY HAVE SAVAGES GUARDIN IT. LIKE CAVEMEN HAMMERING ON A MISSILE WITH A ROCK
THIS IS THE SECURITY?
WHUMP
BLUNT-FORCE TRAUMA WILL SUFFICE
PICKING UP AUDIO. EARPIECE IS DOING ITS BEST TO TRANSLATE BUT HE IS TALKING IN A VERY OLD DIALECT. I STILL GET THE GIST... HE'S READY TO KILL ANYTHING THAT MOVES.

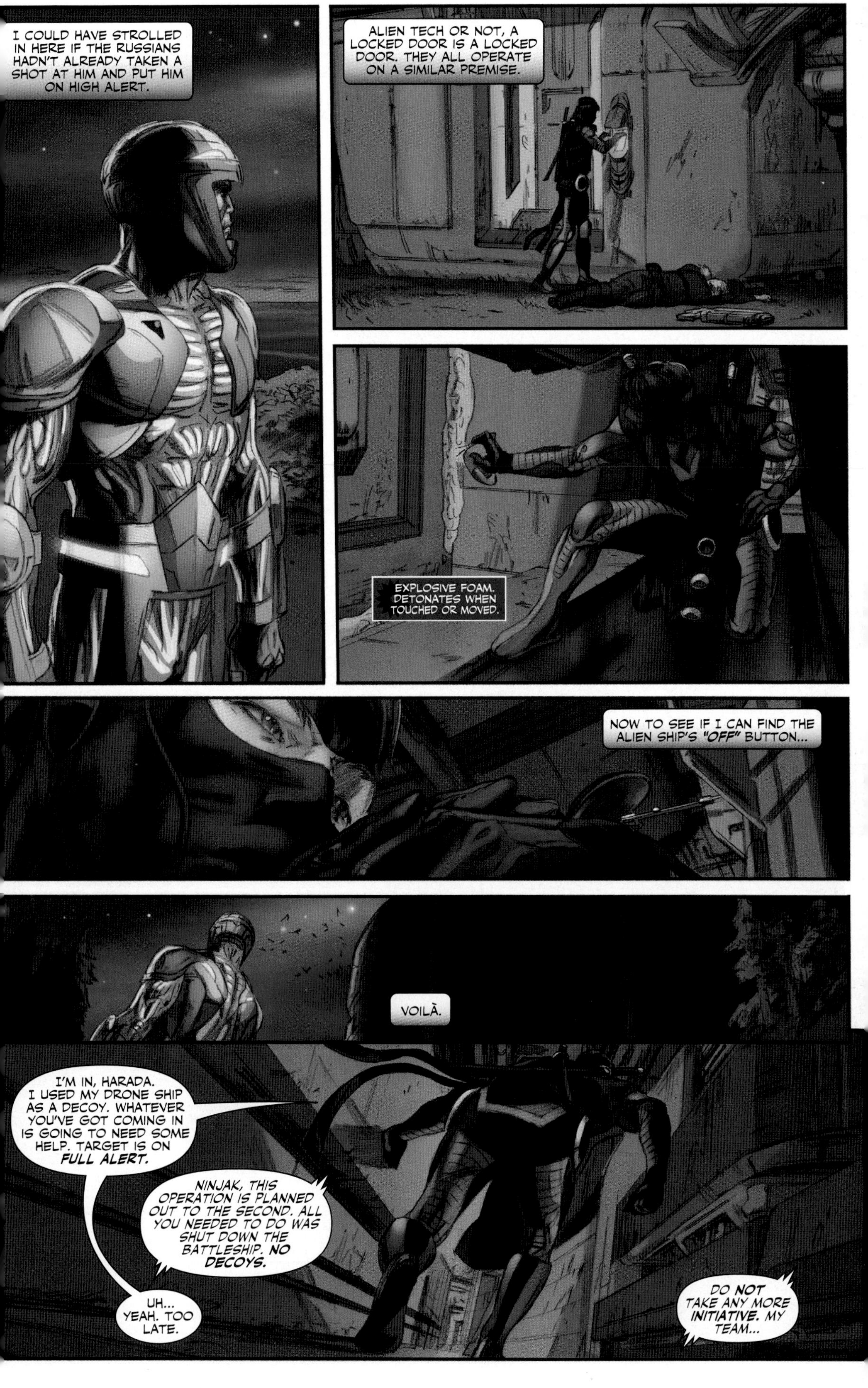

I COULD HAVE STROLLED IN HERE IF THE RUSSIANS HADN'T ALREADY TAKEN A SHOT AT HIM AND PUT HIM ON HIGH ALERT.
ALIEN TECH OR NOT, A LOCKED DOOR IS A LOCKED DOOR. THEY ALL OPERATE ON A SIMILAR PREMISE.
EXPLOSIVE FOAM. DETONATES WHEN TOUCHED OR MOVED.
NOW TO SEE IF I CAN FIND THE ALIEN SHIP'S *"OFF"* BUTTON...
VOILÀ.
I'M IN, HARADA. I USED MY DRONE SHIP AS A DECOY. WHATEVER YOU'VE GOT COMING IN IS GOING TO NEED SOME HELP. TARGET IS ON ***FULL ALERT.***
NINJAK, THIS OPERATION IS PLANNED OUT TO THE SECOND. ALL YOU NEEDED TO DO WAS SHUT DOWN THE BATTLESHIP. **NO DECOYS.**
UH... YEAH. TOO LATE.
DO **NOT** TAKE ANY MORE **INITIATIVE.** MY TEAM...

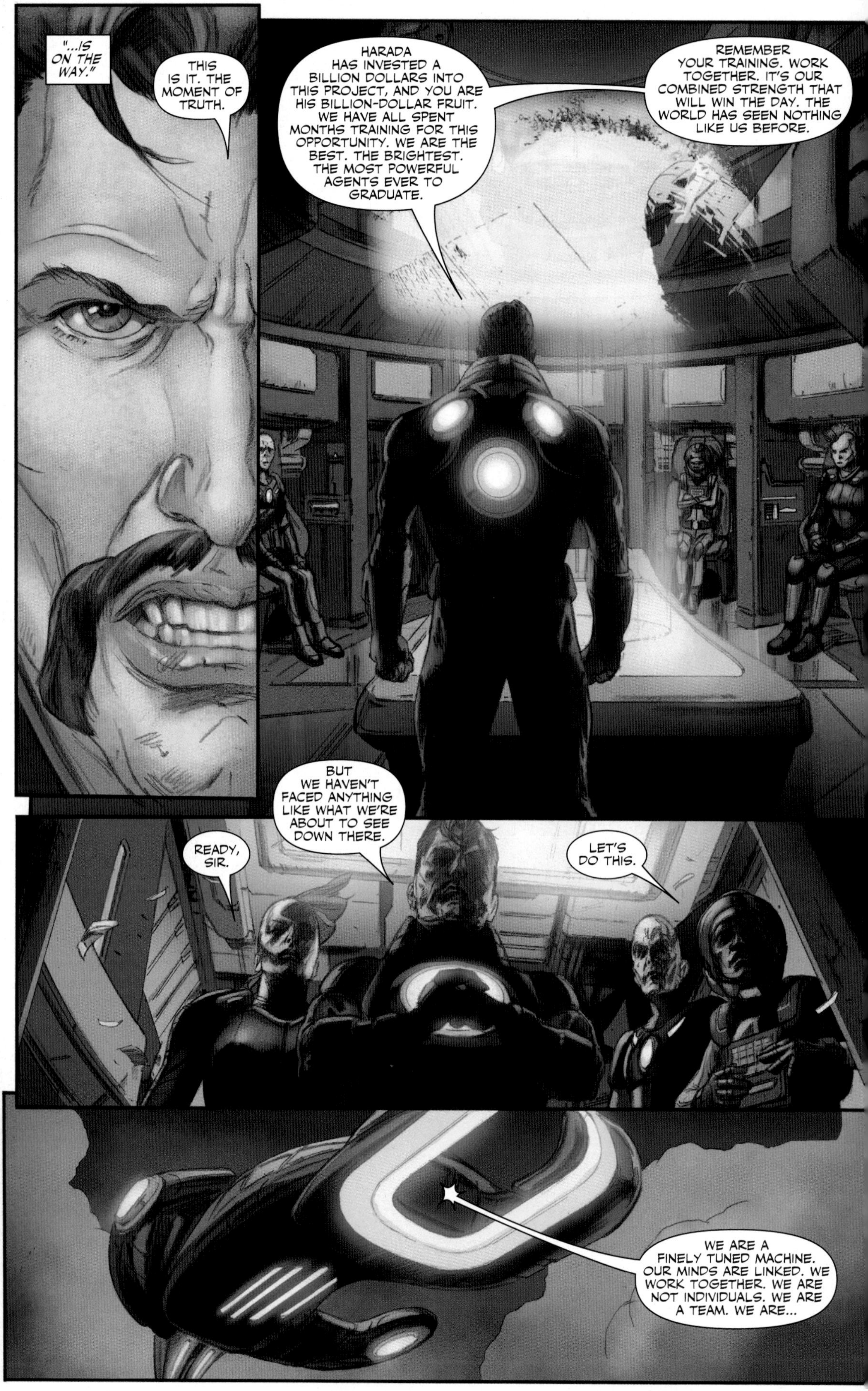
"...IS ON THE WAY."
THIS IS IT. THE MOMENT OF TRUTH.
HARADA HAS INVESTED A BILLION DOLLARS INTO THIS PROJECT, AND YOU ARE HIS BILLION-DOLLAR FRUIT. WE HAVE ALL SPENT MONTHS TRAINING FOR THIS OPPORTUNITY. WE ARE THE BEST. THE BRIGHTEST. THE MOST POWERFUL AGENTS EVER TO GRADUATE.
REMEMBER YOUR TRAINING. WORK TOGETHER. IT'S OUR COMBINED STRENGTH THAT WILL WIN THE DAY. THE WORLD HAS SEEN NOTHING LIKE US BEFORE.
READY, SIR.
BUT WE HAVEN'T FACED ANYTHING LIKE WHAT WE'RE ABOUT TO SEE DOWN THERE.
LET'S DO THIS.
WE ARE A FINELY TUNED MACHINE. OUR MINDS ARE LINKED. WE WORK TOGETHER. WE ARE NOT INDIVIDUALS. WE ARE A TEAM. WE ARE...

UNITY!

CODENAME: MIRROR. COMBAT EXPERT. CAN MIRROR AND MIMIC THE FIGHTING STYLE AND CAPABILITIES OF ANY OPPONENT HE FACES. AS ADEPT AS HE IS AT COMBAT, HE HAS A MENTAL BLOCK THAT KEEPS HIM FROM BEING ABLE TO EITHER SPEAK OR HEAR.

CODENAME: BOMB. THE MUSCLE. ABLE TO INCREASE HER MUSCLE-MASS INCREMENTALLY VIA THE UNIQUE CONNECTION HER MIND HAS WITH HER BODY. CAN CONVERT ANY MENTAL ENERGY INTO PHYSICAL, KINETIC STRENGTH.

CODENAME: THE CAPTAIN. THE LEADER OF THE GROUP AND OLDEST ON THE TEAM. CAPABLE OF CREATING A MENTAL LINK THAT UNITES THE ENTIRE TEAM. IN ADDITION, HE USES ENHANCED VOICE-COMMANDS THAT ARE IMPOSSIBLE NOT TO OBEY.

CODENAME: ETHER. TECHNOLOGY EXPERT. ABLE TO MENTALLY DOWNLOAD ANY INFORMATION THAT IS STORED ELECTRONICALLY. SOCIALLY INEPT AND RELATIVELY UNSKILLED IN COMBAT, BUT HIS INTELLECT HELPS HIM COMPENSATE.

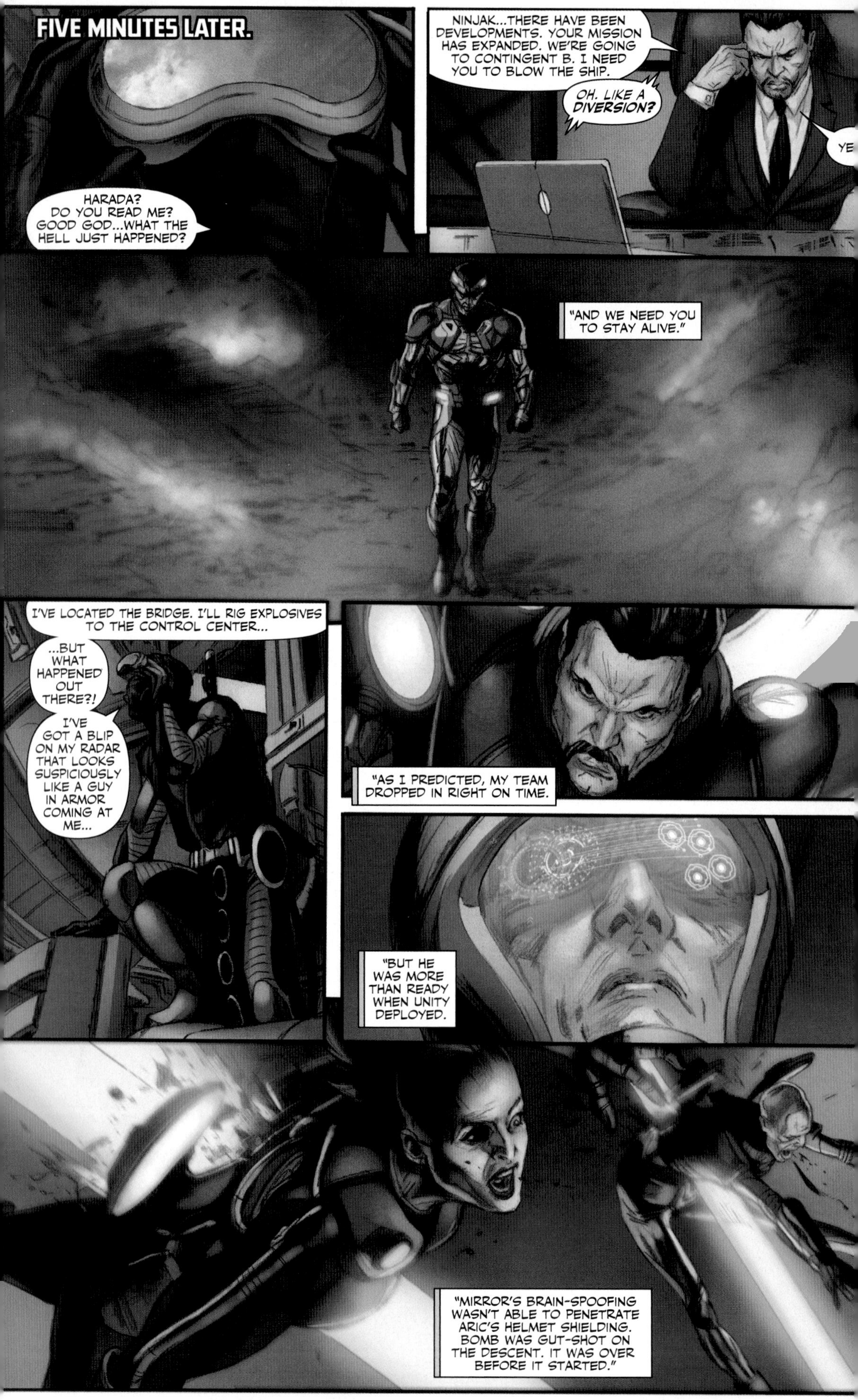
FIVE MINUTES LATER.
HARADA? DO YOU READ ME? GOOD GOD...WHAT THE HELL JUST HAPPENED?
NINJAK...THERE HAVE BEEN DEVELOPMENTS. YOUR MISSION HAS EXPANDED. WE'RE GOING TO CONTINGENT B. I NEED YOU TO BLOW THE SHIP.
OH. LIKE A DIVERSION?
"AND WE NEED YOU TO STAY ALIVE."
I'VE LOCATED THE BRIDGE. I'LL RIG EXPLOSIVES TO THE CONTROL CENTER...
...BUT WHAT HAPPENED OUT THERE?!
I'VE GOT A BLIP ON MY RADAR THAT LOOKS SUSPICIOUSLY LIKE A GUY IN ARMOR COMING AT ME...
"AS I PREDICTED, MY TEAM DROPPED IN RIGHT ON TIME.
"BUT HE WAS MORE THAN READY WHEN UNITY DEPLOYED.
"MIRROR'S BRAIN-SPOOFING WASN'T ABLE TO PENETRATE ARIC'S HELMET SHIELDING. BOMB WAS GUT-SHOT ON THE DESCENT. IT WAS OVER BEFORE IT STARTED."

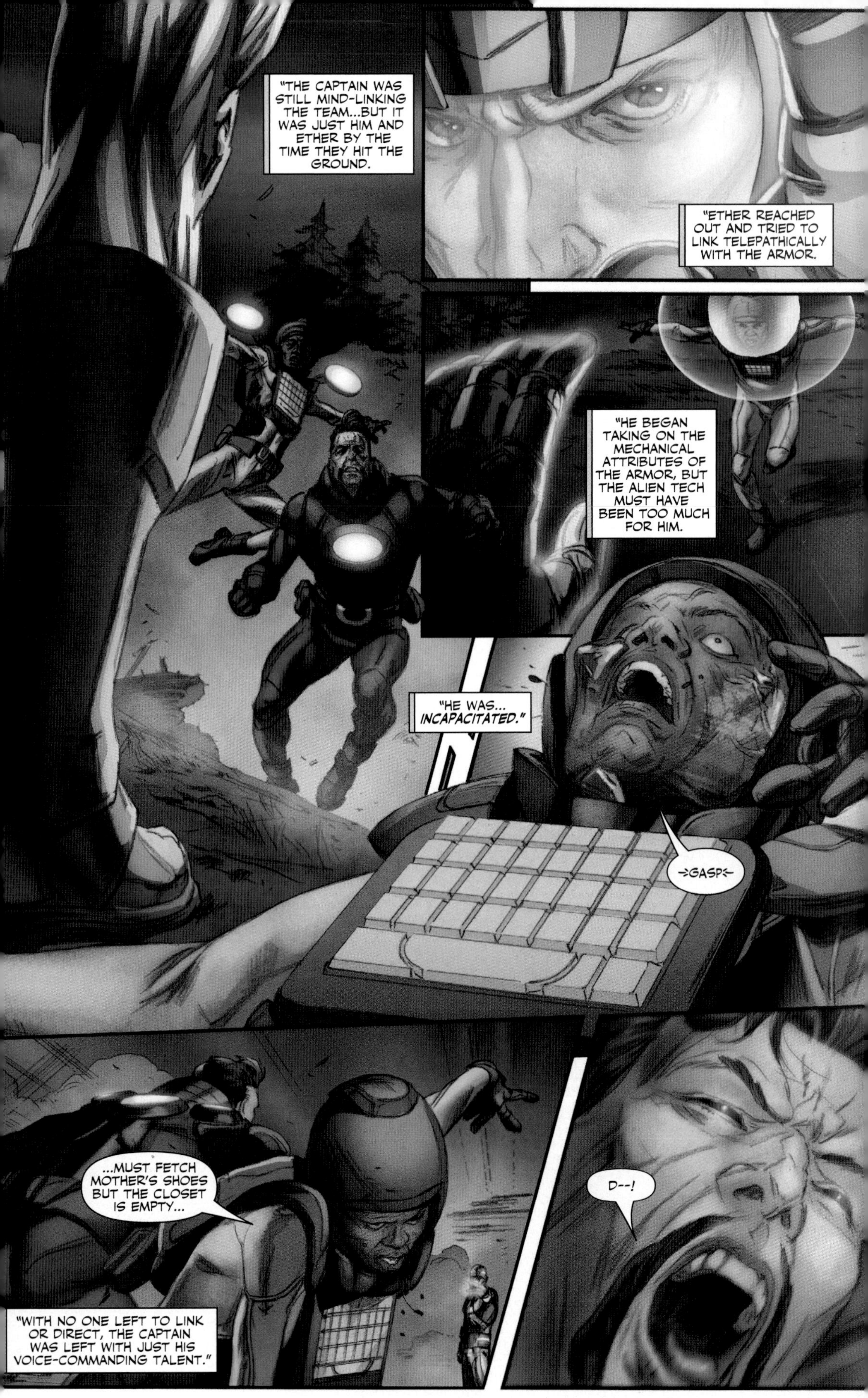
"THE CAPTAIN WAS STILL MIND-LINKING THE TEAM...BUT IT WAS JUST HIM AND ETHER BY THE TIME THEY HIT THE GROUND.
"ETHER REACHED OUT AND TRIED TO LINK TELEPATHICALLY WITH THE ARMOR.
"HE BEGAN TAKING ON THE MECHANICAL ATTRIBUTES OF THE ARMOR, BUT THE ALIEN TECH MUST HAVE BEEN TOO MUCH FOR HIM.
"HE WAS... *INCAPACITATED.*"
>GASP<
...MUST FETCH MOTHER'S SHOES BUT THE CLOSET IS EMPTY...
"WITH NO ONE LEFT TO LINK OR DIRECT, THE CAPTAIN WAS LEFT WITH JUST HIS VOICE-COMMANDING TALENT."
D--!

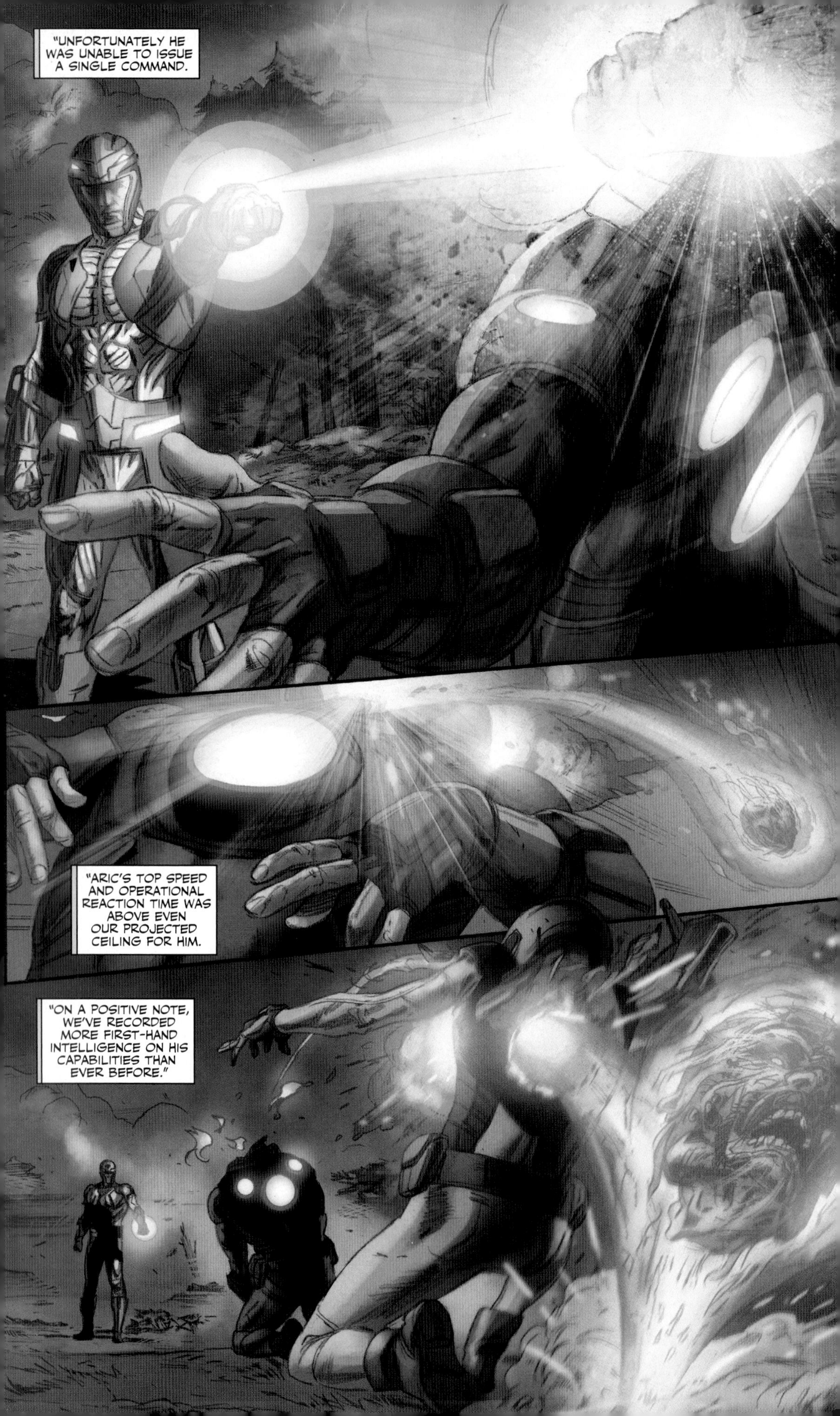
"UNFORTUNATELY HE WAS UNABLE TO ISSUE A SINGLE COMMAND.
"ARIC'S TOP SPEED AND OPERATIONAL REACTION TIME WAS ABOVE EVEN OUR PROJECTED CEILING FOR HIM.
"ON A POSITIVE NOTE, WE'VE RECORDED MORE FIRST-HAND INTELLIGENCE ON HIS CAPABILITIES THAN EVER BEFORE."

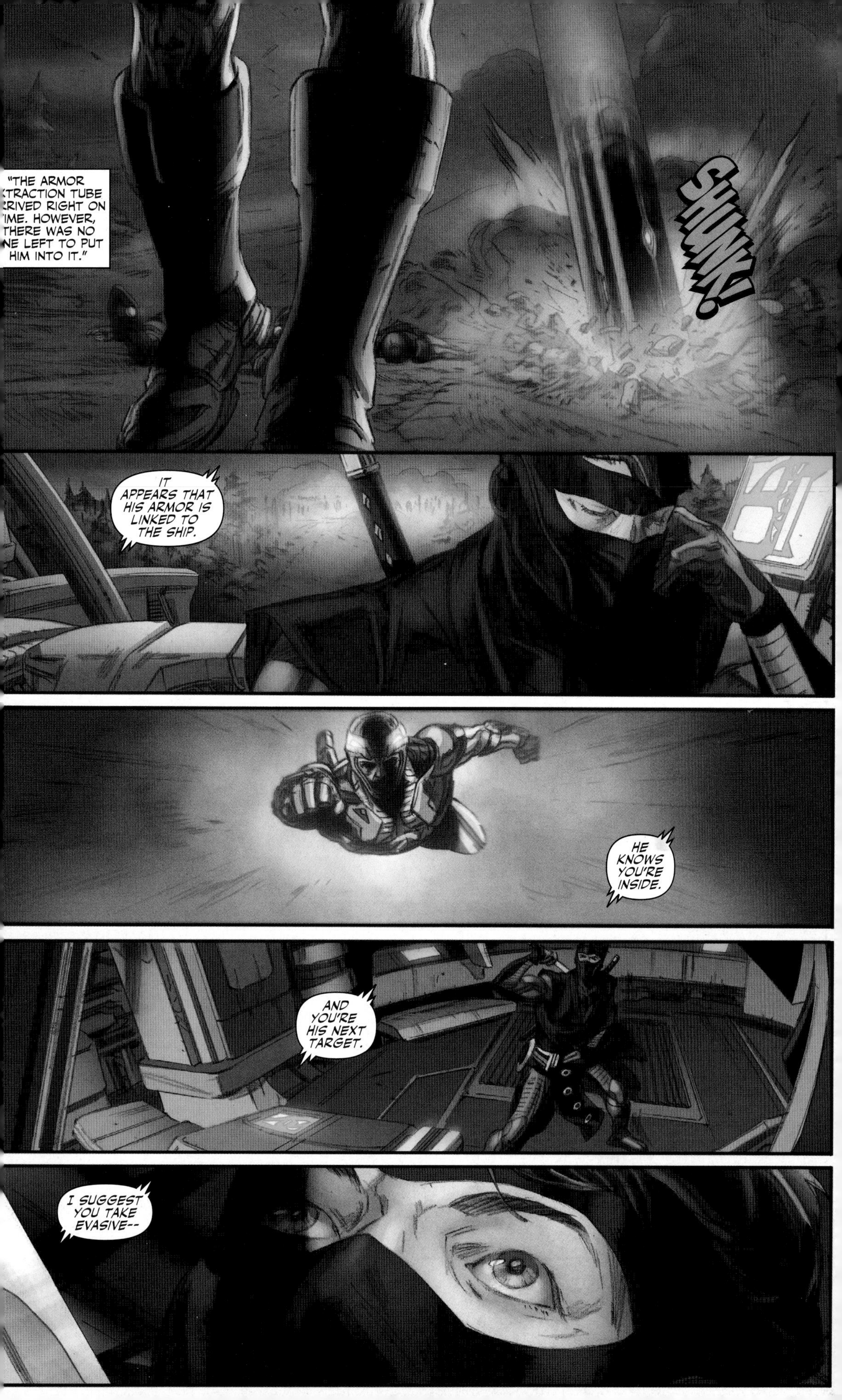
"THE ARMOR
XTRACTION TUBE
RRIVED RIGHT ON
TIME. HOWEVER,
THERE WAS NO
NE LEFT TO PUT
HIM INTO IT."
SHUNK!
IT APPEARS THAT HIS ARMOR IS LINKED TO THE SHIP.
HE KNOWS YOU'RE INSIDE.
AND YOU'RE HIS NEXT TARGET.
I SUGGEST YOU TAKE EVASIVE--

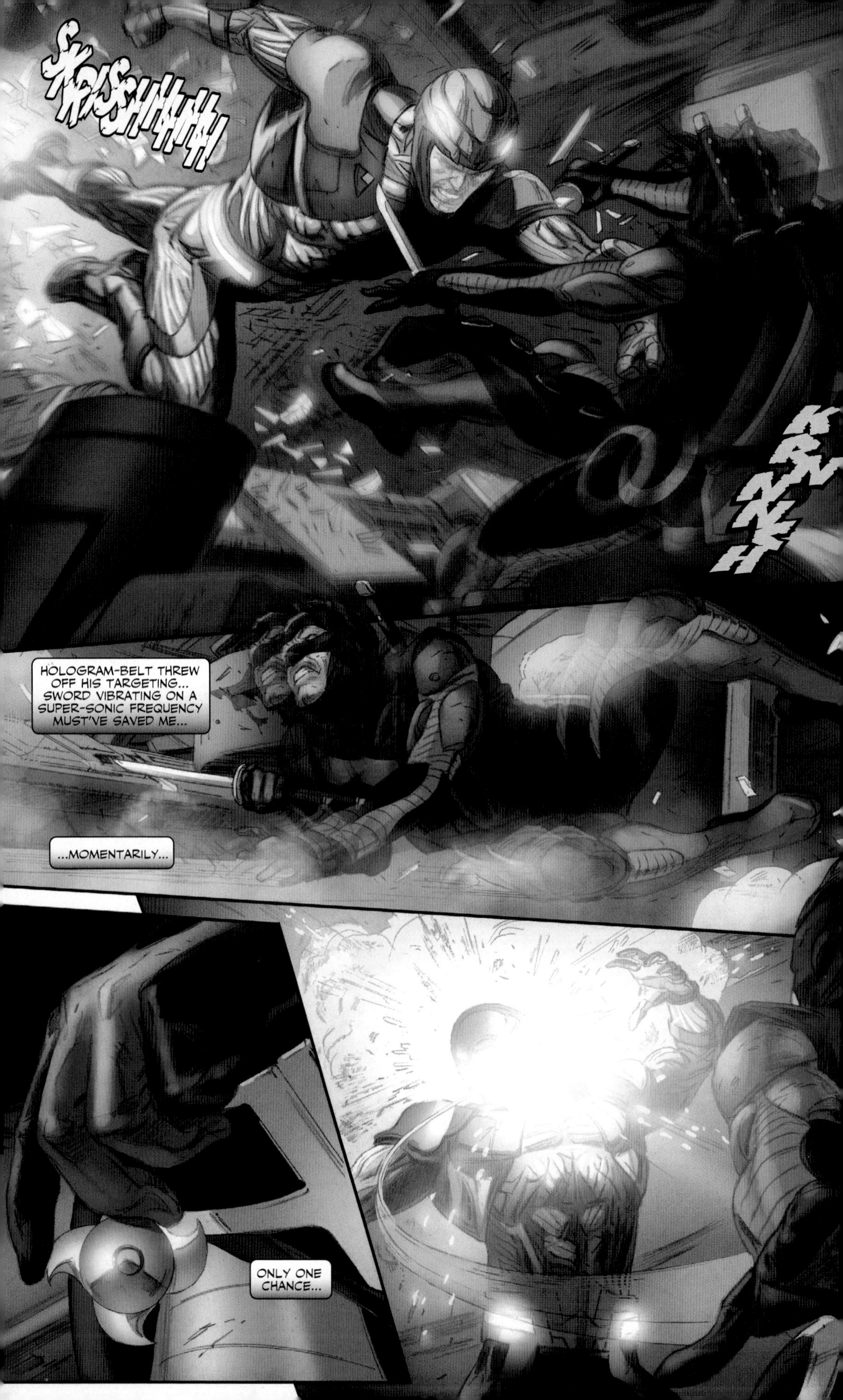
SKRISHHHHH!
KRNNKH
HOLOGRAM-BELT THREW OFF HIS TARGETING... SWORD VIBRATING ON A SUPER-SONIC FREQUENCY MUST'VE SAVED ME...
...MOMENTARILY...
ONLY ONE CHANCE...

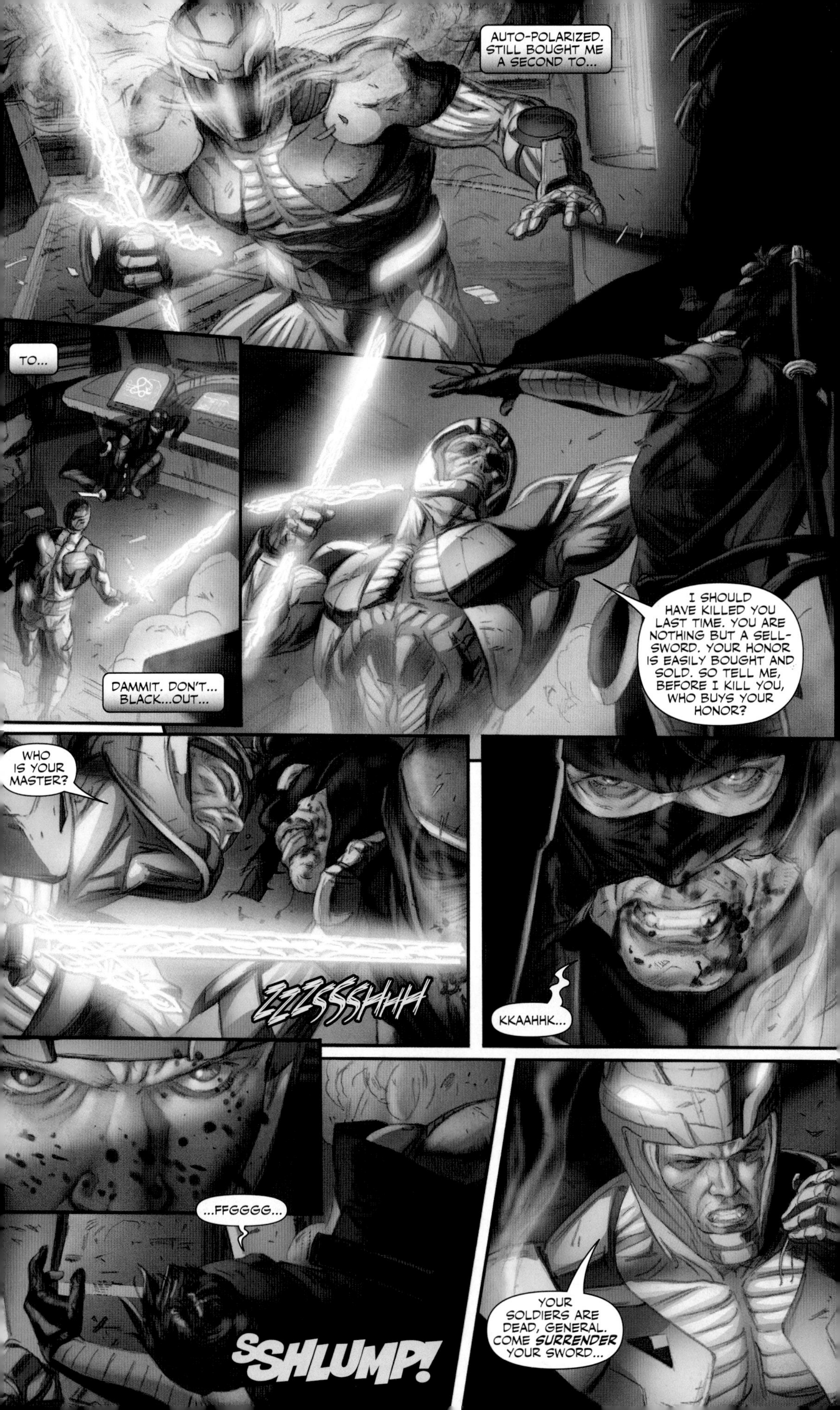

AUTO-POLARIZED. STILL BOUGHT ME A SECOND TO...
TO...
DAMMIT. DON'T... BLACK...OUT...
I SHOULD HAVE KILLED YOU LAST TIME. YOU ARE NOTHING BUT A SELL-SWORD. YOUR HONOR IS EASILY BOUGHT AND SOLD. SO TELL ME, BEFORE I KILL YOU, WHO BUYS YOUR HONOR?
WHO IS YOUR MASTER?
ZZZSSSHHH
KKAAHHK...
...FFGGGG...
SSHLUMP!
YOUR SOLDIERS ARE DEAD, GENERAL. COME SURRENDER YOUR SWORD...

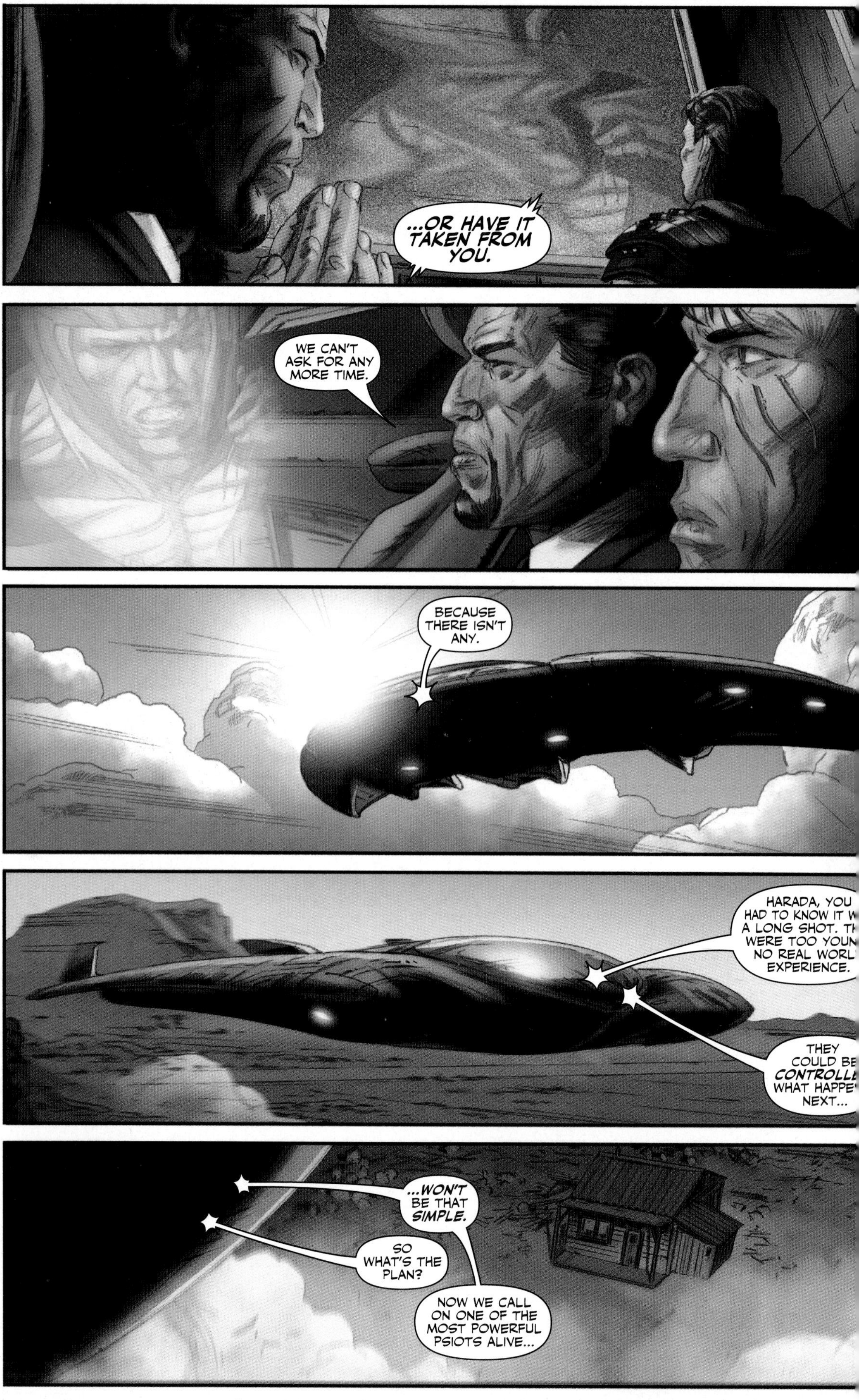
...OR HAVE IT TAKEN FROM YOU.
WE CAN'T ASK FOR ANY MORE TIME.
BECAUSE THERE ISN'T ANY.
HARADA, YOU HAD TO KNOW IT W A LONG SHOT. TH WERE TOO YOUN NO REAL WORL EXPERIENCE.
THEY COULD BE CONTROLLE WHAT HAPPE NEXT...
...WON'T BE THAT SIMPLE.
SO WHAT'S THE PLAN?
NOW WE CALL ON ONE OF THE MOST POWERFUL PSIOTS ALIVE...

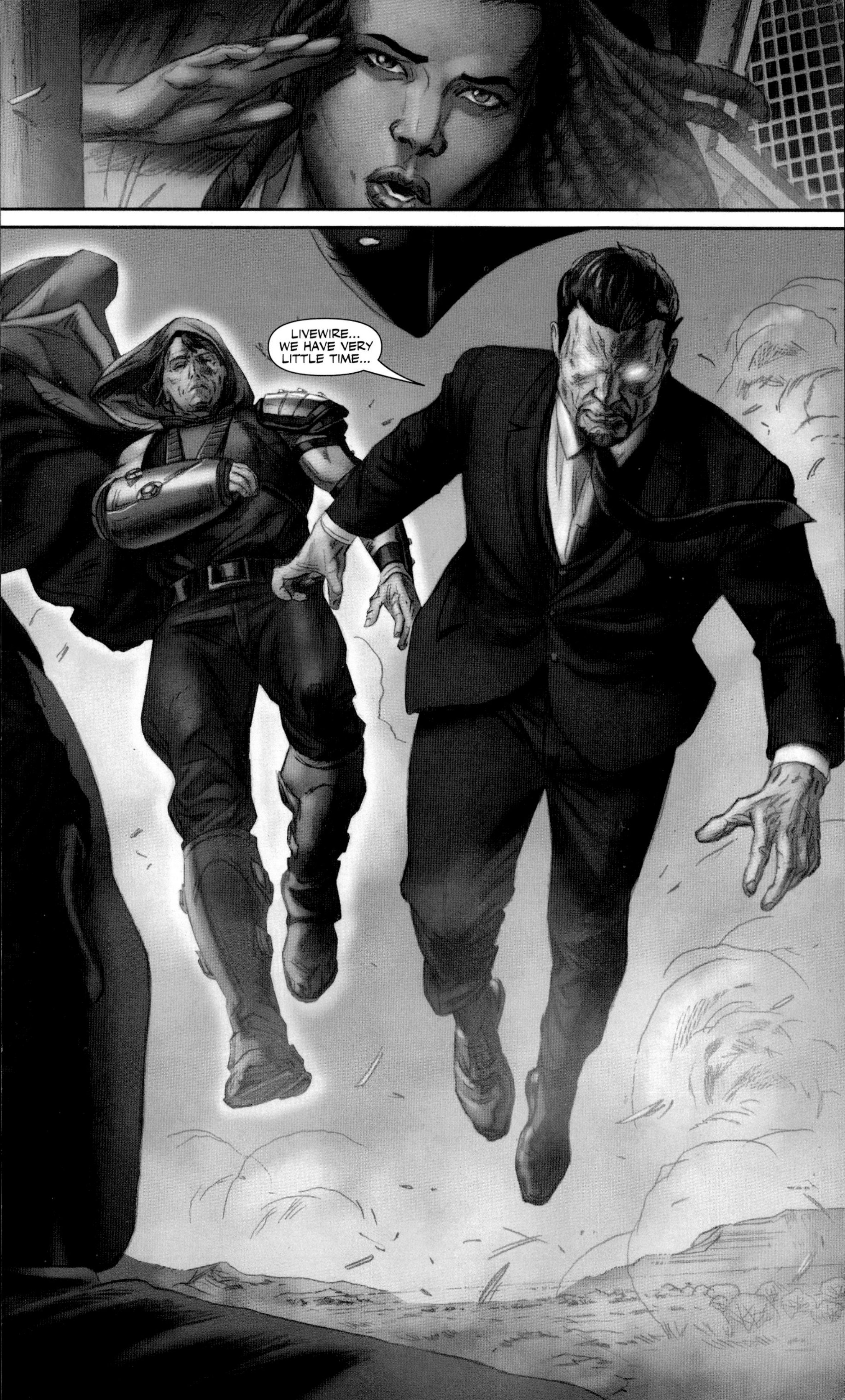
LIVEWIRE... WE HAVE VERY LITTLE TIME...

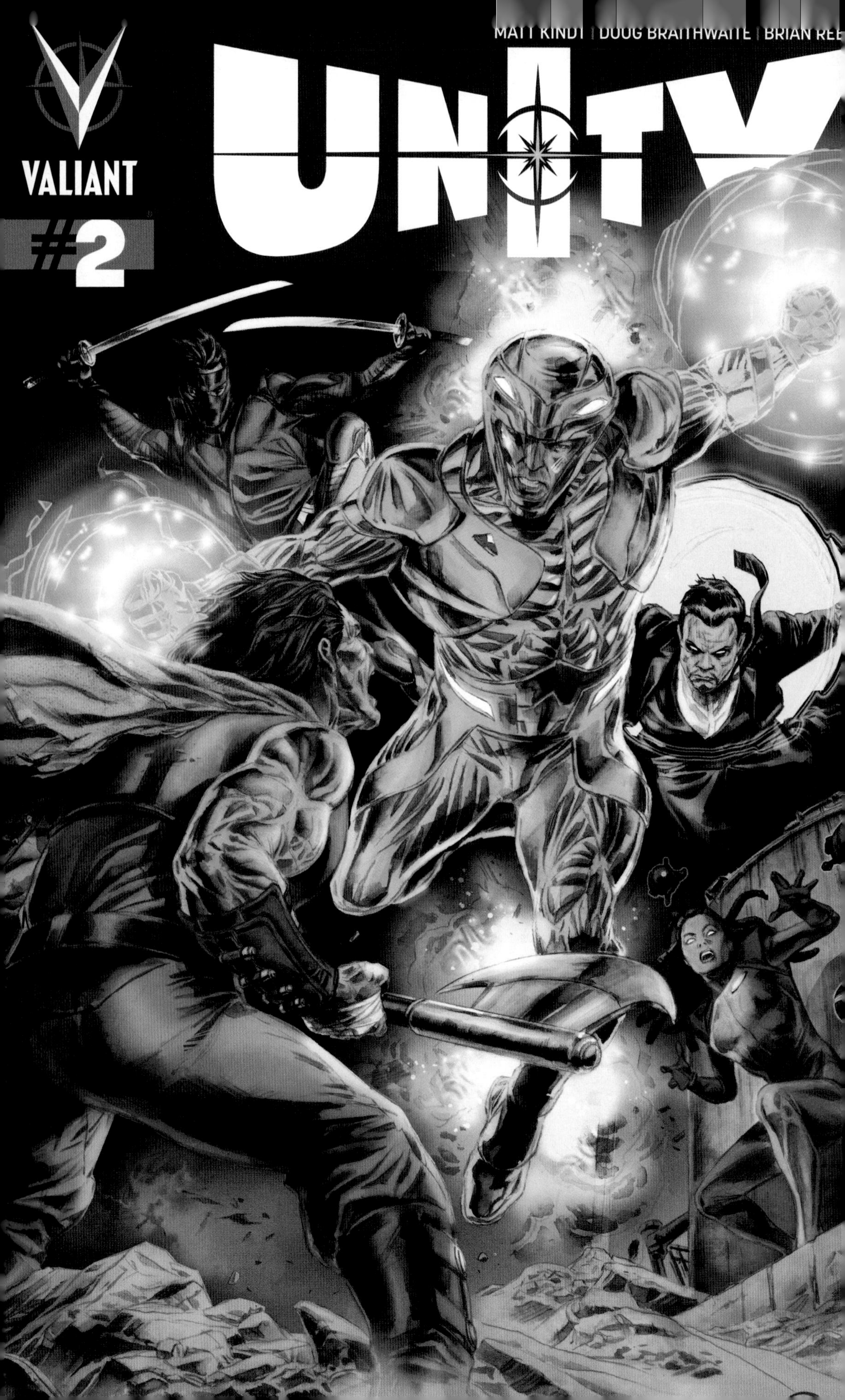
MATT KINDT | DOUG BRAITHWAITE
VALIANT
UNITY
#2

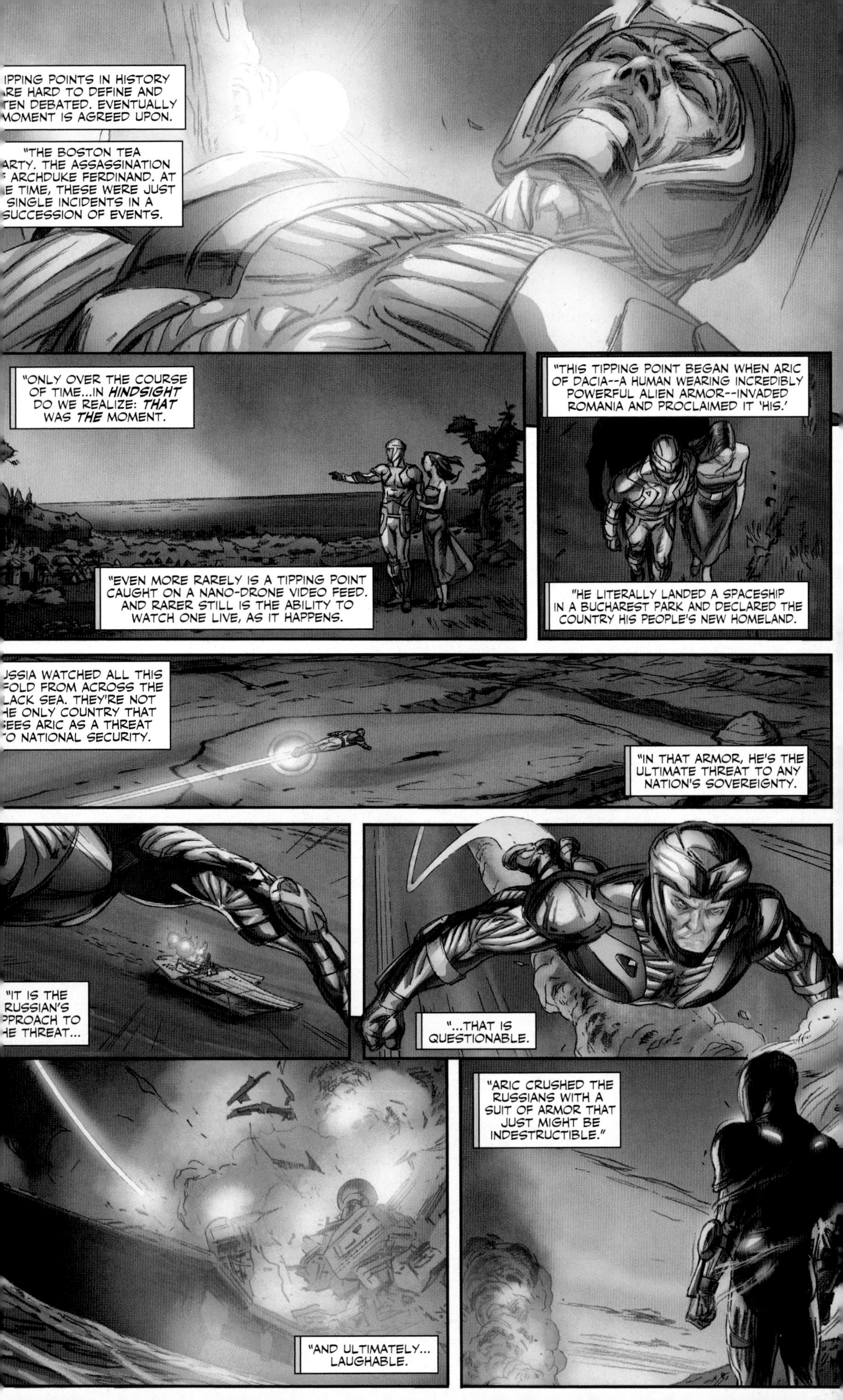

IPPING POINTS IN HISTORY
RE HARD TO DEFINE AND
TEN DEBATED. EVENTUALLY
MOMENT IS AGREED UPON.
"THE BOSTON TEA
ARTY. THE ASSASSINATION
F ARCHDUKE FERDINAND. AT
E TIME, THESE WERE JUST
SINGLE INCIDENTS IN A
SUCCESSION OF EVENTS.
"ONLY OVER THE COURSE OF TIME...IN *HINDSIGHT* DO WE REALIZE: *THAT* WAS *THE* MOMENT.
"EVEN MORE RARELY IS A TIPPING POINT CAUGHT ON A NANO-DRONE VIDEO FEED. AND RARER STILL IS THE ABILITY TO WATCH ONE LIVE, AS IT HAPPENS.
"THIS TIPPING POINT BEGAN WHEN ARIC OF DACIA--A HUMAN WEARING INCREDIBLY POWERFUL ALIEN ARMOR--INVADED ROMANIA AND PROCLAIMED IT 'HIS.'
"HE LITERALLY LANDED A SPACESHIP IN A BUCHAREST PARK AND DECLARED THE COUNTRY HIS PEOPLE'S NEW HOMELAND.
JSSIA WATCHED ALL THIS
FOLD FROM ACROSS THE
LACK SEA. THEY'RE NOT
HE ONLY COUNTRY THAT
EES ARIC AS A THREAT
O NATIONAL SECURITY.
"IN THAT ARMOR, HE'S THE ULTIMATE THREAT TO ANY NATION'S SOVEREIGNTY.
"IT IS THE
RUSSIAN'S
PPROACH TO
HE THREAT...
"...THAT IS QUESTIONABLE.
"AND ULTIMATELY... LAUGHABLE.
"ARIC CRUSHED THE RUSSIANS WITH A SUIT OF ARMOR THAT JUST MIGHT BE INDESTRUCTIBLE."

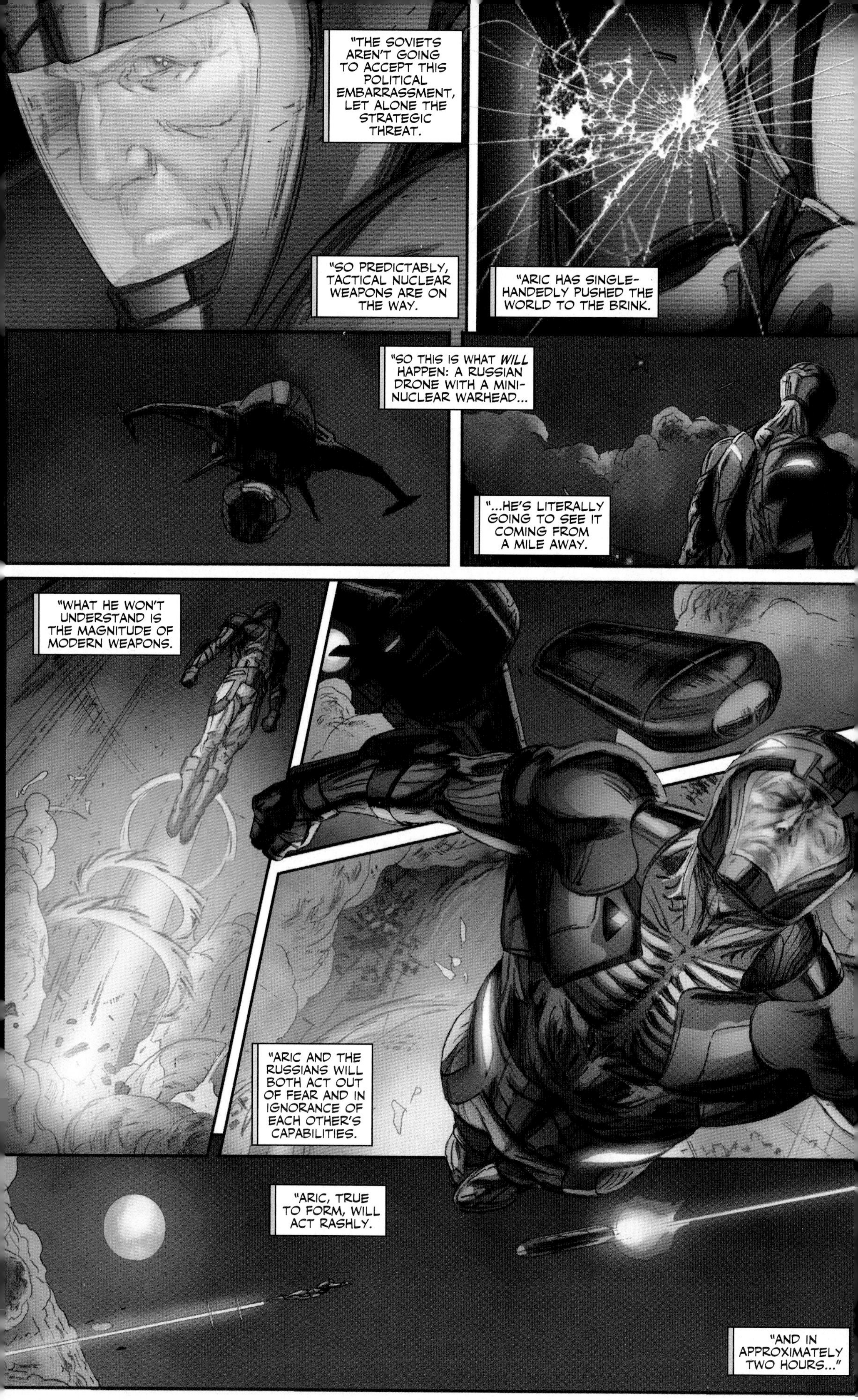
"THE SOVIETS AREN'T GOING TO ACCEPT THIS POLITICAL EMBARRASSMENT, LET ALONE THE STRATEGIC THREAT.
"SO PREDICTABLY, TACTICAL NUCLEAR WEAPONS ARE ON THE WAY.
"ARIC HAS SINGLE-HANDEDLY PUSHED THE WORLD TO THE BRINK.
"SO THIS IS WHAT *WILL* HAPPEN: A RUSSIAN DRONE WITH A MINI-NUCLEAR WARHEAD...
"...HE'S LITERALLY GOING TO SEE IT COMING FROM A MILE AWAY.
"WHAT HE WON'T UNDERSTAND IS THE MAGNITUDE OF MODERN WEAPONS.
"ARIC AND THE RUSSIANS WILL BOTH ACT OUT OF FEAR AND IN IGNORANCE OF EACH OTHER'S CAPABILITIES.
"ARIC, TRUE TO FORM, WILL ACT RASHLY.
"AND IN APPROXIMATELY TWO HOURS..."

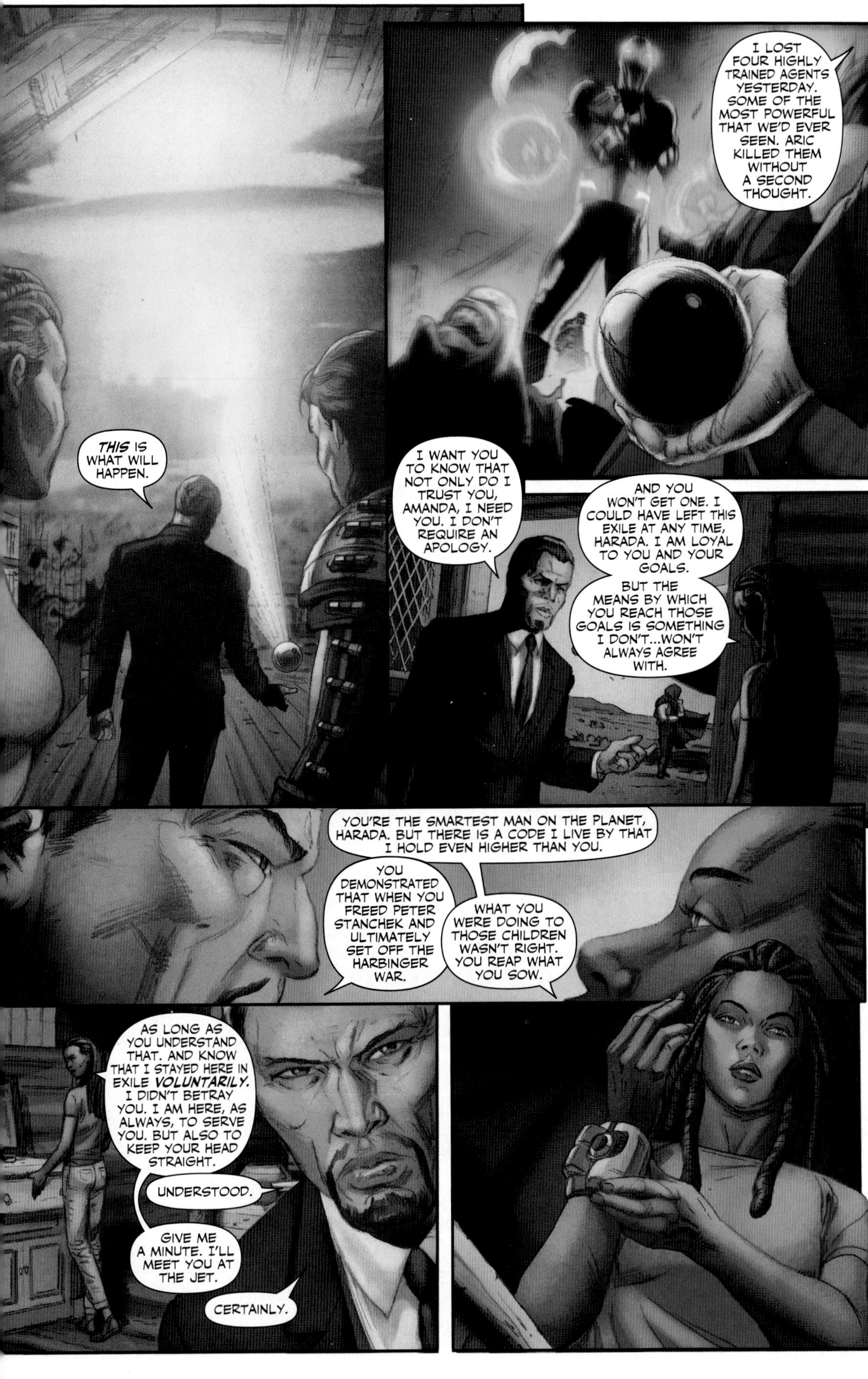
I LOST FOUR HIGHLY TRAINED AGENTS YESTERDAY. SOME OF THE MOST POWERFUL THAT WE'D EVER SEEN. ARIC KILLED THEM WITHOUT A SECOND THOUGHT.
THIS IS WHAT WILL HAPPEN.
I WANT YOU TO KNOW THAT NOT ONLY DO I TRUST YOU, AMANDA, I NEED YOU. I DON'T REQUIRE AN APOLOGY.
AND YOU WON'T GET ONE. I COULD HAVE LEFT THIS EXILE AT ANY TIME, HARADA. I AM LOYAL TO YOU AND YOUR GOALS.
BUT THE MEANS BY WHICH YOU REACH THOSE GOALS IS SOMETHING I DON'T...WON'T ALWAYS AGREE WITH.
YOU'RE THE SMARTEST MAN ON THE PLANET, HARADA. BUT THERE IS A CODE I LIVE BY THAT I HOLD EVEN HIGHER THAN YOU.
YOU DEMONSTRATED THAT WHEN YOU FREED PETER STANCHEK AND ULTIMATELY SET OFF THE HARBINGER WAR.
WHAT YOU WERE DOING TO THOSE CHILDREN WASN'T RIGHT. YOU REAP WHAT YOU SOW.
AS LONG AS YOU UNDERSTAND THAT. AND KNOW THAT I STAYED HERE IN EXILE VOLUNTARILY. I DIDN'T BETRAY YOU. I AM HERE, AS ALWAYS, TO SERVE YOU. BUT ALSO TO KEEP YOUR HEAD STRAIGHT.
UNDERSTOOD.
GIVE ME A MINUTE. I'LL MEET YOU AT THE JET.
CERTAINLY.

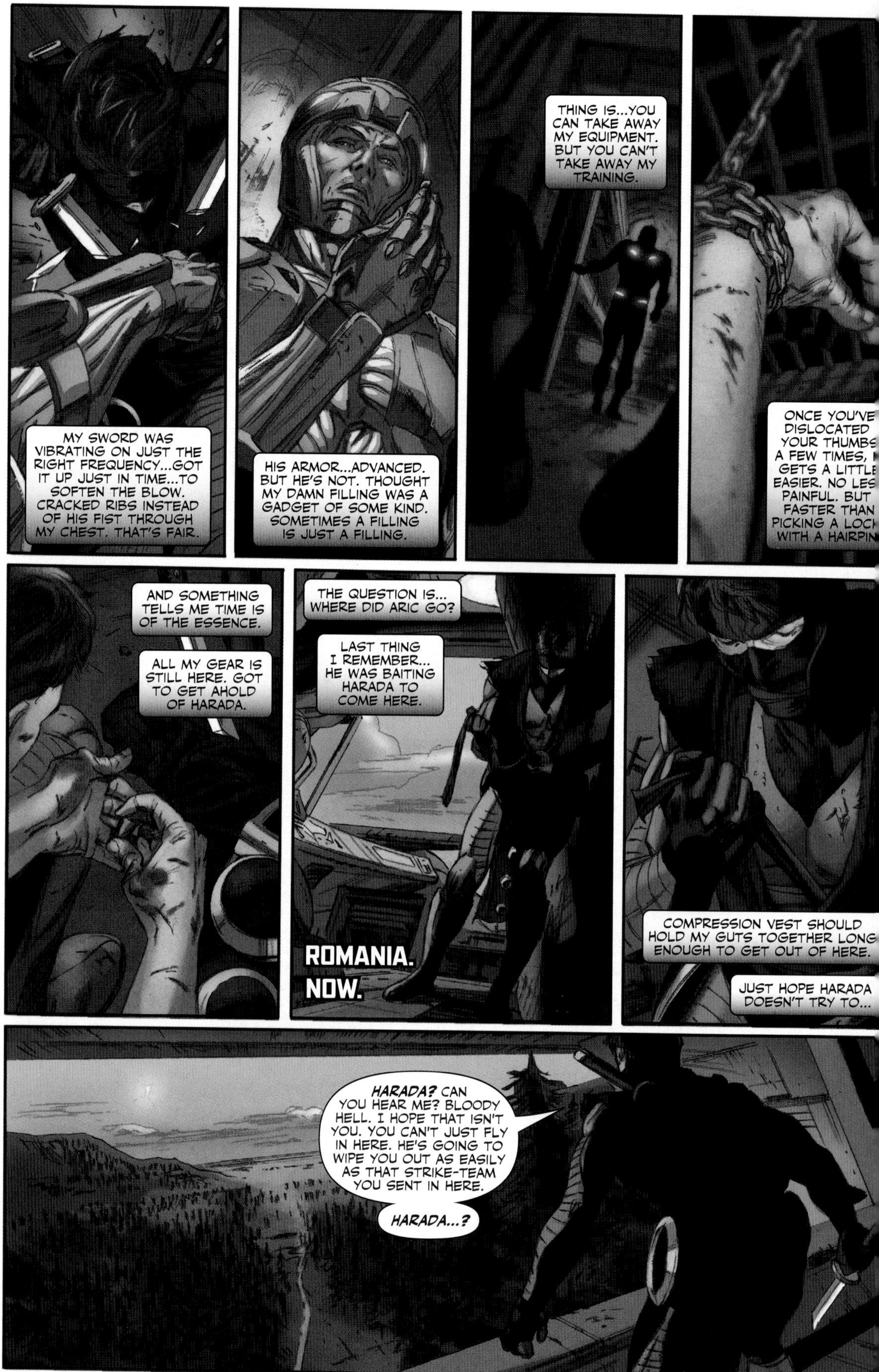
MY SWORD WAS VIBRATING ON JUST THE RIGHT FREQUENCY...GOT IT UP JUST IN TIME...TO SOFTEN THE BLOW. CRACKED RIBS INSTEAD OF HIS FIST THROUGH MY CHEST. THAT'S FAIR.
HIS ARMOR...ADVANCED. BUT HE'S NOT. THOUGHT MY DAMN FILLING WAS A GADGET OF SOME KIND. SOMETIMES A FILLING IS JUST A FILLING.
THING IS...YOU CAN TAKE AWAY MY EQUIPMENT. BUT YOU CAN'T TAKE AWAY MY TRAINING.
ONCE YOU'VE DISLOCATED YOUR THUMBS A FEW TIMES, GETS A LITTLE EASIER. NO LES PAINFUL. BUT FASTER THAN PICKING A LOCK WITH A HAIRPIN
AND SOMETHING TELLS ME TIME IS OF THE ESSENCE.
ALL MY GEAR IS STILL HERE. GOT TO GET AHOLD OF HARADA.
THE QUESTION IS... WHERE DID ARIC GO?
LAST THING I REMEMBER... HE WAS BAITING HARADA TO COME HERE.
ROMANIA. NOW.
COMPRESSION VEST SHOULD HOLD MY GUTS TOGETHER LONG ENOUGH TO GET OUT OF HERE.
JUST HOPE HARADA DOESN'T TRY TO...
HARADA? CAN YOU HEAR ME? BLOODY HELL. I HOPE THAT ISN'T YOU. YOU CAN'T JUST FLY IN HERE. HE'S GOING TO WIPE YOU OUT AS EASILY AS THAT STRIKE-TEAM YOU SENT IN HERE.
HARADA...?

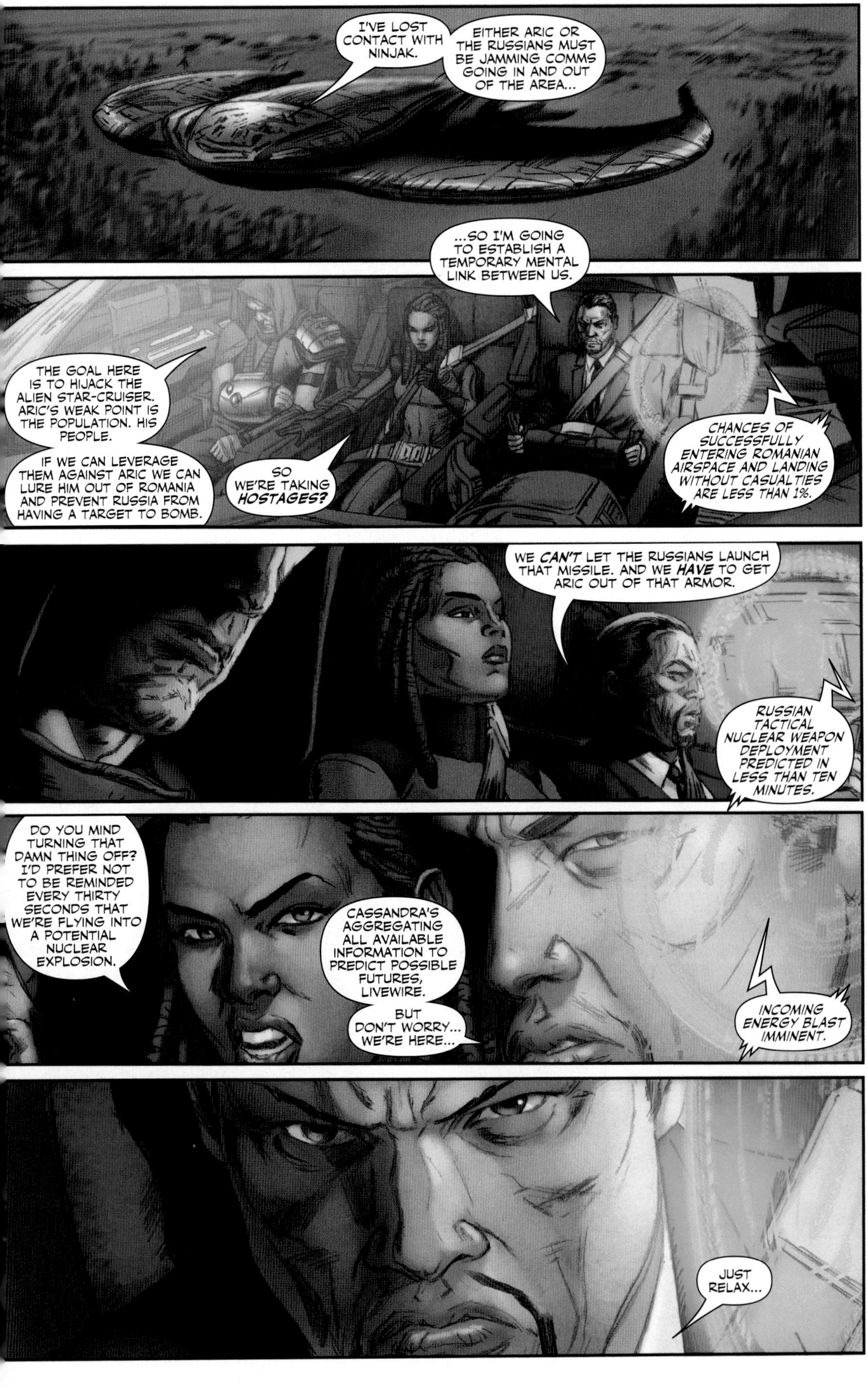
I'VE LOST CONTACT WITH NINJAK.
EITHER ARIC OR THE RUSSIANS MUST BE JAMMING COMMS GOING IN AND OUT OF THE AREA...
...SO I'M GOING TO ESTABLISH A TEMPORARY MENTAL LINK BETWEEN US.
THE GOAL HERE IS TO HIJACK THE ALIEN STAR-CRUISER. ARIC'S WEAK POINT IS THE POPULATION. HIS PEOPLE.
IF WE CAN LEVERAGE THEM AGAINST ARIC WE CAN LURE HIM OUT OF ROMANIA AND PREVENT RUSSIA FROM HAVING A TARGET TO BOMB.
SO WE'RE TAKING ***HOSTAGES?***
CHANCES OF SUCCESSFULLY ENTERING ROMANIAN AIRSPACE AND LANDING WITHOUT CASUALTIES ARE LESS THAN 1%.
WE ***CAN'T*** LET THE RUSSIANS LAUNCH THAT MISSILE. AND WE ***HAVE*** TO GET ARIC OUT OF THAT ARMOR.
RUSSIAN TACTICAL NUCLEAR WEAPON DEPLOYMENT PREDICTED IN LESS THAN TEN MINUTES.
DO YOU MIND TURNING THAT DAMN THING OFF? I'D PREFER NOT TO BE REMINDED EVERY THIRTY SECONDS THAT WE'RE FLYING INTO A POTENTIAL NUCLEAR EXPLOSION.
CASSANDRA'S AGGREGATING ALL AVAILABLE INFORMATION TO PREDICT POSSIBLE FUTURES, LIVEWIRE.
BUT DON'T WORRY... WE'RE HERE...
INCOMING ENERGY BLAST IMMINENT.
JUST RELAX...

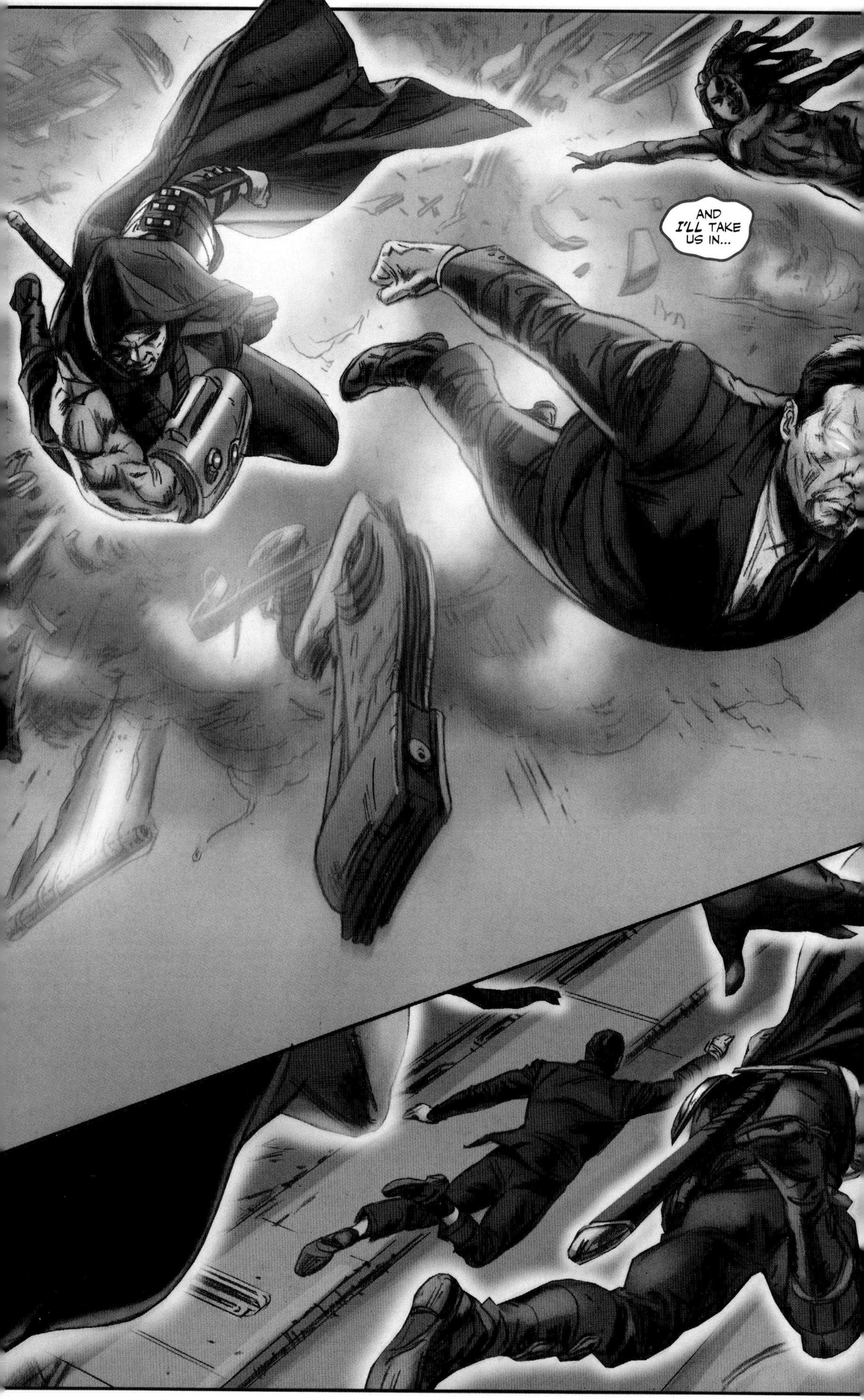
AND I'LL TAKE US IN...

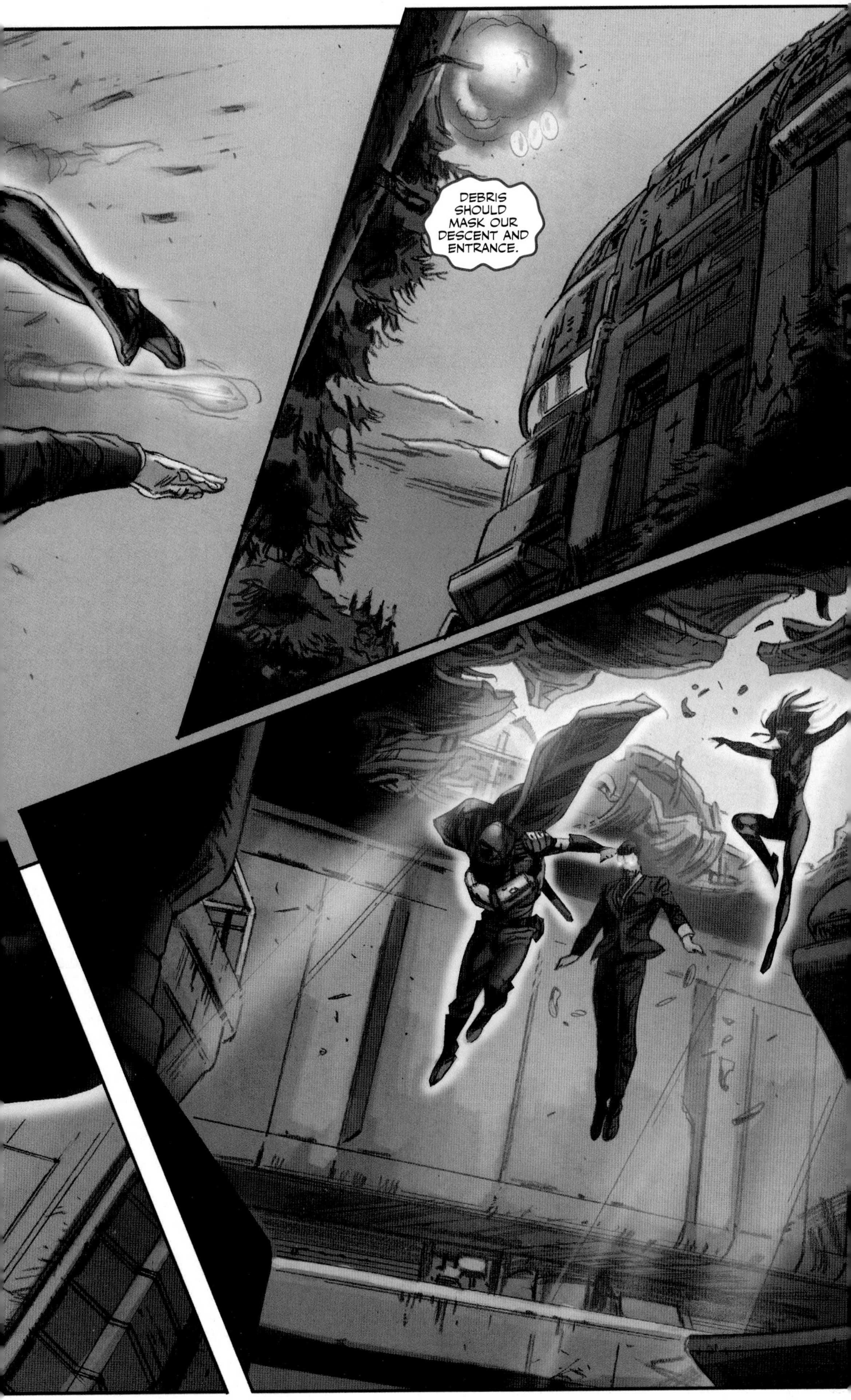
DEBRIS SHOULD MASK OUR DESCENT AND ENTRANCE.

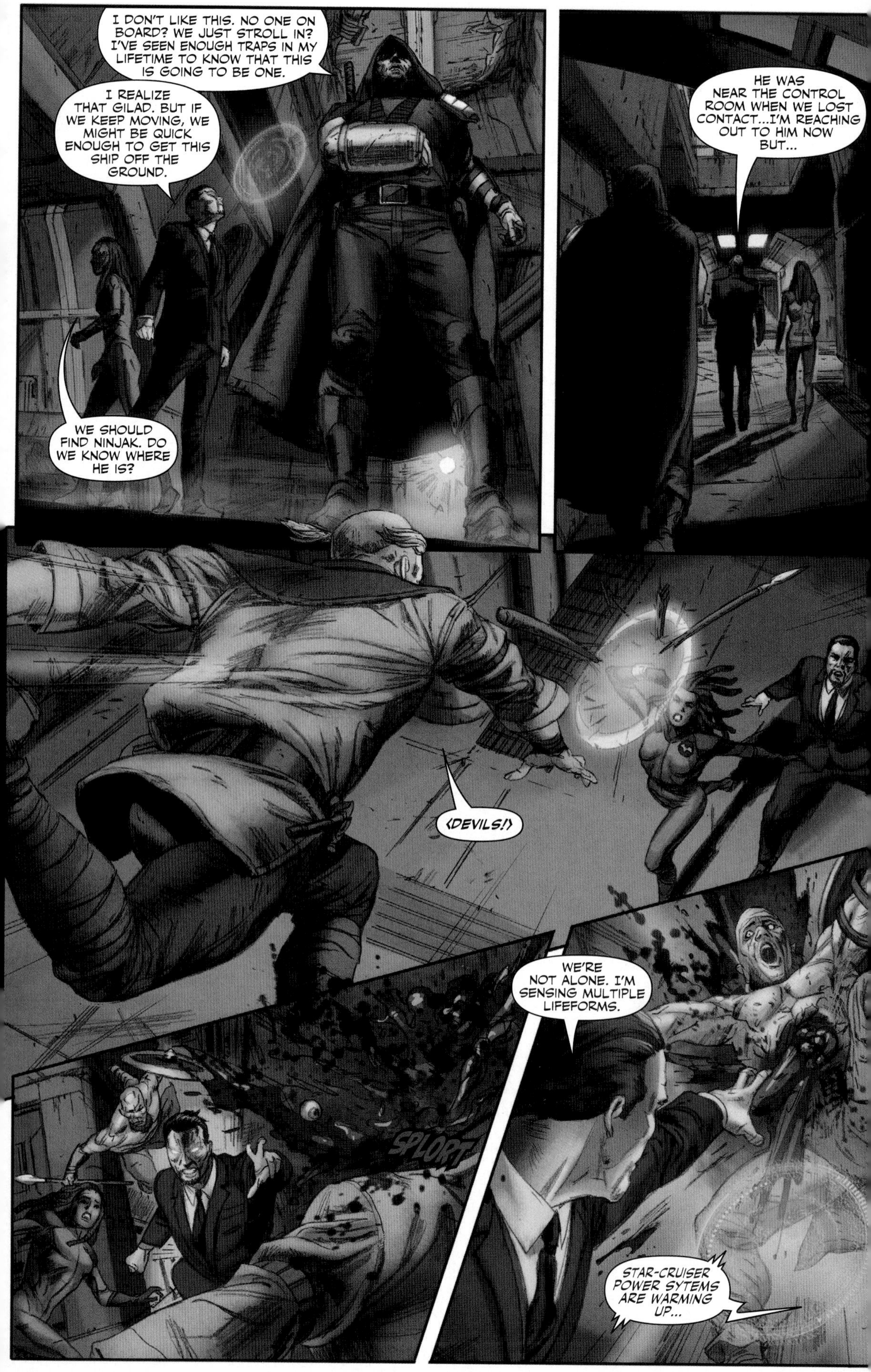
I DON'T LIKE THIS. NO ONE ON BOARD? WE JUST STROLL IN? I'VE SEEN ENOUGH TRAPS IN MY LIFETIME TO KNOW THAT THIS IS GOING TO BE ONE.
I REALIZE THAT GILAD. BUT IF WE KEEP MOVING, WE MIGHT BE QUICK ENOUGH TO GET THIS SHIP OFF THE GROUND.
WE SHOULD FIND NINJAK. DO WE KNOW WHERE HE IS?
HE WAS NEAR THE CONTROL ROOM WHEN WE LOST CONTACT...I'M REACHING OUT TO HIM NOW BUT...
‹DEVILS!›
SPLORT
WE'RE NOT ALONE. I'M SENSING MULTIPLE LIFEFORMS.
STAR-CRUISER POWER SYTEMS ARE WARMING UP...

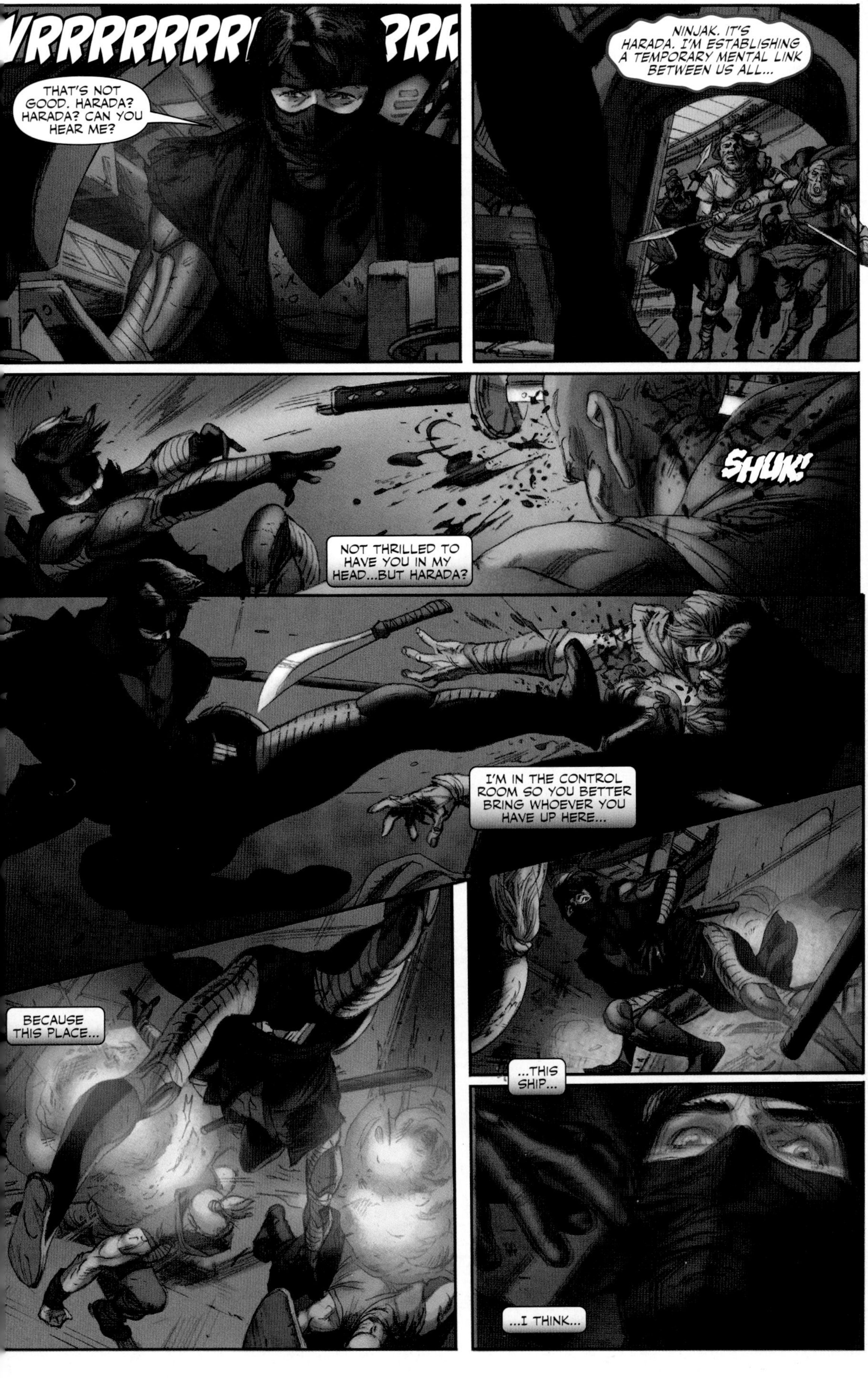
VRRRRRRRRR ?RR
THAT'S NOT GOOD. HARADA? HARADA? CAN YOU HEAR ME?
NINJAK. IT'S HARADA. I'M ESTABLISHING A TEMPORARY MENTAL LINK BETWEEN US ALL...
SHUK!
NOT THRILLED TO HAVE YOU IN MY HEAD...BUT HARADA?
I'M IN THE CONTROL ROOM SO YOU BETTER BRING WHOEVER YOU HAVE UP HERE...
BECAUSE THIS PLACE...
...THIS SHIP...
...I THINK...

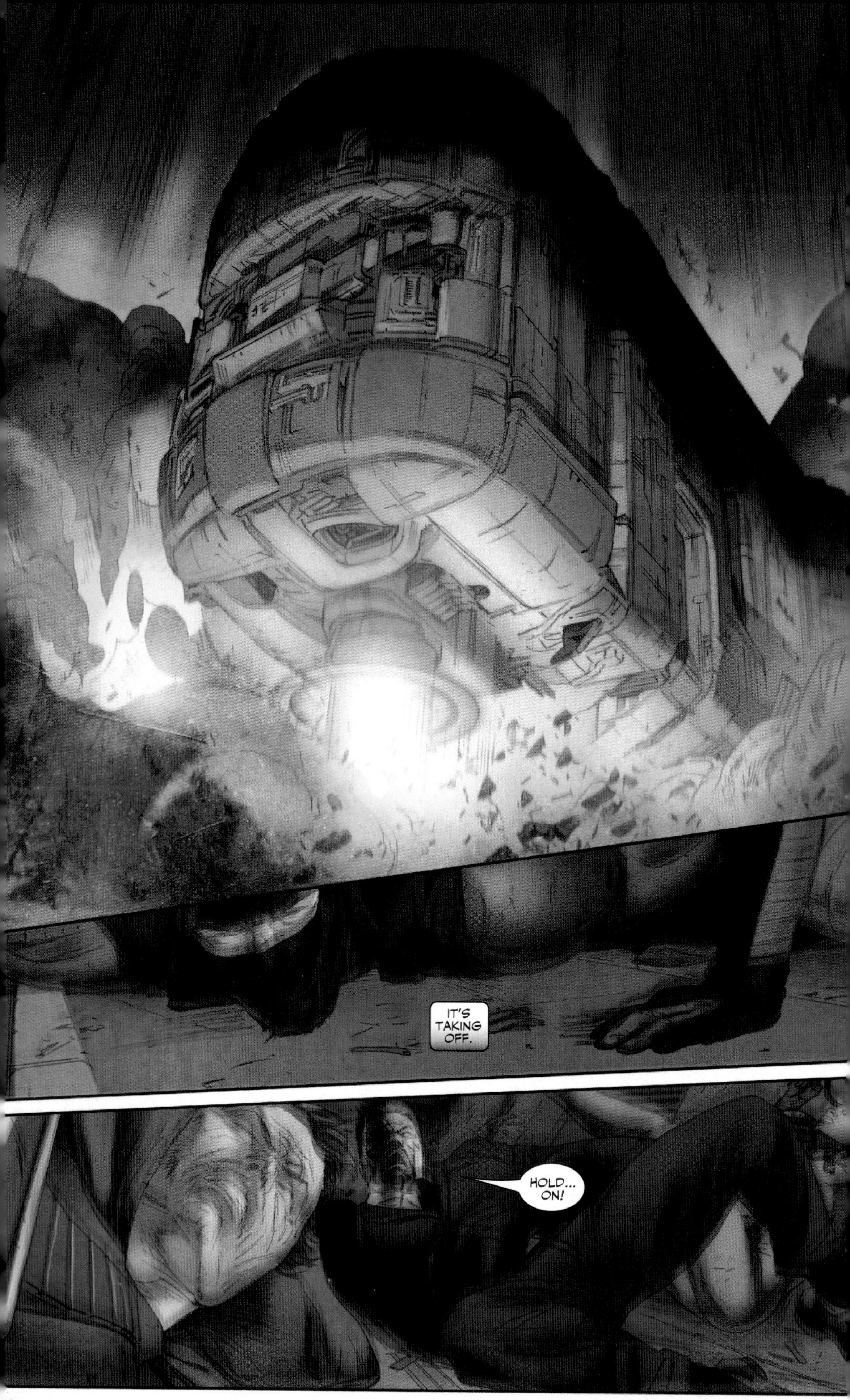
IT'S TAKING OFF.
HOLD... ON!

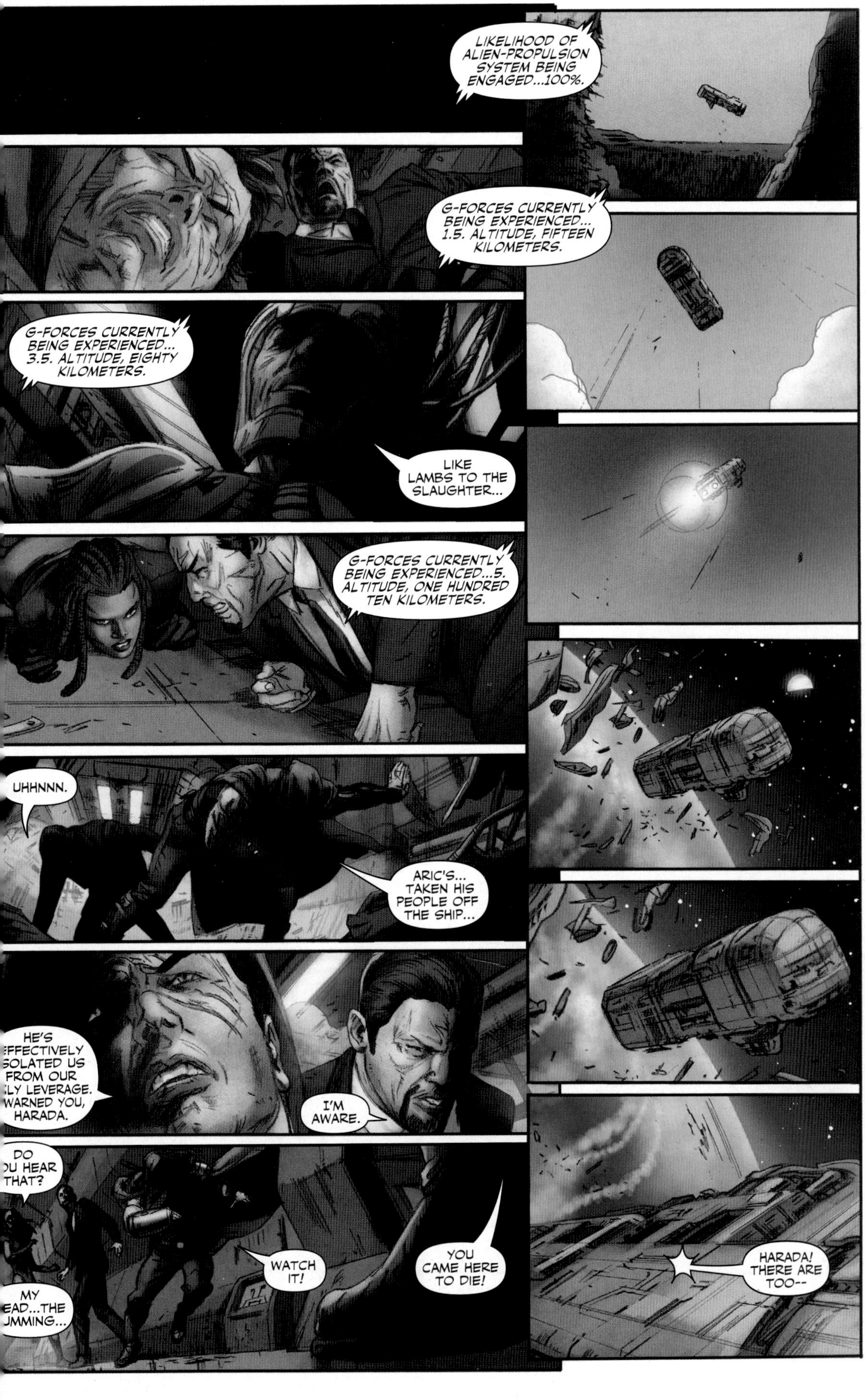

LIKELIHOOD OF ALIEN-PROPULSION SYSTEM BEING ENGAGED...100%.
G-FORCES CURRENTLY BEING EXPERIENCED... 1.5. ALTITUDE, FIFTEEN KILOMETERS.
G-FORCES CURRENTLY BEING EXPERIENCED... 3.5. ALTITUDE, EIGHTY KILOMETERS.
LIKE LAMBS TO THE SLAUGHTER...
G-FORCES CURRENTLY BEING EXPERIENCED...5. ALTITUDE, ONE HUNDRED TEN KILOMETERS.
UHHNNN.
ARIC'S... TAKEN HIS PEOPLE OFF THE SHIP...
HE'S EFFECTIVELY ISOLATED US FROM OUR LY LEVERAGE. WARNED YOU, HARADA.
I'M AWARE.
DO OU HEAR THAT?
MY EAD...THE UMMING...
WATCH IT!
YOU CAME HERE TO DIE!
HARADA! THERE ARE TOO--

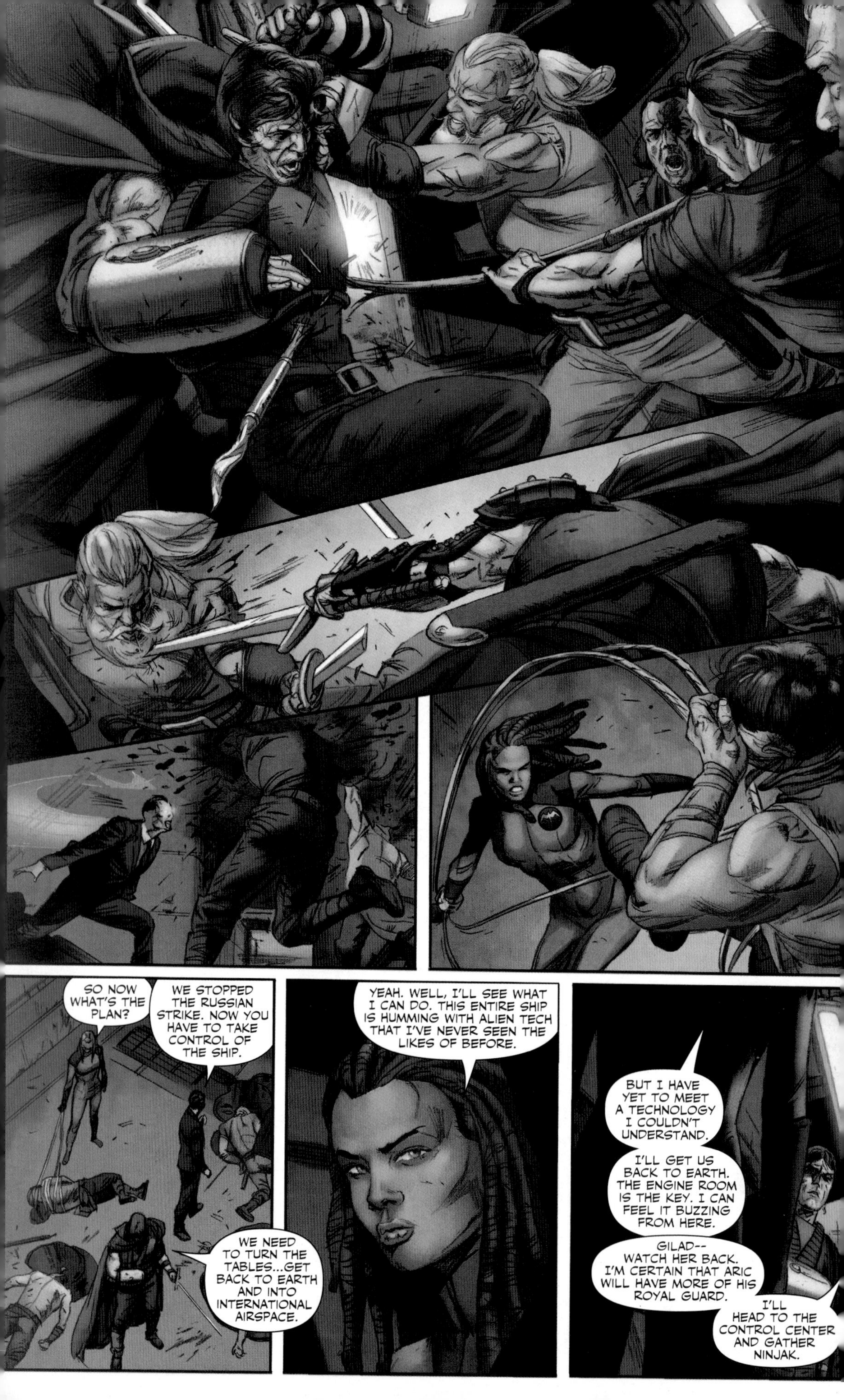
SO NOW WHAT'S THE PLAN?
WE STOPPED THE RUSSIAN STRIKE. NOW YOU HAVE TO TAKE CONTROL OF THE SHIP.
WE NEED TO TURN THE TABLES...GET BACK TO EARTH AND INTO INTERNATIONAL AIRSPACE.
YEAH. WELL, I'LL SEE WHAT I CAN DO. THIS ENTIRE SHIP IS HUMMING WITH ALIEN TECH THAT I'VE NEVER SEEN THE LIKES OF BEFORE.
BUT I HAVE YET TO MEET A TECHNOLOGY I COULDN'T UNDERSTAND.
I'LL GET US BACK TO EARTH. THE ENGINE ROOM IS THE KEY. I CAN FEEL IT BUZZING FROM HERE.
GILAD-- WATCH HER BACK. I'M CERTAIN THAT ARIC WILL HAVE MORE OF HIS ROYAL GUARD.
I'LL HEAD TO THE CONTROL CENTER AND GATHER NINJAK.

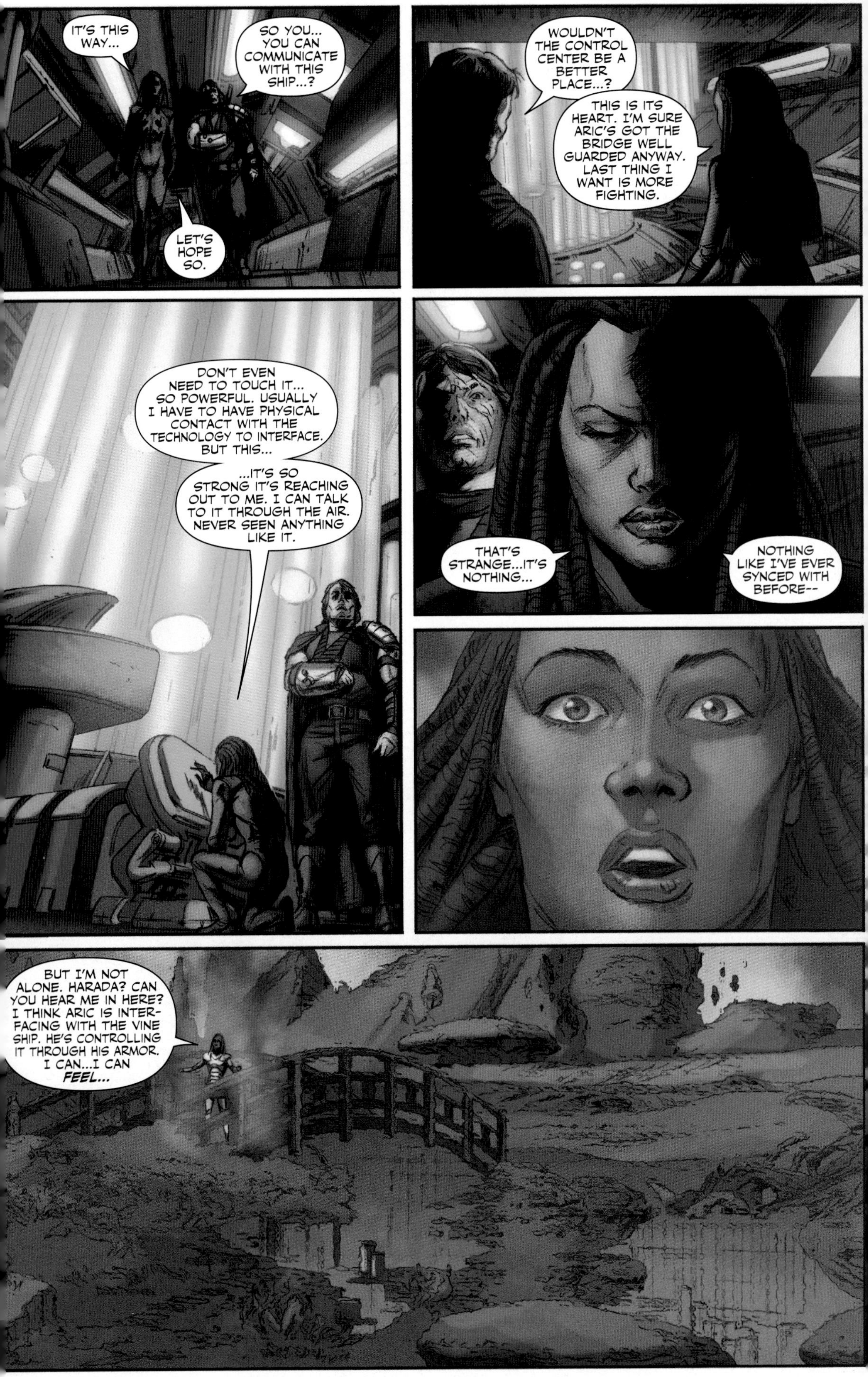

IT'S THIS WAY...
SO YOU... YOU CAN COMMUNICATE WITH THIS SHIP...?
LET'S HOPE SO.
WOULDN'T THE CONTROL CENTER BE A BETTER PLACE...?
THIS IS ITS HEART. I'M SURE ARIC'S GOT THE BRIDGE WELL GUARDED ANYWAY. LAST THING I WANT IS MORE FIGHTING.
DON'T EVEN NEED TO TOUCH IT... SO POWERFUL. USUALLY I HAVE TO HAVE PHYSICAL CONTACT WITH THE TECHNOLOGY TO INTERFACE. BUT THIS...
...IT'S SO STRONG IT'S REACHING OUT TO ME. I CAN TALK TO IT THROUGH THE AIR. NEVER SEEN ANYTHING LIKE IT.
THAT'S STRANGE...IT'S NOTHING...
NOTHING LIKE I'VE EVER SYNCED WITH BEFORE--
BUT I'M NOT ALONE. HARADA? CAN YOU HEAR ME IN HERE? I THINK ARIC IS INTER-FACING WITH THE VINE SHIP. HE'S CONTROLLING IT THROUGH HIS ARMOR. I CAN...I CAN ***FEEL...***

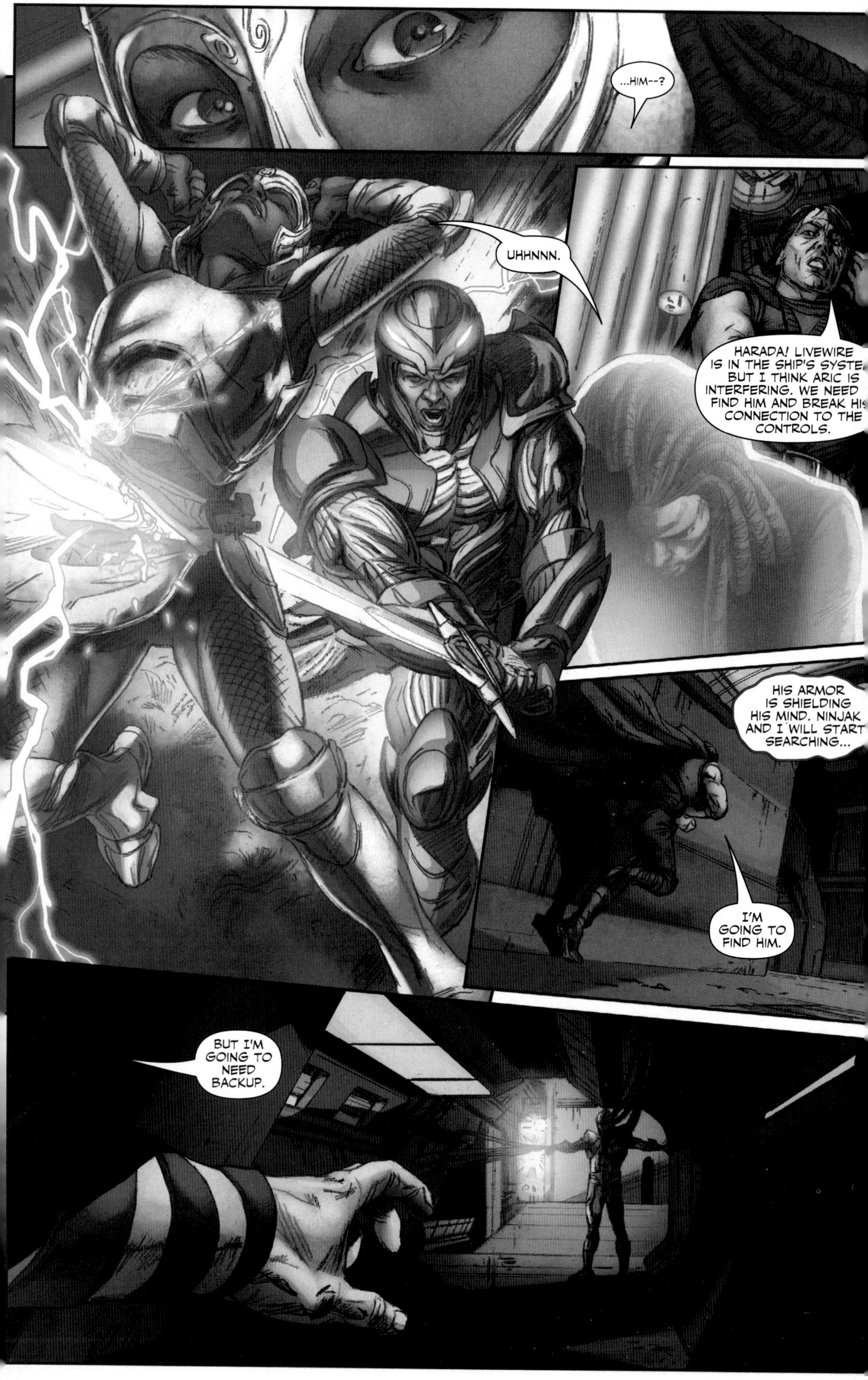
...HIM--?
UHHNNN.
HARADA! LIVEWIRE IS IN THE SHIP'S SYSTE BUT I THINK ARIC IS INTERFERING. WE NEED FIND HIM AND BREAK HIS CONNECTION TO THE CONTROLS.
HIS ARMOR IS SHIELDING HIS MIND. NINJAK AND I WILL START SEARCHING...
I'M GOING TO FIND HIM.
BUT I'M GOING TO NEED BACKUP.

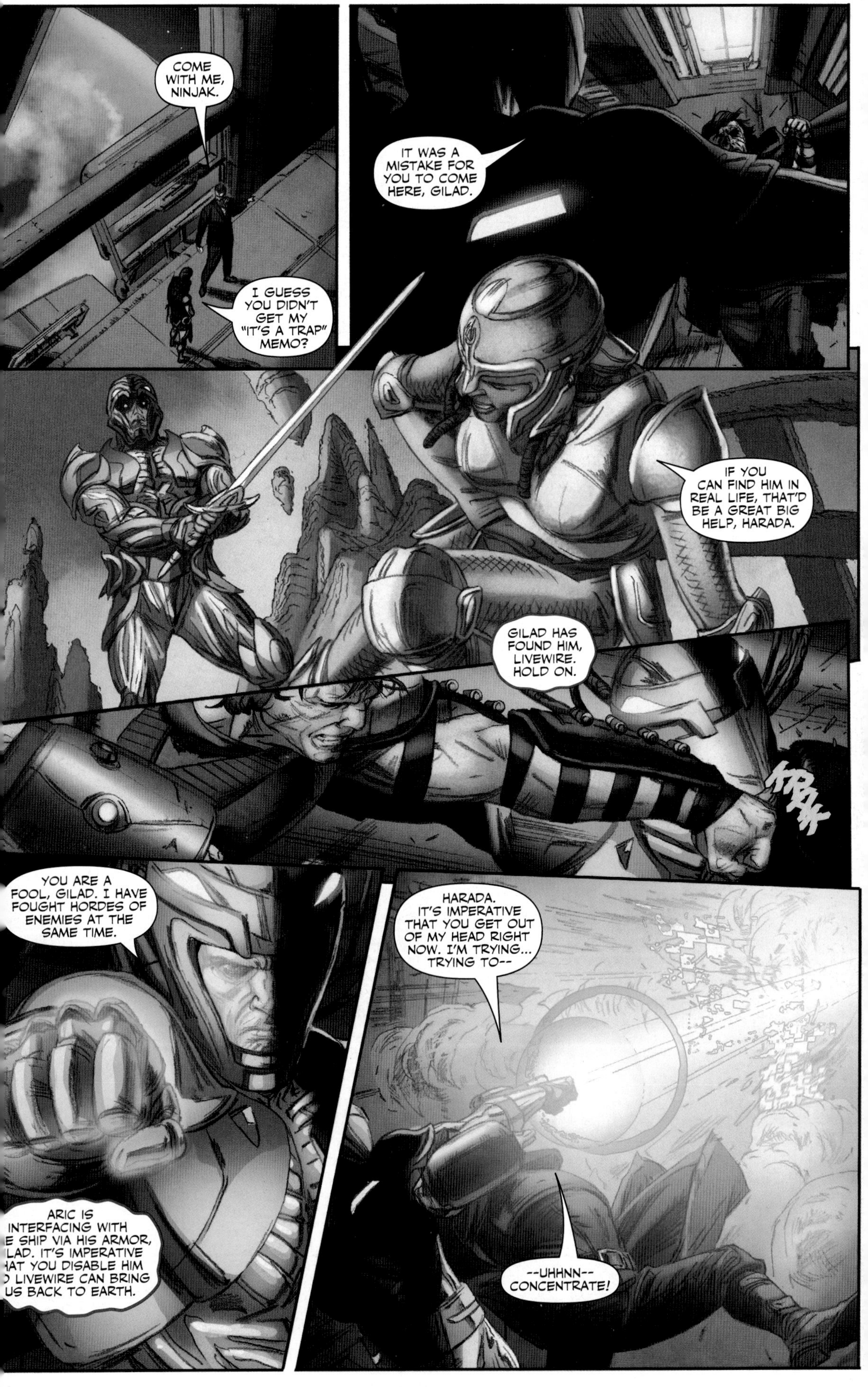
COME WITH ME, NINJAK.
I GUESS YOU DIDN'T GET MY "IT'S A TRAP" MEMO?
IT WAS A MISTAKE FOR YOU TO COME HERE, GILAD.
IF YOU CAN FIND HIM IN REAL LIFE, THAT'D BE A GREAT BIG HELP, HARADA.
GILAD HAS FOUND HIM, LIVEWIRE. HOLD ON.
KRAK
YOU ARE A FOOL, GILAD. I HAVE FOUGHT HORDES OF ENEMIES AT THE SAME TIME.
ARIC IS INTERFACING WITH E SHIP VIA HIS ARMOR, LAD. IT'S IMPERATIVE HAT YOU DISABLE HIM LIVEWIRE CAN BRING US BACK TO EARTH.
HARADA. IT'S IMPERATIVE THAT YOU GET OUT OF MY HEAD RIGHT NOW. I'M TRYING... TRYING TO--
--UHHNN-- CONCENTRATE!

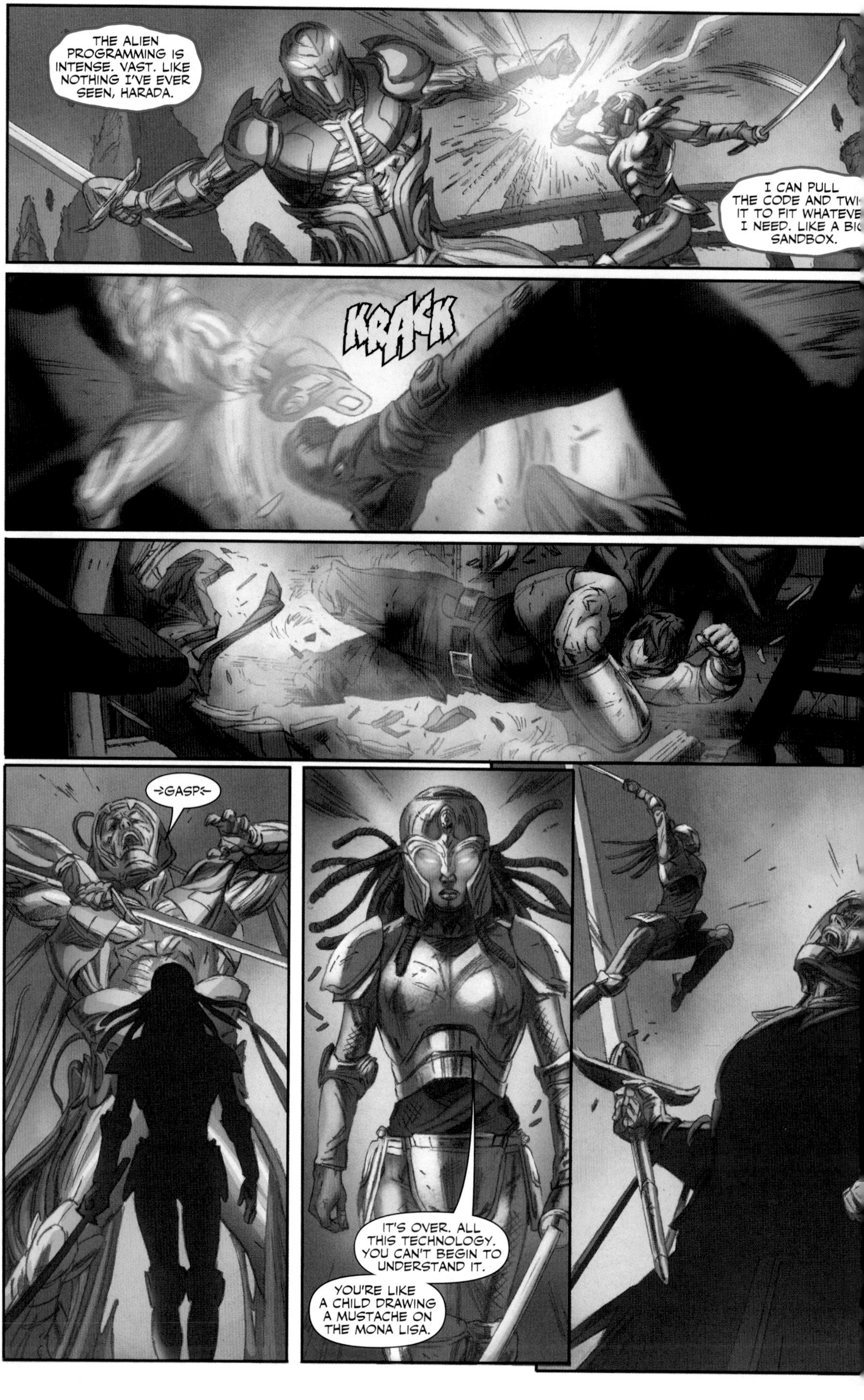

THE ALIEN PROGRAMMING IS INTENSE. VAST. LIKE NOTHING I'VE EVER SEEN, HARADA.
I CAN PULL THE CODE AND TWI IT TO FIT WHATEVE I NEED. LIKE A BI SANDBOX.
KRAKK
GASP
IT'S OVER. ALL THIS TECHNOLOGY. YOU CAN'T BEGIN TO UNDERSTAND IT.
YOU'RE LIKE A CHILD DRAWING A MUSTACHE ON THE MONA LISA.

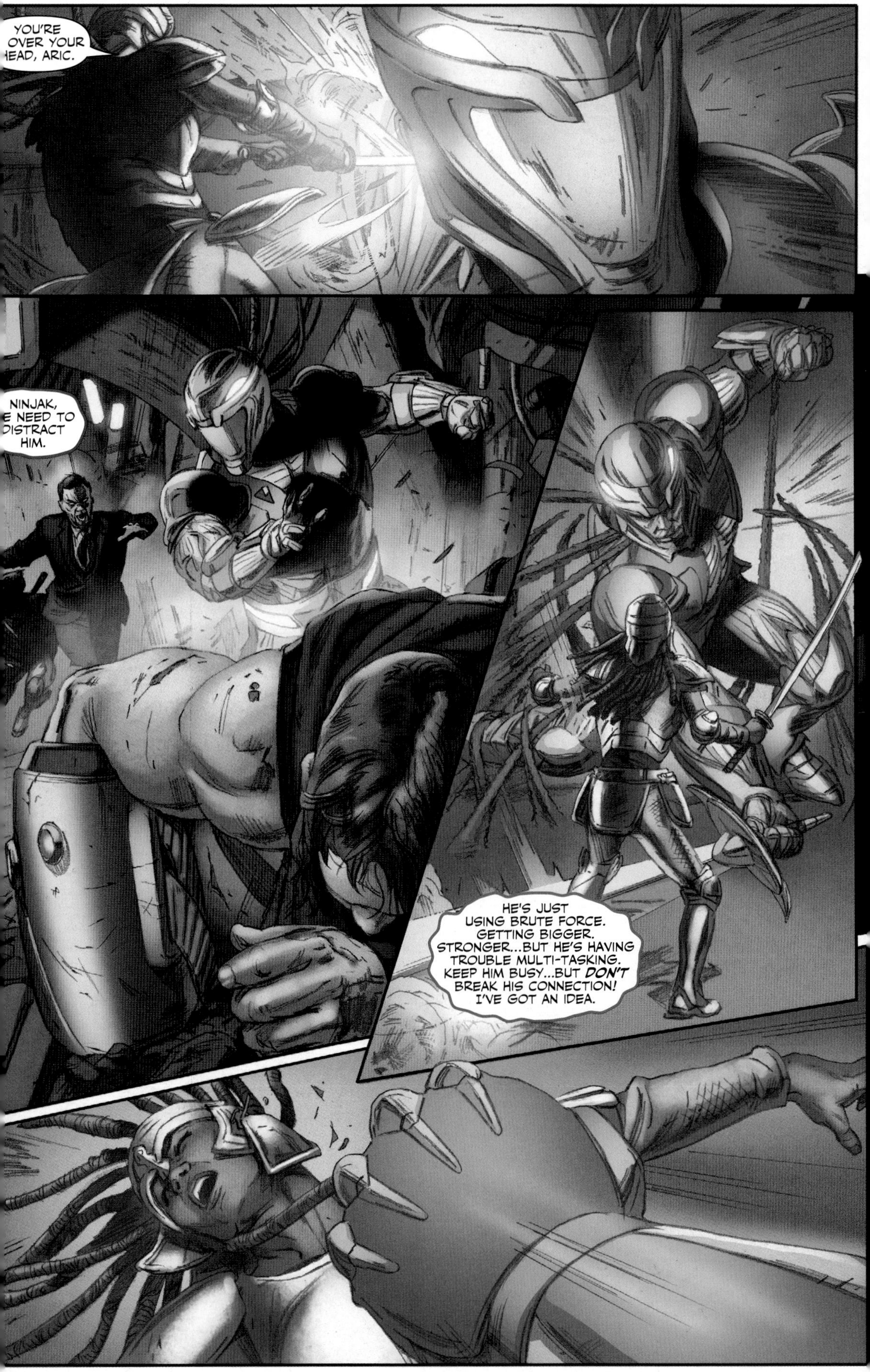

YOU'RE OVER YOUR HEAD, ARIC.
NINJAK, E NEED TO DISTRACT HIM.
HE'S JUST USING BRUTE FORCE. GETTING BIGGER. STRONGER...BUT HE'S HAVING TROUBLE MULTI-TASKING. KEEP HIM BUSY...BUT *DON'T* BREAK HIS CONNECTION! I'VE GOT AN IDEA.

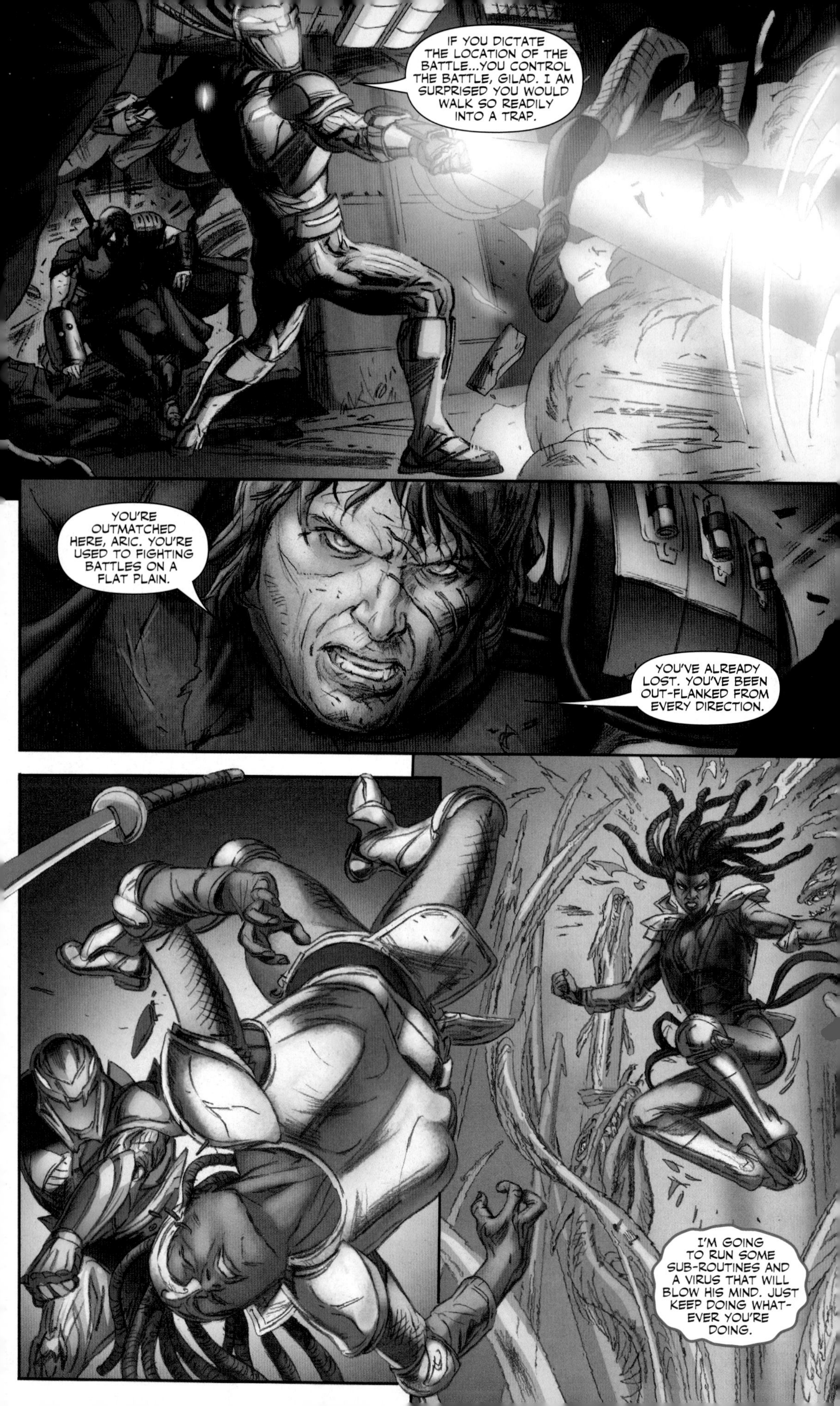
IF YOU DICTATE THE LOCATION OF THE BATTLE...YOU CONTROL THE BATTLE, GILAD. I AM SURPRISED YOU WOULD WALK SO READILY INTO A TRAP.
YOU'RE OUTMATCHED HERE, ARIC. YOU'RE USED TO FIGHTING BATTLES ON A FLAT PLAIN.
YOU'VE ALREADY LOST. YOU'VE BEEN OUT-FLANKED FROM EVERY DIRECTION.
I'M GOING TO RUN SOME SUB-ROUTINES AND A VIRUS THAT WILL BLOW HIS MIND. JUST KEEP DOING WHAT-EVER YOU'RE DOING.

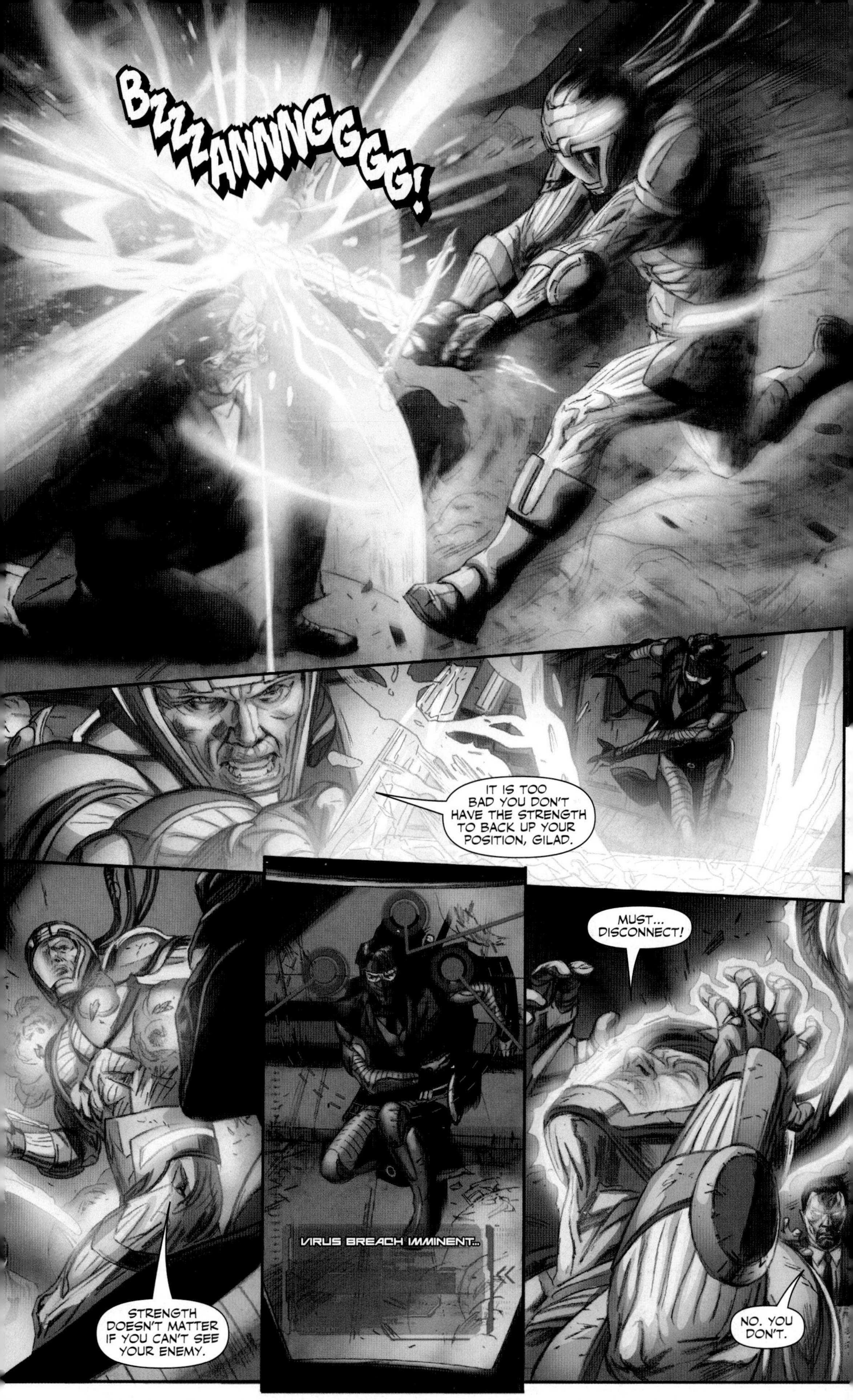
BZZZANNNGGGG!
IT IS TOO BAD YOU DON'T HAVE THE STRENGTH TO BACK UP YOUR POSITION, GILAD.
STRENGTH DOESN'T MATTER IF YOU CAN'T SEE YOUR ENEMY.
VIRUS BREACH IMMINENT...
MUST... DISCONNECT!
NO. YOU DON'T.

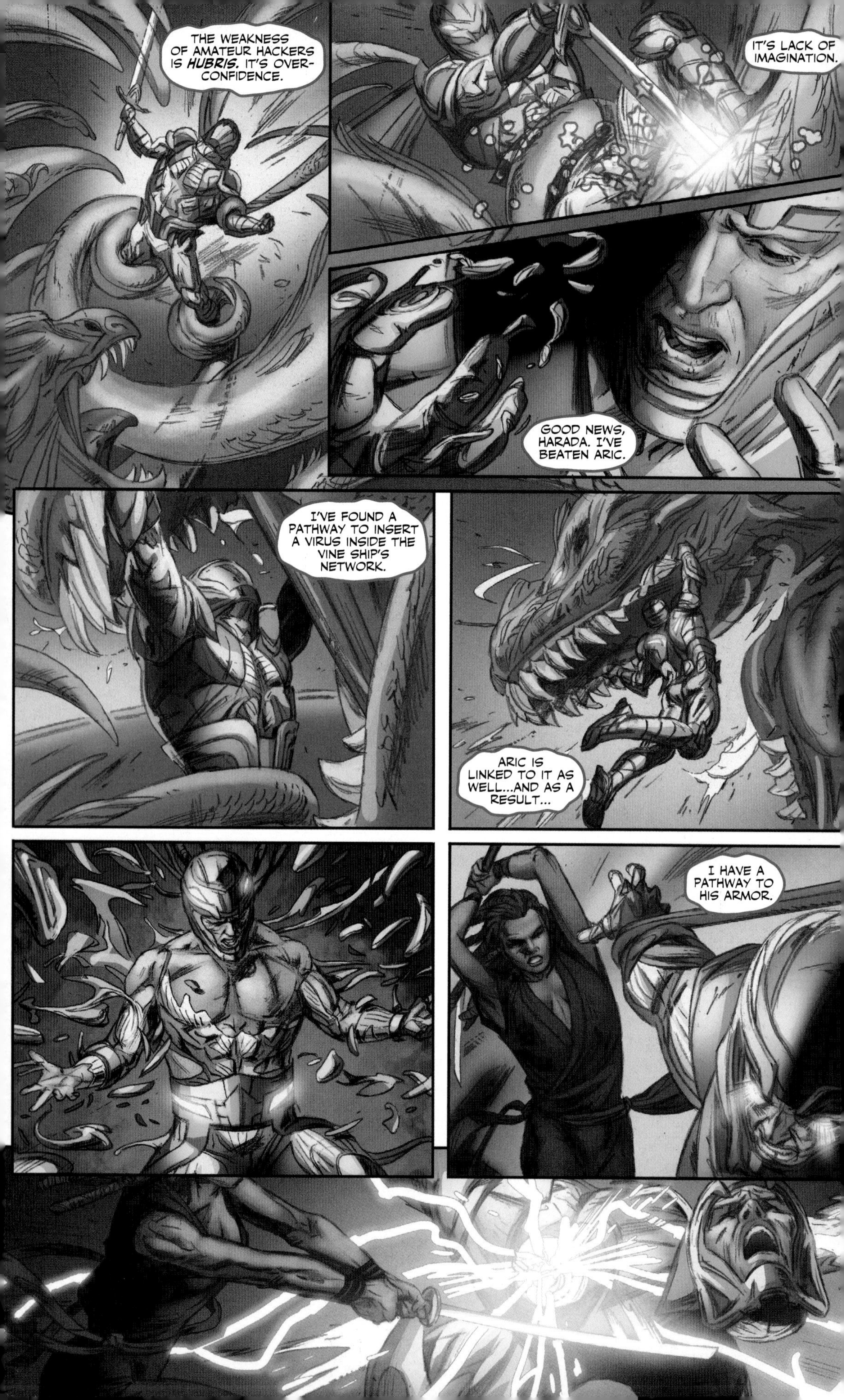
THE WEAKNESS OF AMATEUR HACKERS IS *HUBRIS.* IT'S OVER-CONFIDENCE.
IT'S LACK OF IMAGINATION.
GOOD NEWS, HARADA. I'VE BEATEN ARIC.
I'VE FOUND A PATHWAY TO INSERT A VIRUS INSIDE THE VINE SHIP'S NETWORK.
ARIC IS LINKED TO IT AS WELL...AND AS A RESULT...
I HAVE A PATHWAY TO HIS ARMOR.

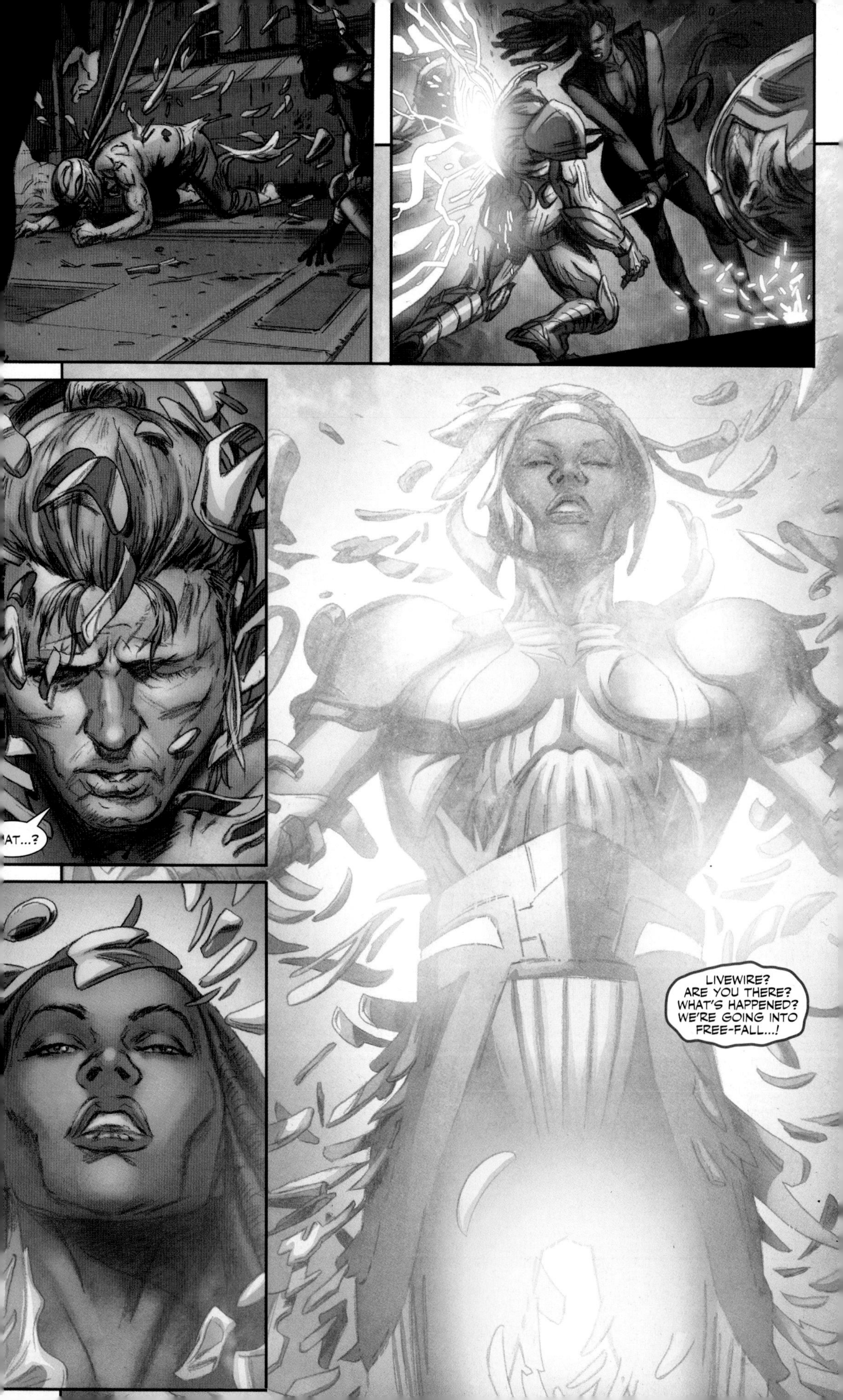
AT...?
LIVEWIRE? ARE YOU THERE? WHAT'S HAPPENED? WE'RE GOING INTO FREE-FALL...!

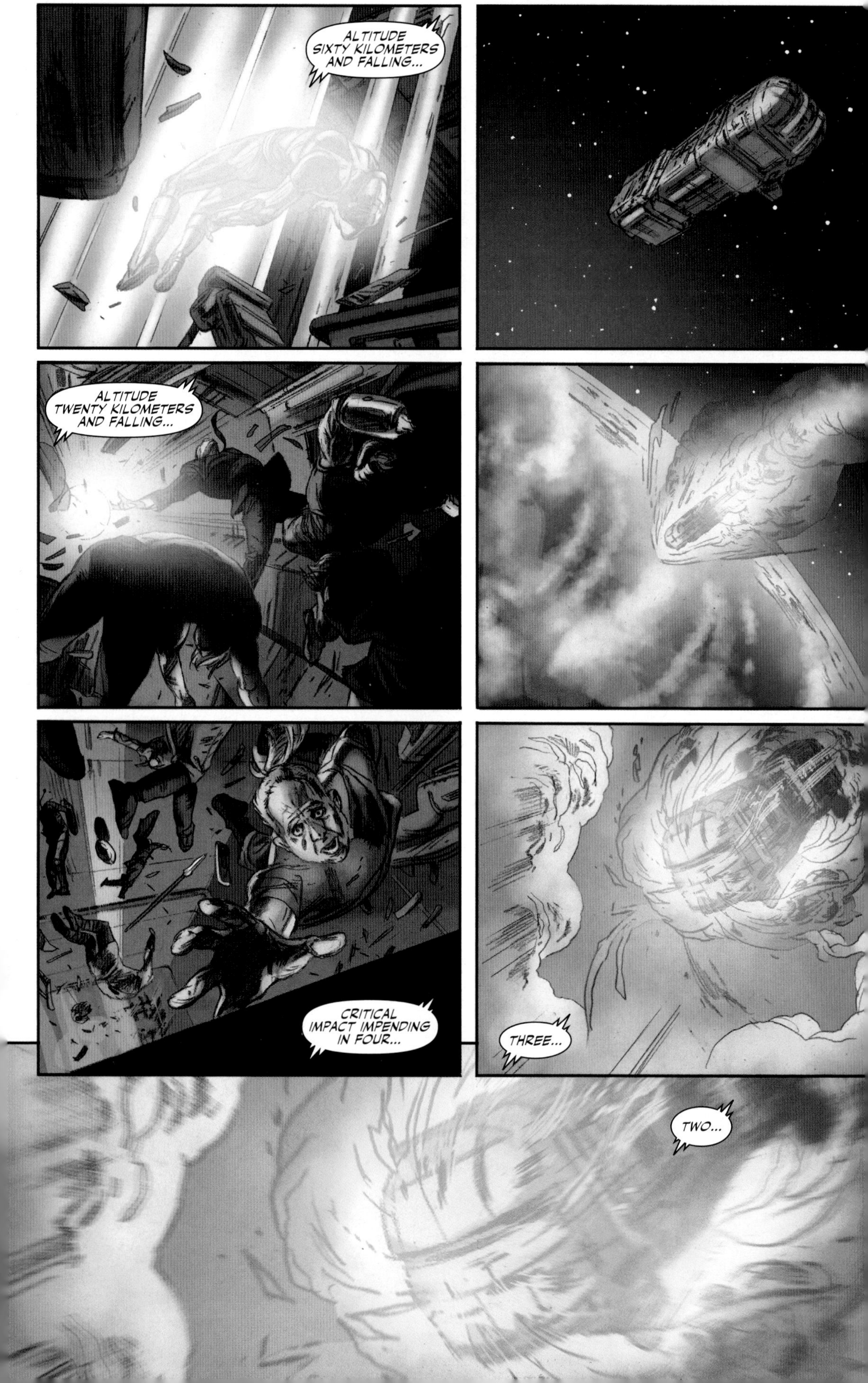
ALTITUDE SIXTY KILOMETERS AND FALLING...
ALTITUDE TWENTY KILOMETERS AND FALLING...
CRITICAL IMPACT IMPENDING IN FOUR...
THREE...
TWO...

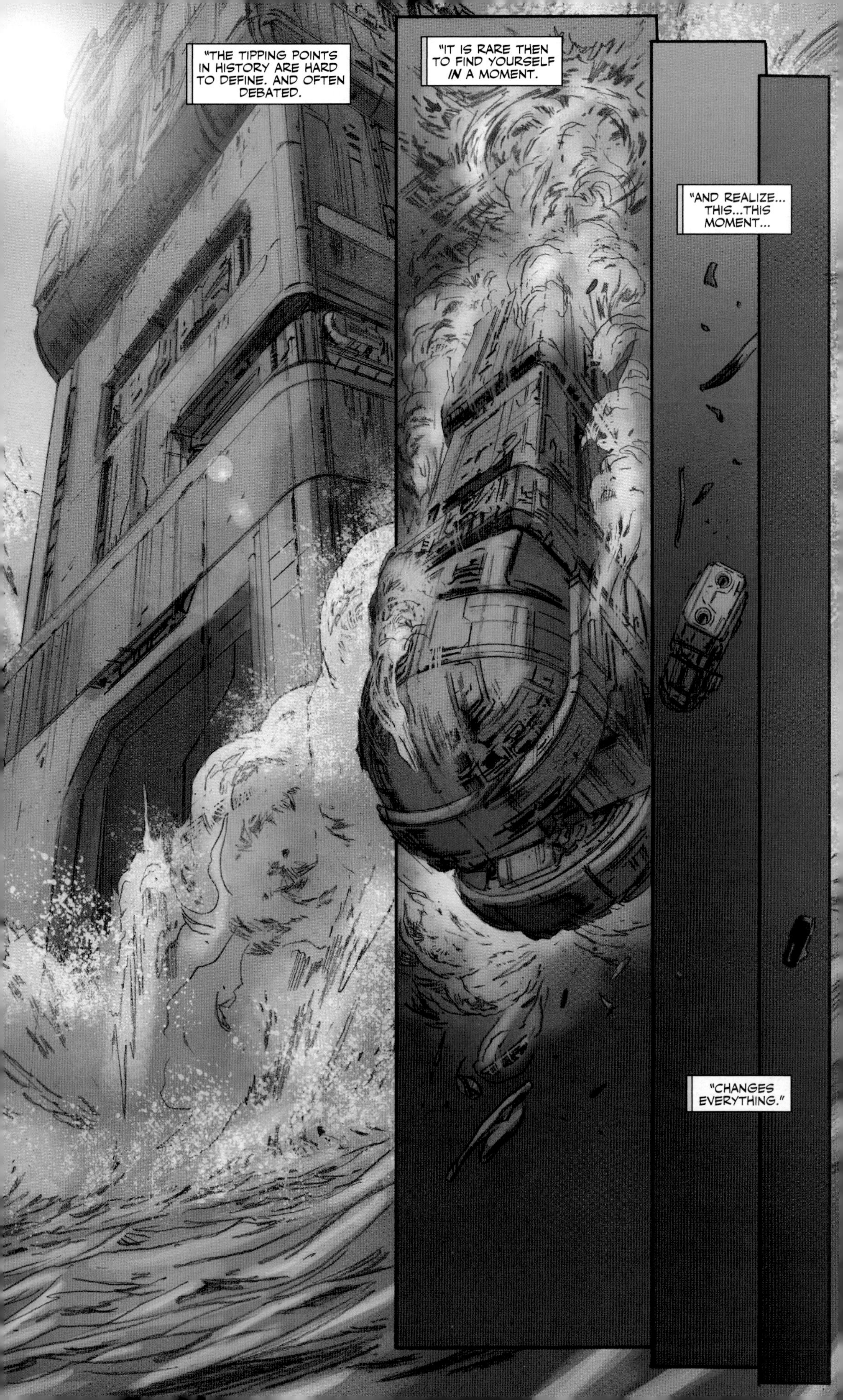
"THE TIPPING POINTS IN HISTORY ARE HARD TO DEFINE. AND OFTEN DEBATED.
"IT IS RARE THEN TO FIND YOURSELF *IN* A MOMENT.
"AND REALIZE... THIS...THIS MOMENT...
"CHANGES EVERYTHING."

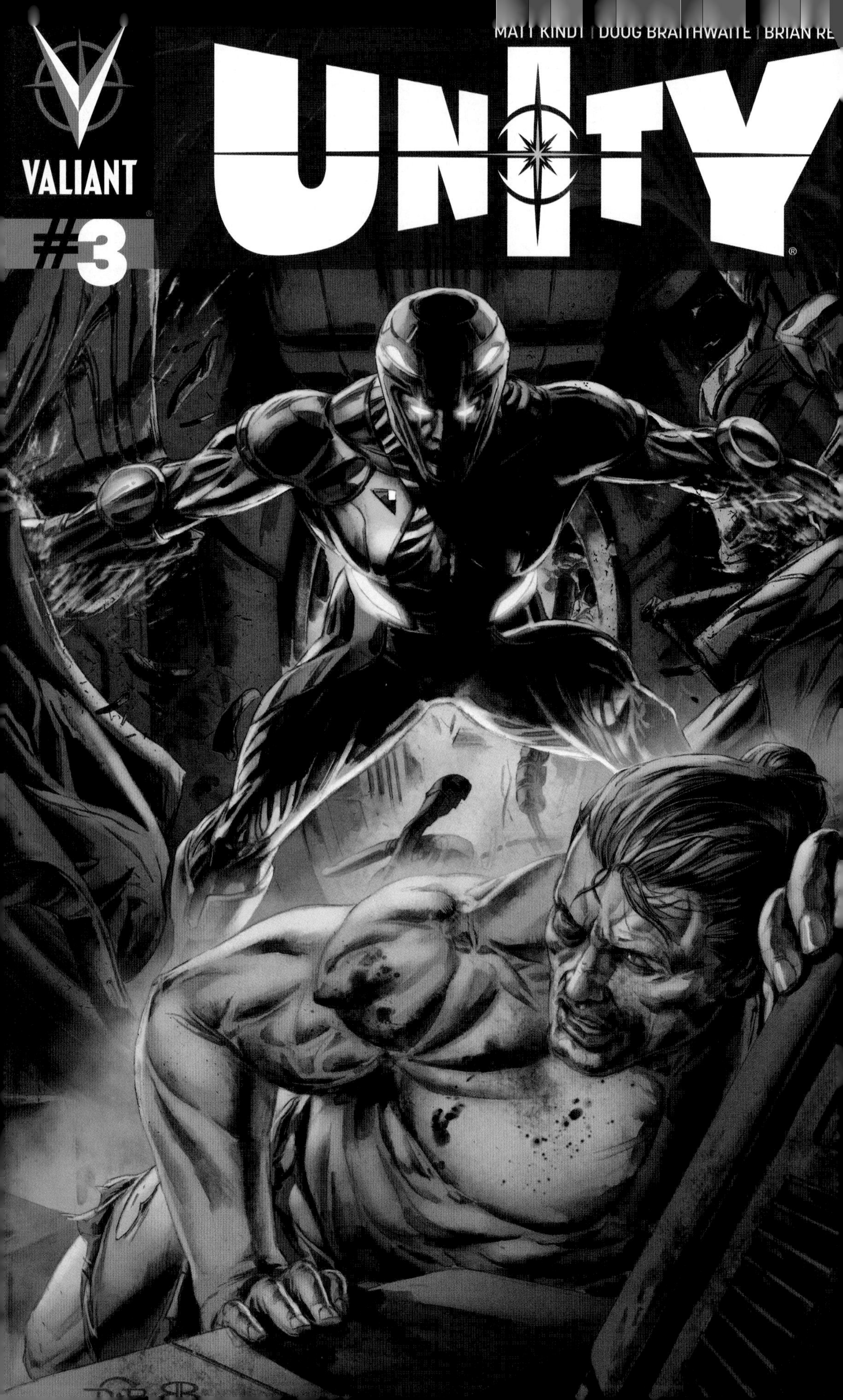
MATT KINDT | DOUG BRAITHWAITE | BRIAN RE
VALIANT
#3
UNITY

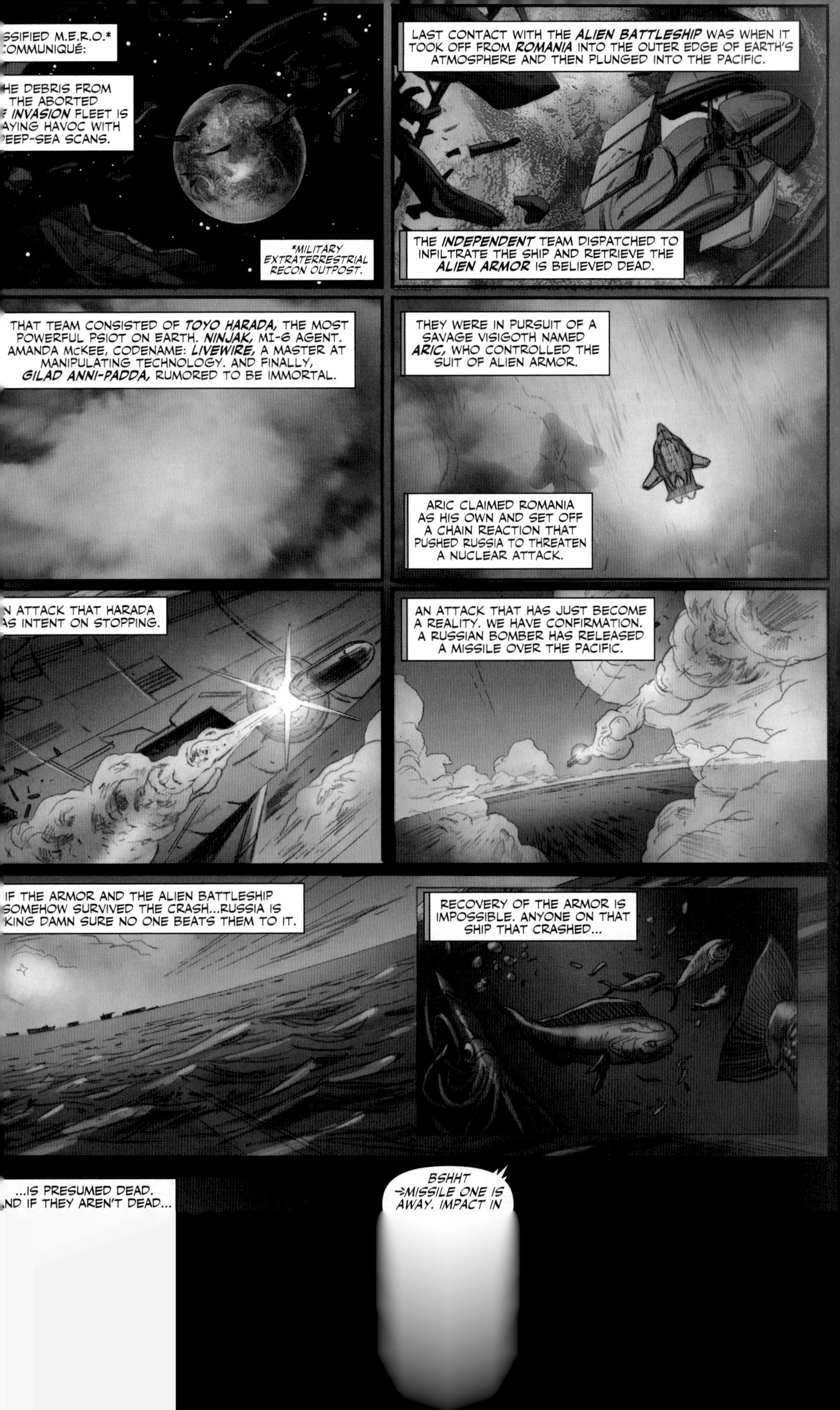

SSIFIED M.E.R.O.* COMMUNIQUÉ:
HE DEBRIS FROM THE ABORTED F INVASION FLEET IS AYING HAVOC WITH EEP-SEA SCANS.
*MILITARY EXTRATERRESTRIAL RECON OUTPOST.
LAST CONTACT WITH THE ALIEN BATTLESHIP WAS WHEN IT TOOK OFF FROM ROMANIA INTO THE OUTER EDGE OF EARTH'S ATMOSPHERE AND THEN PLUNGED INTO THE PACIFIC.
THE INDEPENDENT TEAM DISPATCHED TO INFILTRATE THE SHIP AND RETRIEVE THE ALIEN ARMOR IS BELIEVED DEAD.
THAT TEAM CONSISTED OF TOYO HARADA, THE MOST POWERFUL PSIOT ON EARTH. NINJAK, MI-6 AGENT. AMANDA McKEE, CODENAME: LIVEWIRE, A MASTER AT MANIPULATING TECHNOLOGY. AND FINALLY, GILAD ANNI-PADDA, RUMORED TO BE IMMORTAL.
THEY WERE IN PURSUIT OF A SAVAGE VISIGOTH NAMED ARIC, WHO CONTROLLED THE SUIT OF ALIEN ARMOR.
ARIC CLAIMED ROMANIA AS HIS OWN AND SET OFF A CHAIN REACTION THAT PUSHED RUSSIA TO THREATEN A NUCLEAR ATTACK.
N ATTACK THAT HARADA AS INTENT ON STOPPING.
AN ATTACK THAT HAS JUST BECOME A REALITY. WE HAVE CONFIRMATION. A RUSSIAN BOMBER HAS RELEASED A MISSILE OVER THE PACIFIC.
IF THE ARMOR AND THE ALIEN BATTLESHIP SOMEHOW SURVIVED THE CRASH...RUSSIA IS KING DAMN SURE NO ONE BEATS THEM TO IT.
RECOVERY OF THE ARMOR IS IMPOSSIBLE. ANYONE ON THAT SHIP THAT CRASHED...
...IS PRESUMED DEAD. ND IF THEY AREN'T DEAD...
BSHHT
⇒MISSILE ONE IS AWAY. IMPACT IN

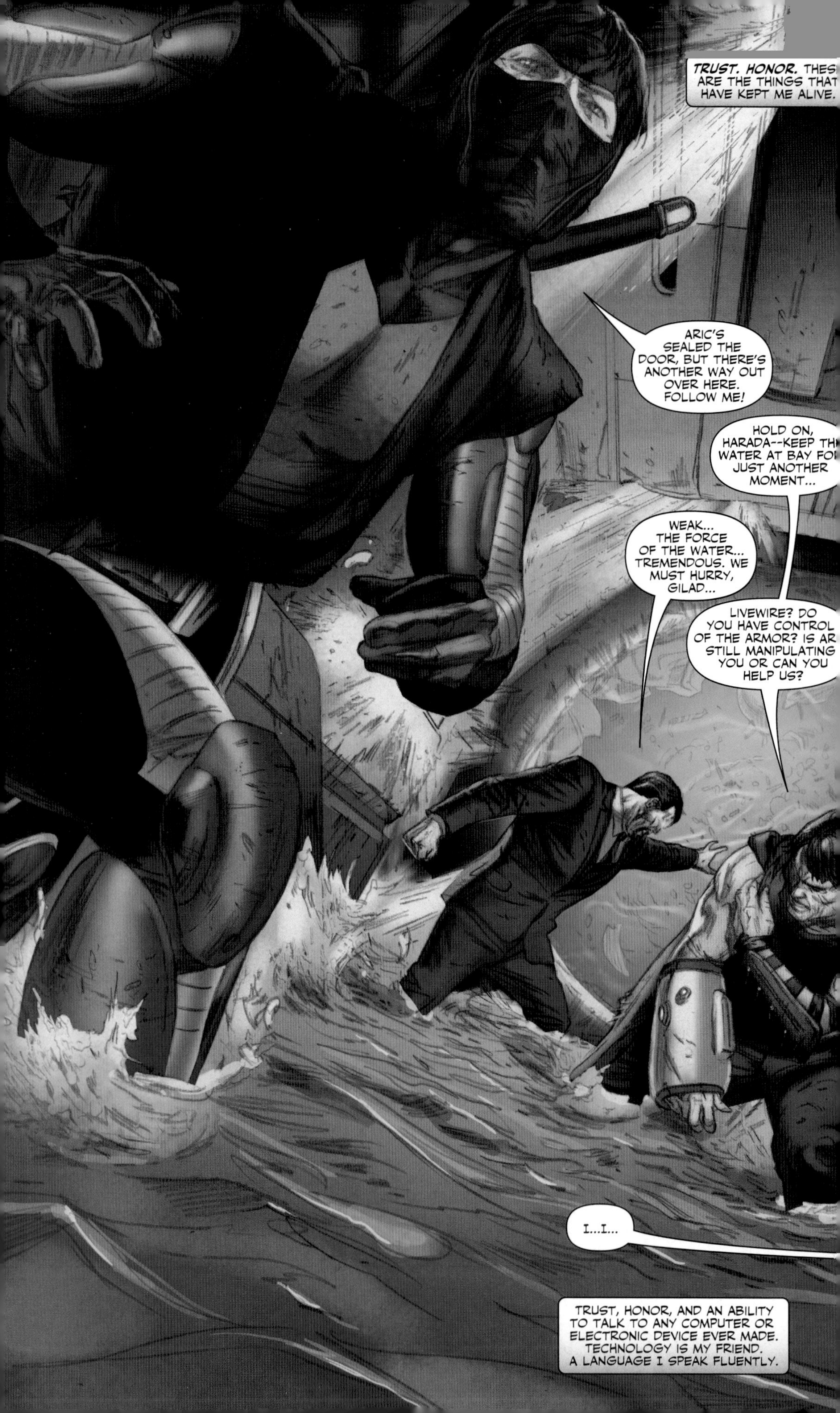
TRUST. HONOR. THES ARE THE THINGS THAT HAVE KEPT ME ALIVE.
ARIC'S SEALED THE DOOR, BUT THERE'S ANOTHER WAY OUT OVER HERE. FOLLOW ME!
HOLD ON, HARADA--KEEP TH WATER AT BAY FO JUST ANOTHER MOMENT...
WEAK... THE FORCE OF THE WATER... TREMENDOUS. WE MUST HURRY, GILAD...
LIVEWIRE? DO YOU HAVE CONTROL OF THE ARMOR? IS AR STILL MANIPULATING YOU OR CAN YOU HELP US?
I...I...
TRUST, HONOR, AND AN ABILITY TO TALK TO ANY COMPUTER OR ELECTRONIC DEVICE EVER MADE. TECHNOLOGY IS MY FRIEND. A LANGUAGE I SPEAK FLUENTLY.

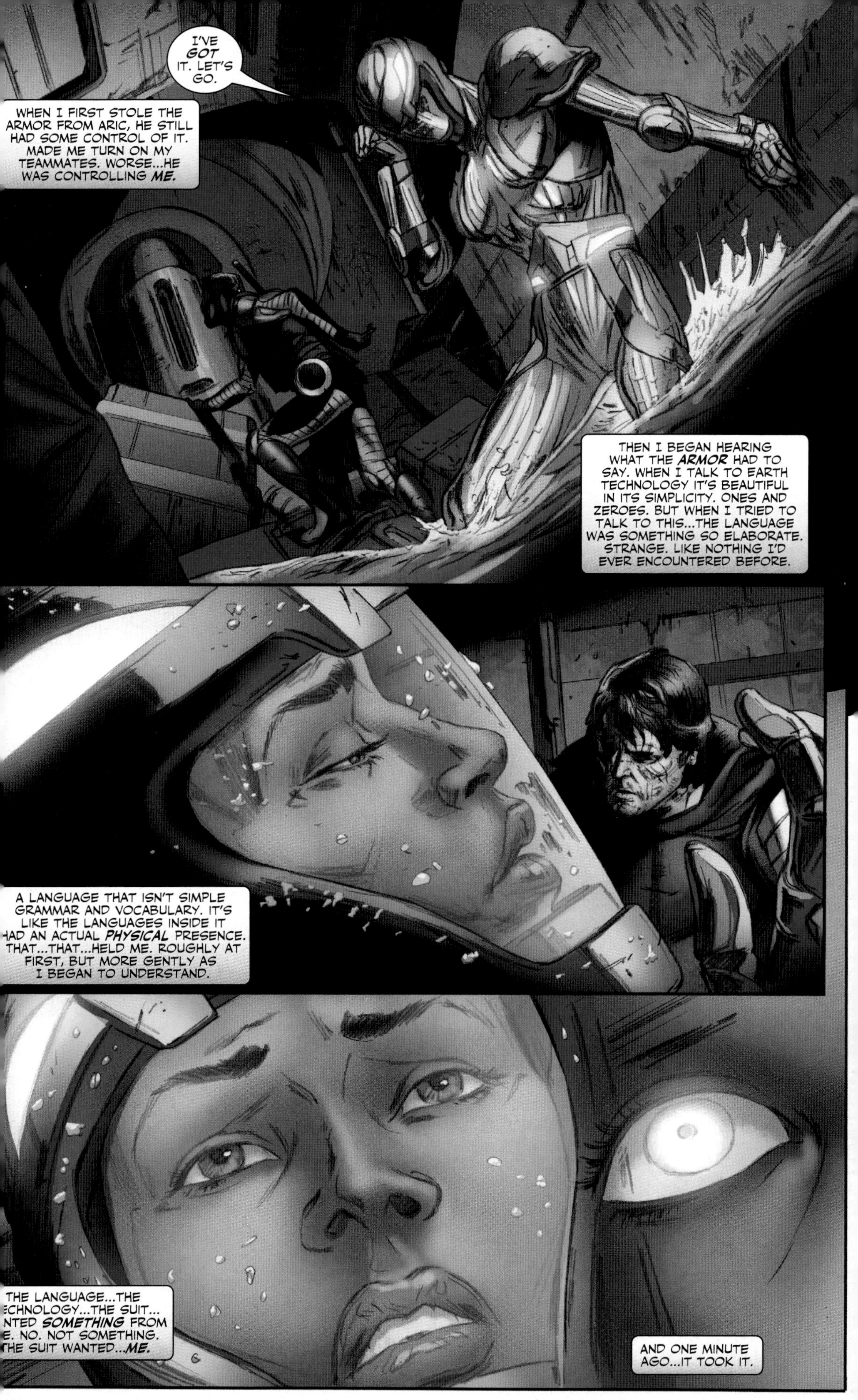
I'VE GOT IT. LET'S GO.
WHEN I FIRST STOLE THE ARMOR FROM ARIC, HE STILL HAD SOME CONTROL OF IT. MADE ME TURN ON MY TEAMMATES. WORSE...HE WAS CONTROLLING ME.
THEN I BEGAN HEARING WHAT THE ARMOR HAD TO SAY. WHEN I TALK TO EARTH TECHNOLOGY IT'S BEAUTIFUL IN ITS SIMPLICITY. ONES AND ZEROES. BUT WHEN I TRIED TO TALK TO THIS...THE LANGUAGE WAS SOMETHING SO ELABORATE. STRANGE. LIKE NOTHING I'D EVER ENCOUNTERED BEFORE.
A LANGUAGE THAT ISN'T SIMPLE GRAMMAR AND VOCABULARY. IT'S LIKE THE LANGUAGES INSIDE IT HAD AN ACTUAL PHYSICAL PRESENCE. THAT...THAT...HELD ME. ROUGHLY AT FIRST, BUT MORE GENTLY AS I BEGAN TO UNDERSTAND.
THE LANGUAGE...THE ECHNOLOGY...THE SUIT... NTED SOMETHING FROM E. NO. NOT SOMETHING. THE SUIT WANTED...ME.
AND ONE MINUTE AGO...IT TOOK IT.

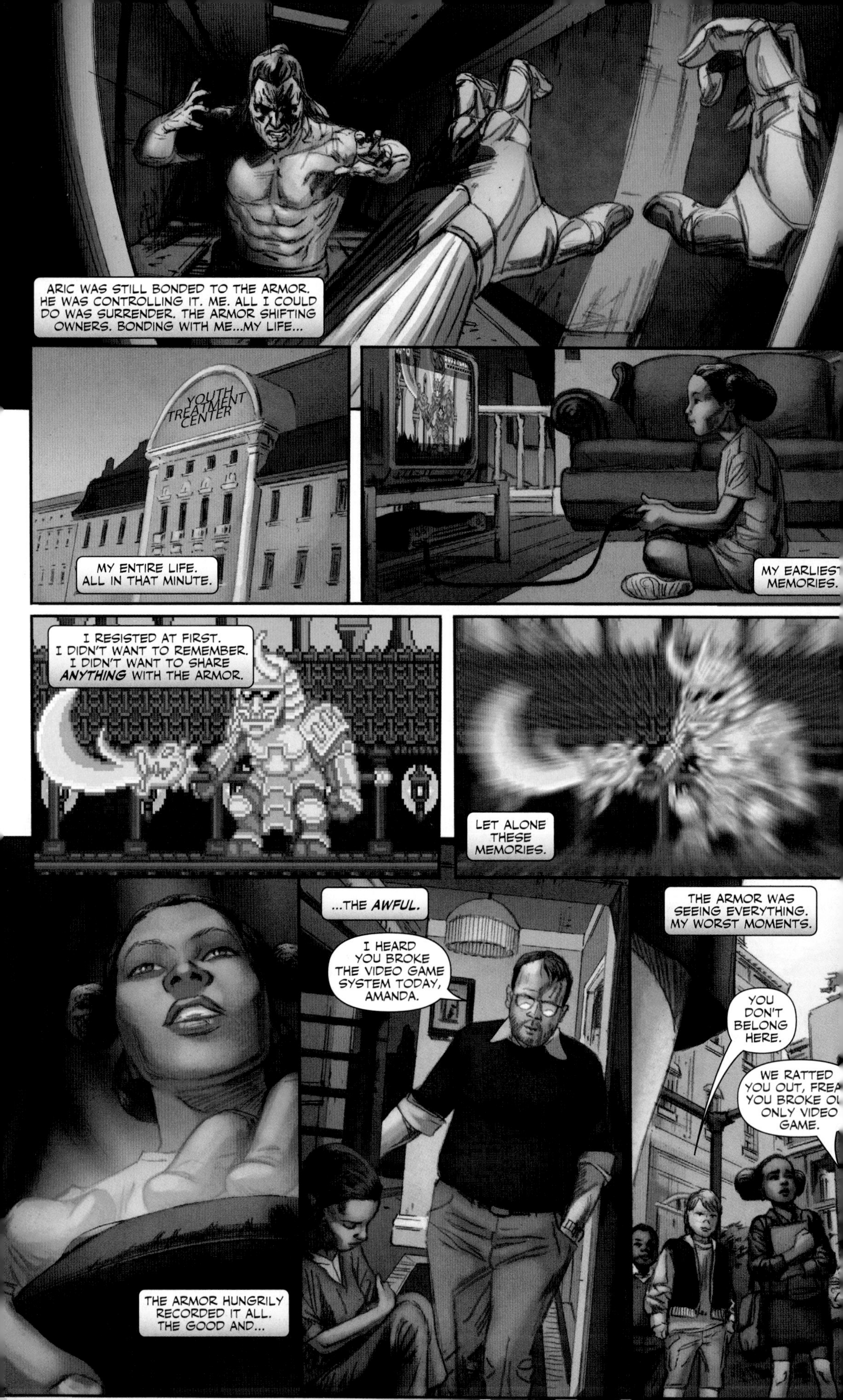
ARIC WAS STILL BONDED TO THE ARMOR. HE WAS CONTROLLING IT. ME. ALL I COULD DO WAS SURRENDER. THE ARMOR SHIFTING OWNERS. BONDING WITH ME...MY LIFE...
YOUTH TREATMENT CENTER
MY ENTIRE LIFE. ALL IN THAT MINUTE.
MY EARLIEST MEMORIES.
I RESISTED AT FIRST. I DIDN'T WANT TO REMEMBER. I DIDN'T WANT TO SHARE *ANYTHING* WITH THE ARMOR.
LET ALONE THESE MEMORIES.
THE ARMOR HUNGRILY RECORDED IT ALL. THE GOOD AND...
...THE *AWFUL.*
I HEARD YOU BROKE THE VIDEO GAME SYSTEM TODAY, AMANDA.
THE ARMOR WAS SEEING EVERYTHING. MY WORST MOMENTS.
YOU DON'T BELONG HERE.
WE RATTED YOU OUT, FREA
YOU BROKE OU
ONLY VIDEO GAME.

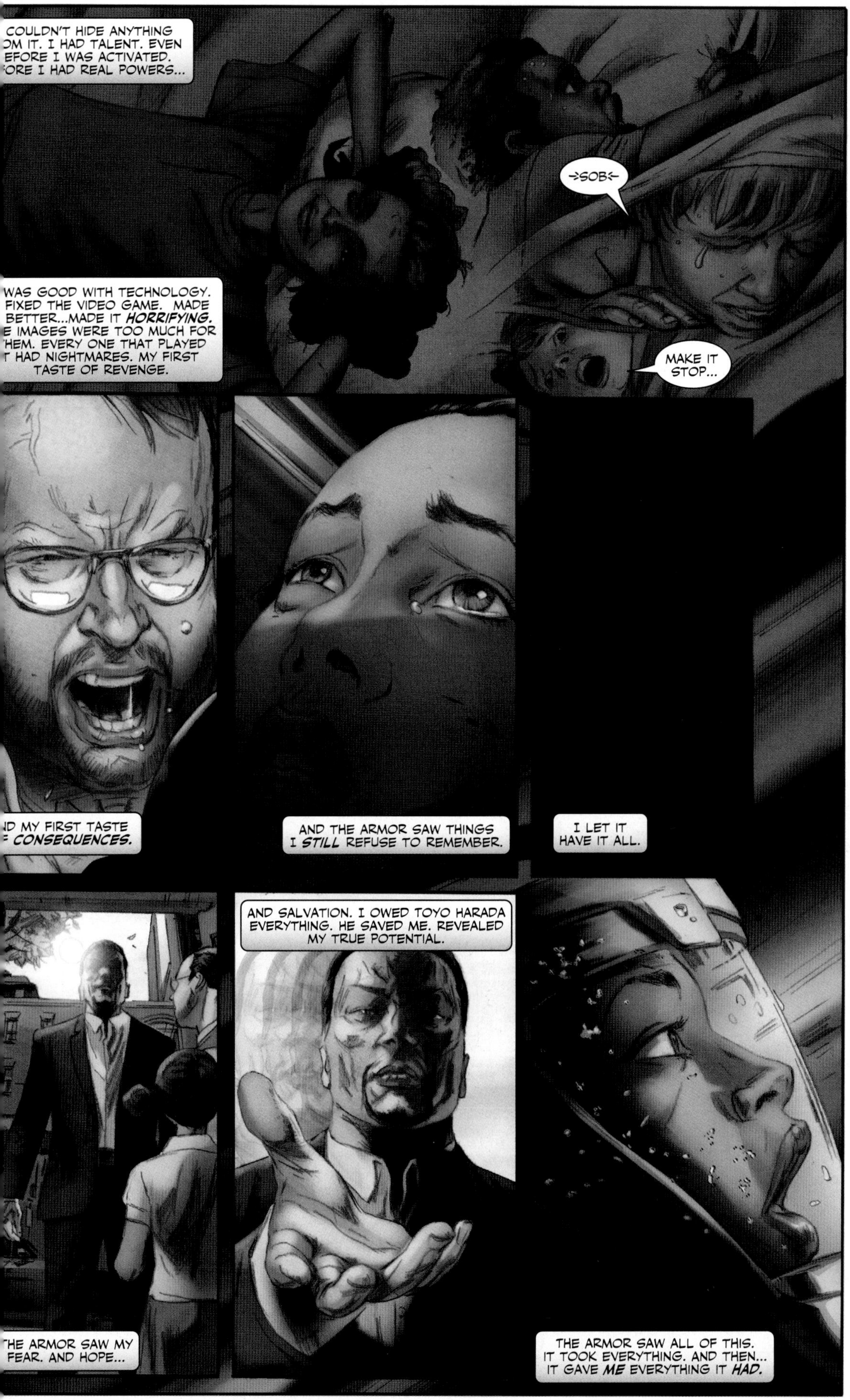
COULDN'T HIDE ANYTHING OM IT. I HAD TALENT. EVEN EFORE I WAS ACTIVATED. FORE I HAD REAL POWERS...
>SOB<
WAS GOOD WITH TECHNOLOGY. FIXED THE VIDEO GAME. MADE BETTER...MADE IT HORRIFYING. E IMAGES WERE TOO MUCH FOR HEM. EVERY ONE THAT PLAYED T HAD NIGHTMARES. MY FIRST TASTE OF REVENGE.
MAKE IT STOP...
D MY FIRST TASTE CONSEQUENCES.
AND THE ARMOR SAW THINGS I STILL REFUSE TO REMEMBER.
I LET IT HAVE IT ALL.
HE ARMOR SAW MY FEAR. AND HOPE...
AND SALVATION. I OWED TOYO HARADA EVERYTHING. HE SAVED ME. REVEALED MY TRUE POTENTIAL.
THE ARMOR SAW ALL OF THIS. IT TOOK EVERYTHING. AND THEN... IT GAVE ME EVERYTHING IT HAD.

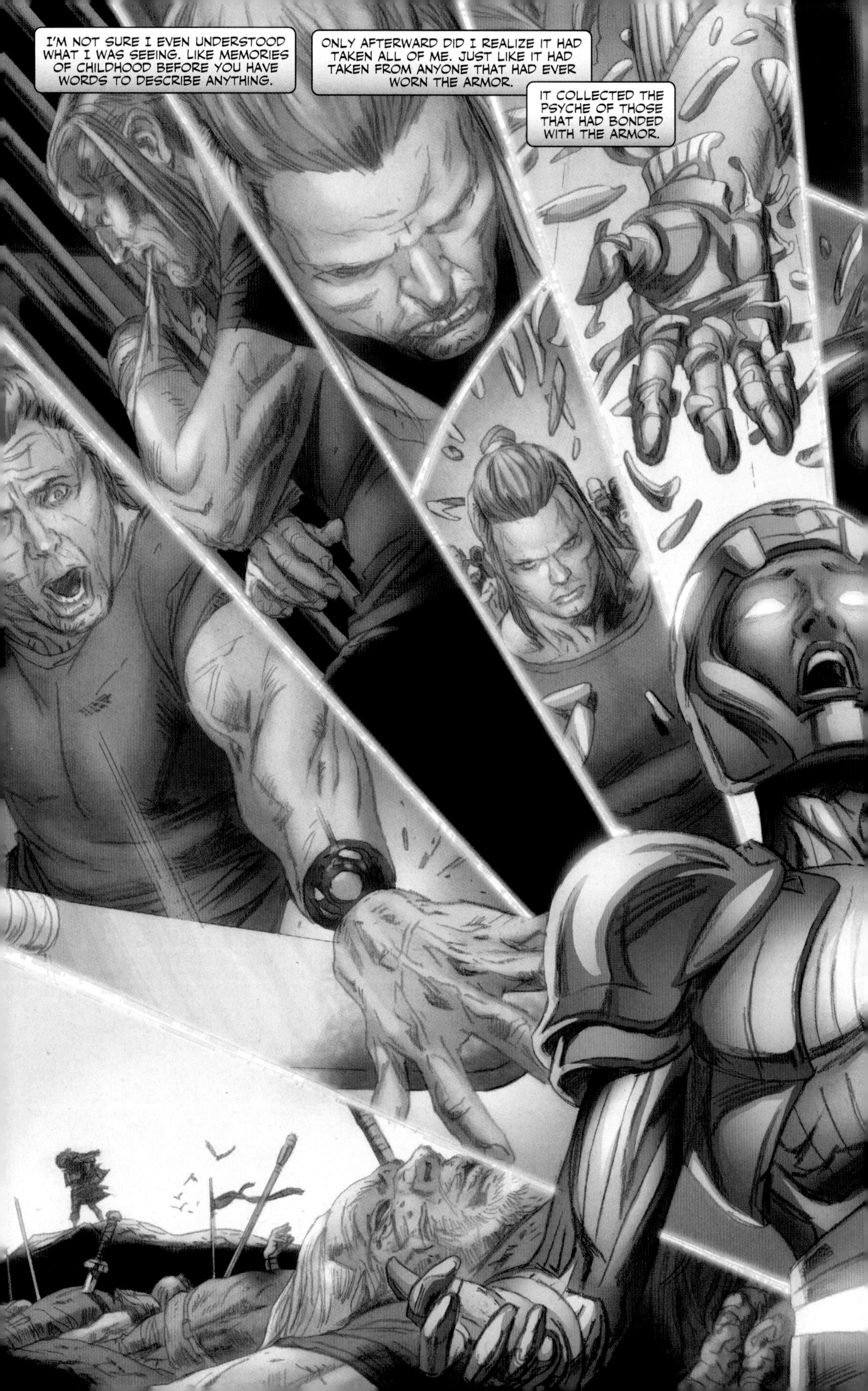
I'M NOT SURE I EVEN UNDERSTOOD WHAT I WAS SEEING. LIKE MEMORIES OF CHILDHOOD BEFORE YOU HAVE WORDS TO DESCRIBE ANYTHING.
ONLY AFTERWARD DID I REALIZE IT HAD TAKEN ALL OF ME. JUST LIKE IT HAD TAKEN FROM ANYONE THAT HAD EVER WORN THE ARMOR.
IT COLLECTED THE PSYCHE OF THOSE THAT HAD BONDED WITH THE ARMOR.

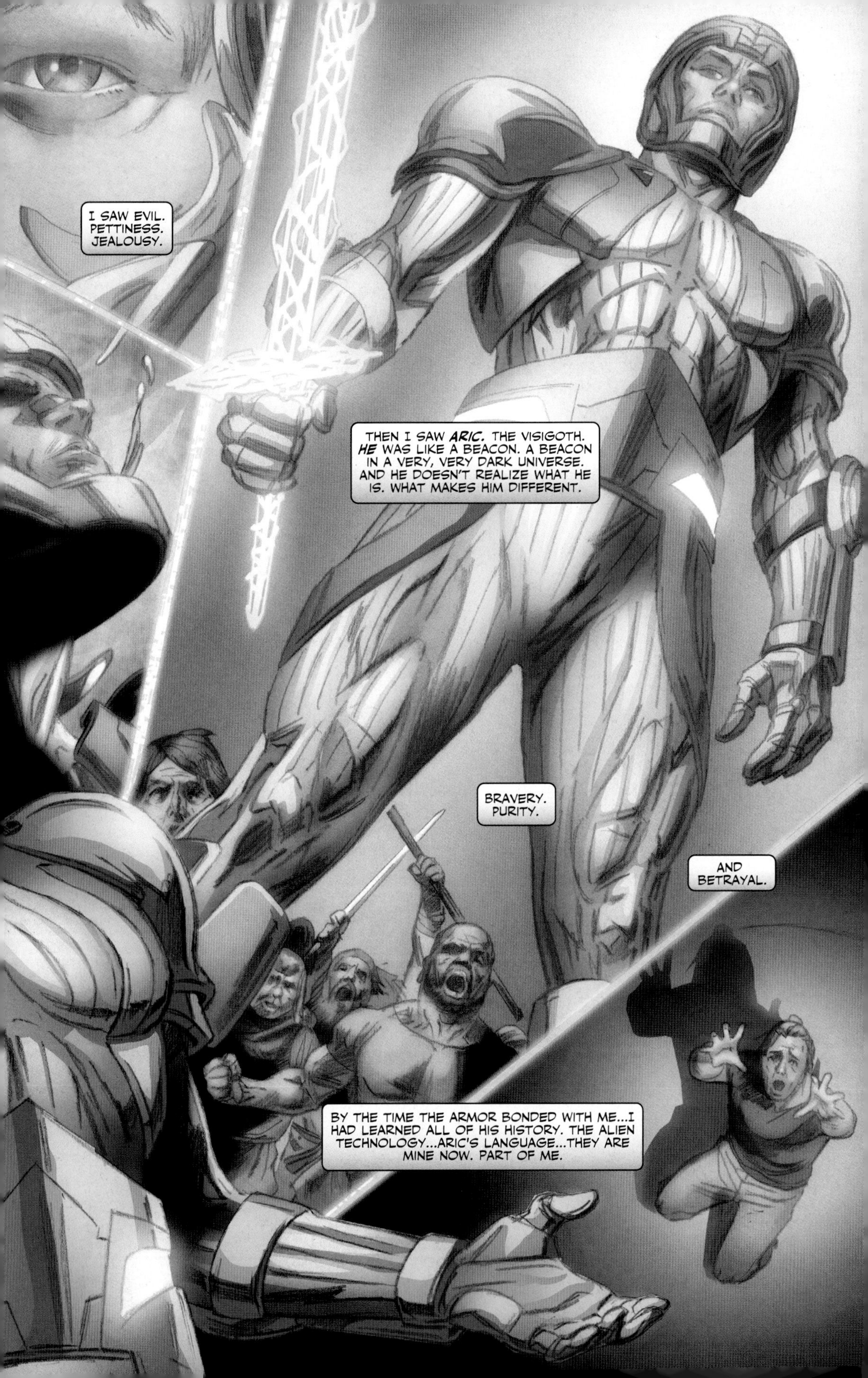
I SAW EVIL. PETTINESS. JEALOUSY.
THEN I SAW *ARIC.* THE VISIGOTH. *HE* WAS LIKE A BEACON. A BEACON IN A VERY, VERY DARK UNIVERSE. AND HE DOESN'T REALIZE WHAT HE IS. WHAT MAKES HIM DIFFERENT.
BRAVERY. PURITY.
AND BETRAYAL.
BY THE TIME THE ARMOR BONDED WITH ME...I HAD LEARNED ALL OF HIS HISTORY. THE ALIEN TECHNOLOGY...ARIC'S LANGUAGE...THEY ARE MINE NOW. PART OF ME.

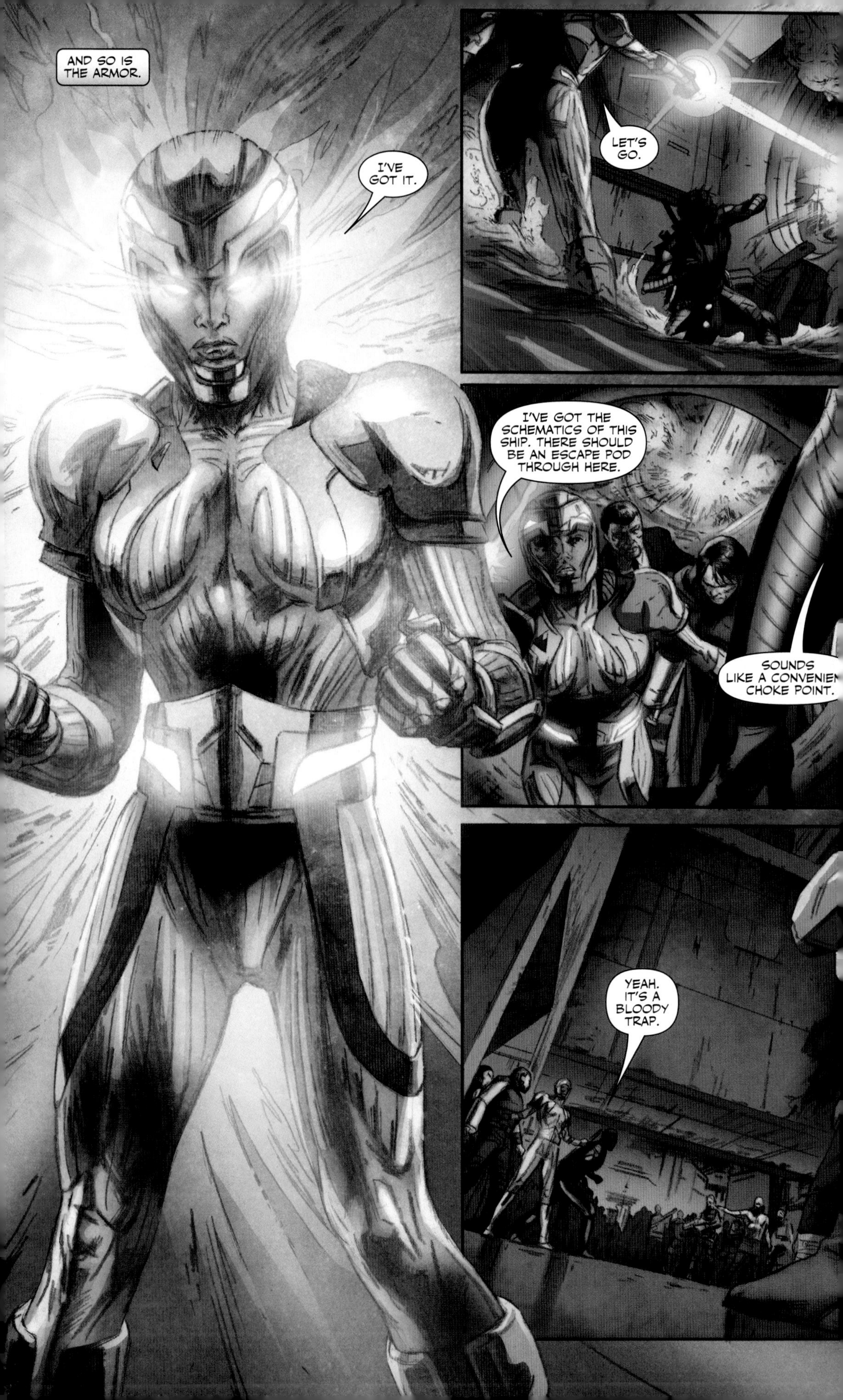
AND SO IS THE ARMOR.
I'VE GOT IT.
LET'S GO.
I'VE GOT THE SCHEMATICS OF THIS SHIP. THERE SHOULD BE AN ESCAPE POD THROUGH HERE.
SOUNDS LIKE A CONVENIEN CHOKE POINT.
YEAH. IT'S A BLOODY TRAP.

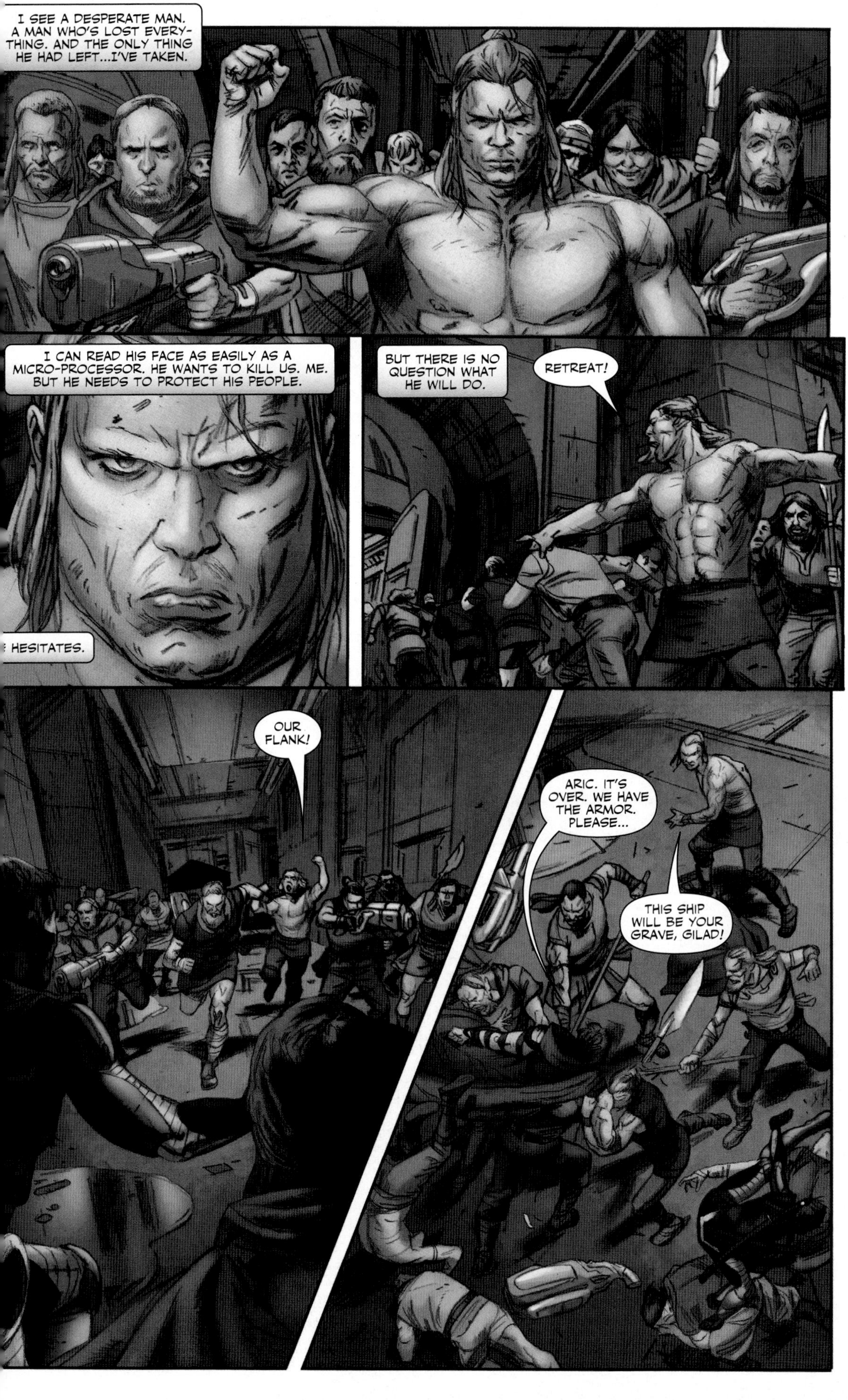
I SEE A DESPERATE MAN. A MAN WHO'S LOST EVERY-THING. AND THE ONLY THING HE HAD LEFT...I'VE TAKEN.
I CAN READ HIS FACE AS EASILY AS A MICRO-PROCESSOR. HE WANTS TO KILL US. ME. BUT HE NEEDS TO PROTECT HIS PEOPLE.
HESITATES.
BUT THERE IS NO QUESTION WHAT HE WILL DO.
RETREAT!
OUR FLANK!
ARIC. IT'S OVER. WE HAVE THE ARMOR. PLEASE...
THIS SHIP WILL BE YOUR GRAVE, GILAD!

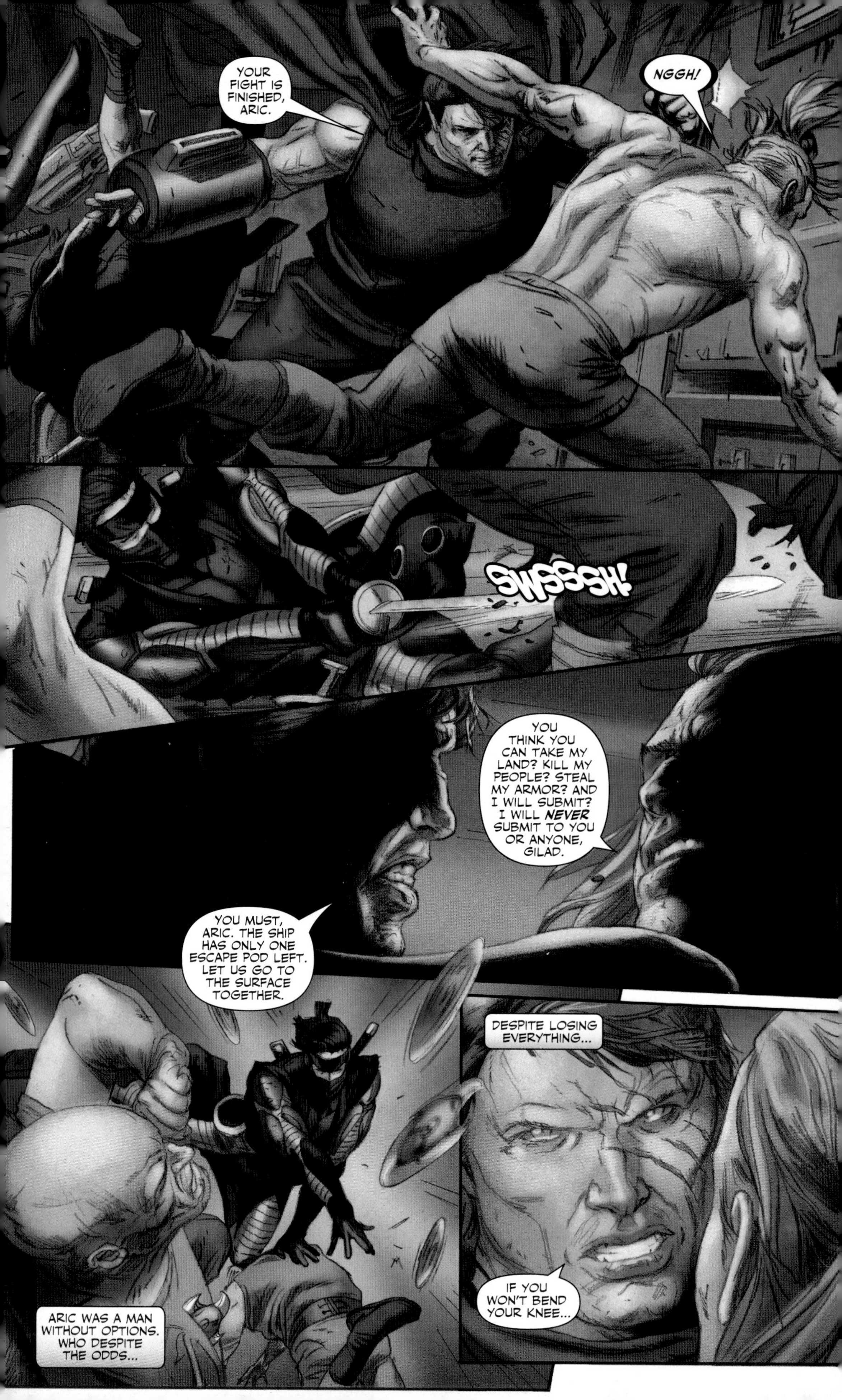
YOUR FIGHT IS FINISHED, ARIC.
NGGH!
SWSSSH!
YOU THINK YOU CAN TAKE MY LAND? KILL MY PEOPLE? STEAL MY ARMOR? AND I WILL SUBMIT? I WILL NEVER SUBMIT TO YOU OR ANYONE, GILAD.
YOU MUST, ARIC. THE SHIP HAS ONLY ONE ESCAPE POD LEFT. LET US GO TO THE SURFACE TOGETHER.
ARIC WAS A MAN WITHOUT OPTIONS. WHO DESPITE THE ODDS...
DESPITE LOSING EVERYTHING...
IF YOU WON'T BEND YOUR KNEE...

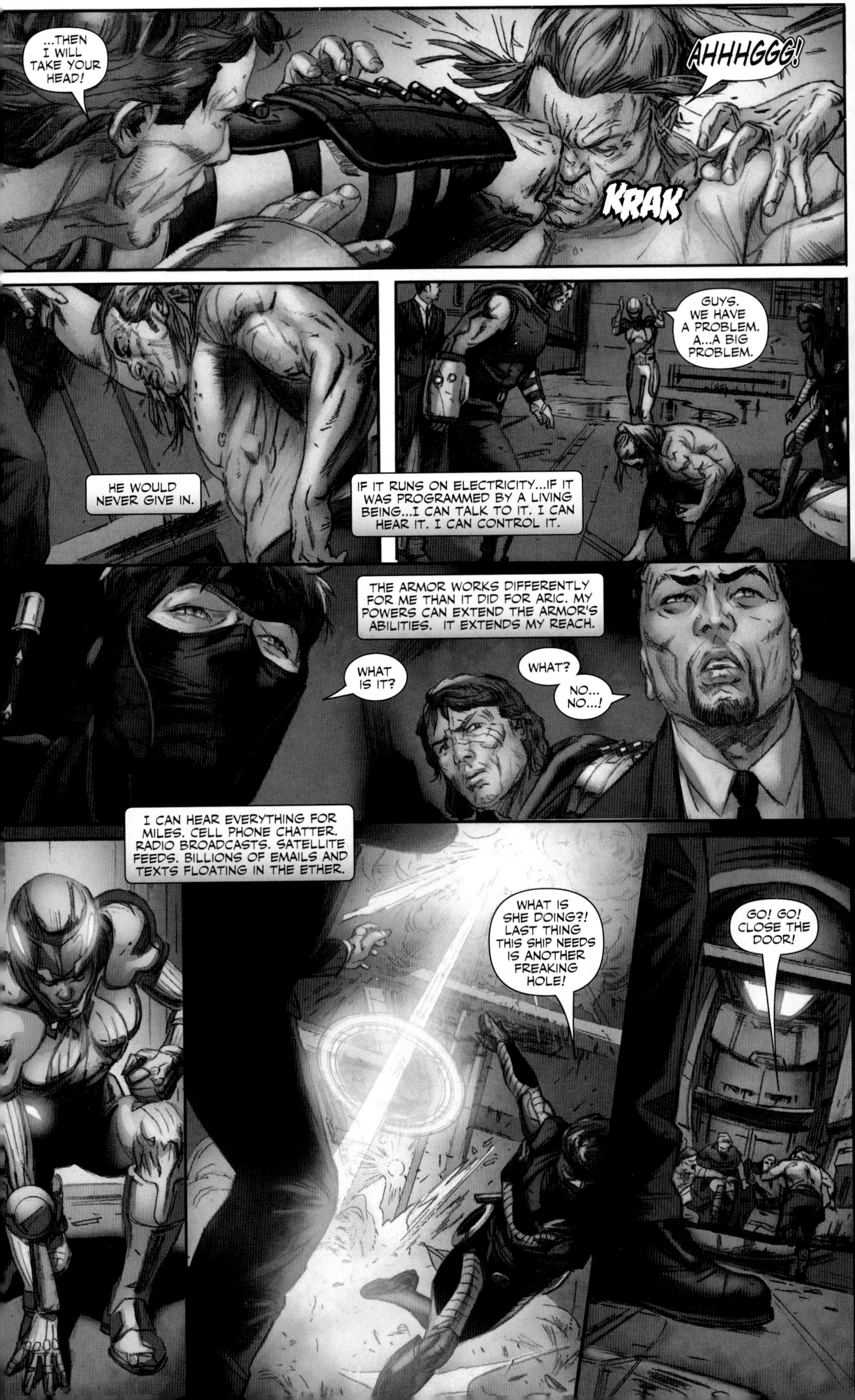
...THEN I WILL TAKE YOUR HEAD!
AHHHGGG!
KRAK
HE WOULD NEVER GIVE IN.
GUYS. WE HAVE A PROBLEM. A...A BIG PROBLEM.
IF IT RUNS ON ELECTRICITY...IF IT WAS PROGRAMMED BY A LIVING BEING...I CAN TALK TO IT. I CAN HEAR IT. I CAN CONTROL IT.
THE ARMOR WORKS DIFFERENTLY FOR ME THAN IT DID FOR ARIC. MY POWERS CAN EXTEND THE ARMOR'S ABILITIES. IT EXTENDS MY REACH.
WHAT IS IT?
WHAT?
NO... NO...!
I CAN HEAR EVERYTHING FOR MILES. CELL PHONE CHATTER. RADIO BROADCASTS. SATELLITE FEEDS. BILLIONS OF EMAILS AND TEXTS FLOATING IN THE ETHER.
WHAT IS SHE DOING?! LAST THING THIS SHIP NEEDS IS ANOTHER FREAKING HOLE!
GO! GO! CLOSE THE DOOR!

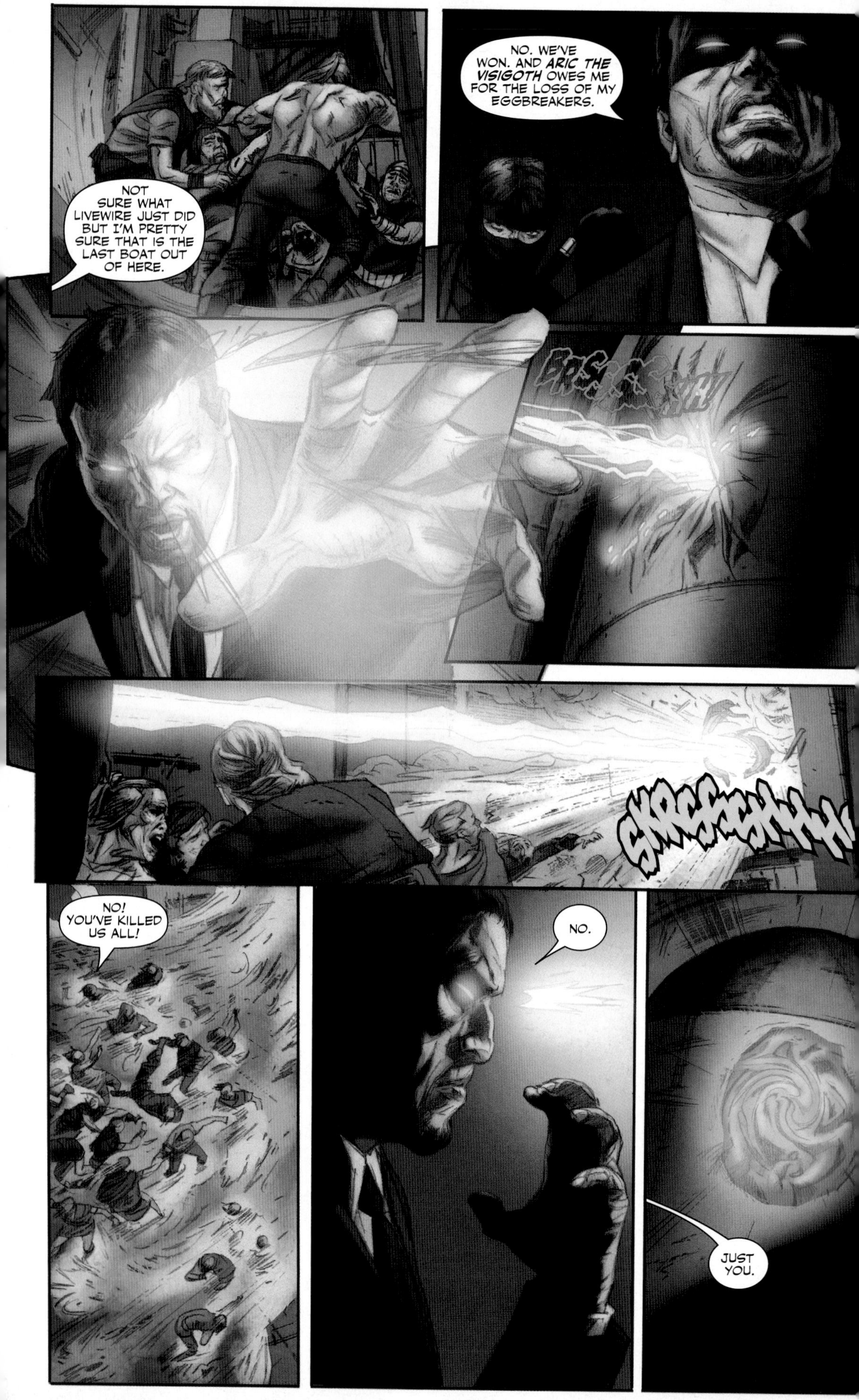
NOT SURE WHAT LIVEWIRE JUST DID BUT I'M PRETTY SURE THAT IS THE LAST BOAT OUT OF HERE.
NO. WE'VE WON. AND ARIC THE VISIGOTH OWES ME FOR THE LOSS OF MY EGGBREAKERS.
SKRCSSCHHHH
NO! YOU'VE KILLED US ALL!
NO.
JUST YOU.

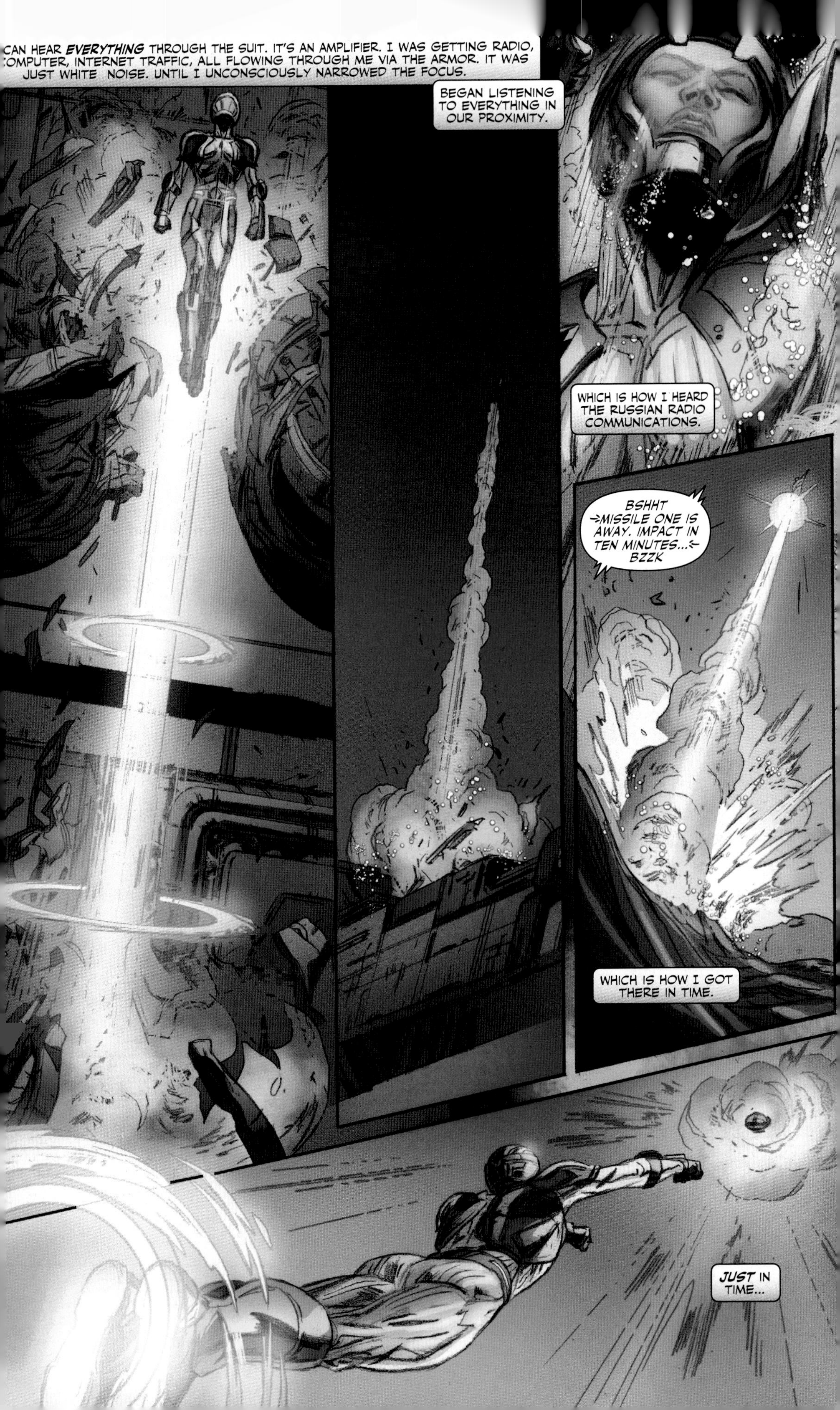

CAN HEAR EVERYTHING THROUGH THE SUIT. IT'S AN AMPLIFIER. I WAS GETTING RADIO, COMPUTER, INTERNET TRAFFIC, ALL FLOWING THROUGH ME VIA THE ARMOR. IT WAS JUST WHITE NOISE. UNTIL I UNCONSCIOUSLY NARROWED THE FOCUS.
BEGAN LISTENING TO EVERYTHING IN OUR PROXIMITY.
WHICH IS HOW I HEARD THE RUSSIAN RADIO COMMUNICATIONS.
BSHHT —MISSILE ONE IS AWAY. IMPACT IN TEN MINUTES...— BZZK
WHICH IS HOW I GOT THERE IN TIME.
JUST IN TIME...

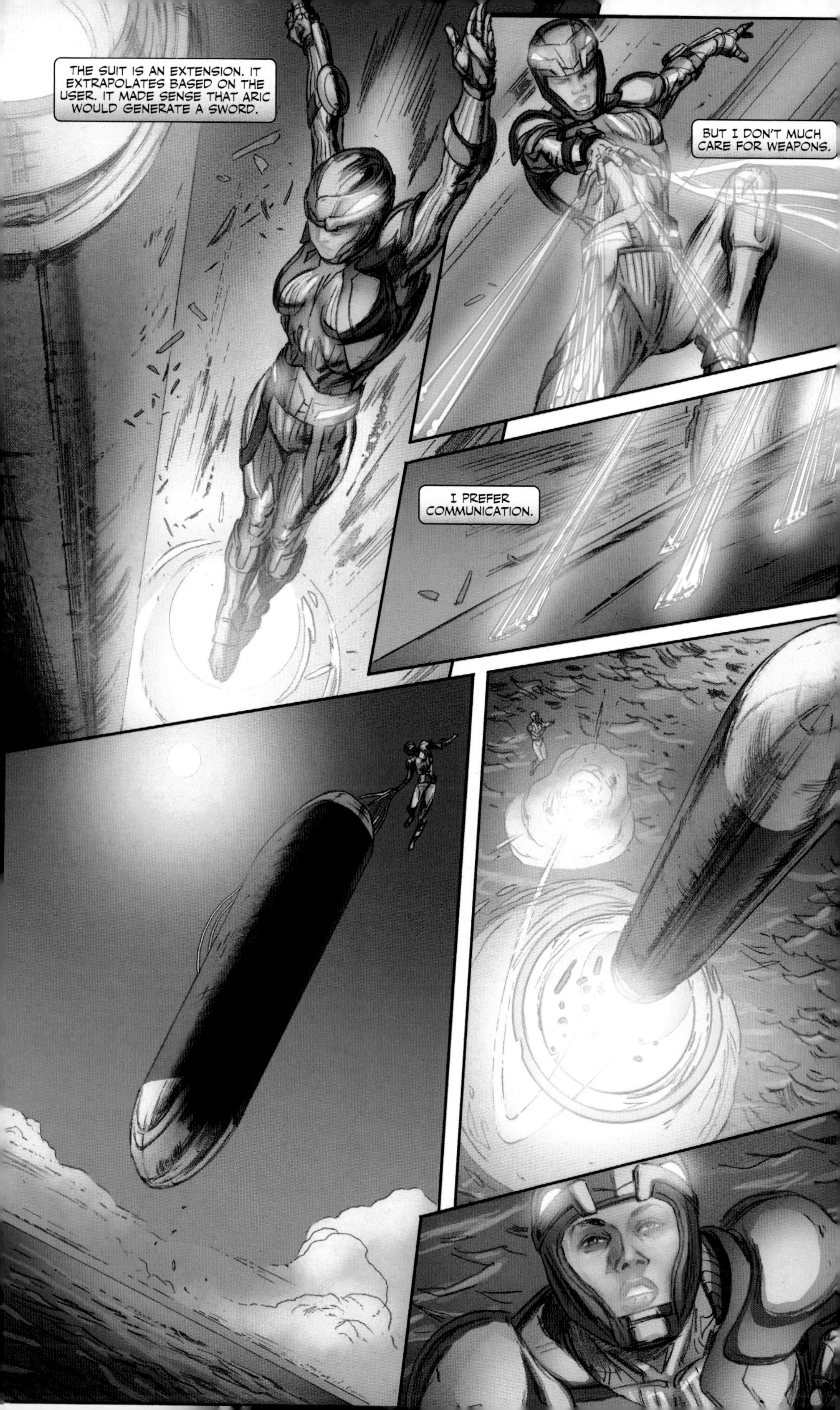
THE SUIT IS AN EXTENSION. IT EXTRAPOLATES BASED ON THE USER. IT MADE SENSE THAT ARIC WOULD GENERATE A SWORD.
BUT I DON'T MUCH CARE FOR WEAPONS.
I PREFER COMMUNICATION.

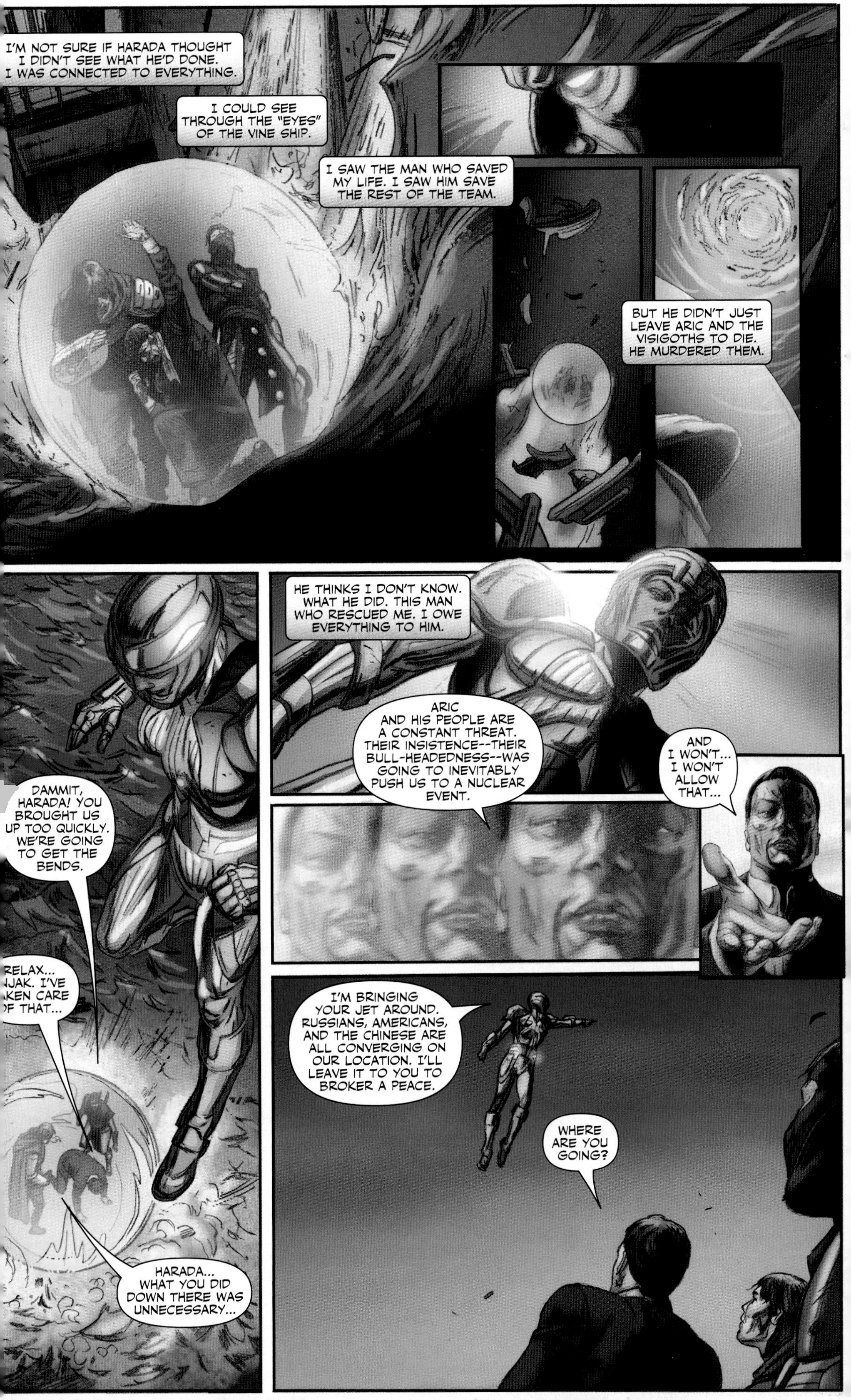
I'M NOT SURE IF HARADA THOUGHT I DIDN'T SEE WHAT HE'D DONE. I WAS CONNECTED TO EVERYTHING.
I COULD SEE THROUGH THE "EYES" OF THE VINE SHIP.
I SAW THE MAN WHO SAVED MY LIFE. I SAW HIM SAVE THE REST OF THE TEAM.
BUT HE DIDN'T JUST LEAVE ARIC AND THE VISIGOTHS TO DIE. HE MURDERED THEM.
DAMMIT, HARADA! YOU BROUGHT US UP TOO QUICKLY. WE'RE GOING TO GET THE BENDS.
RELAX... NJAK. I'VE KEN CARE OF THAT...
HARADA... WHAT YOU DID DOWN THERE WAS UNNECESSARY...
HE THINKS I DON'T KNOW. WHAT HE DID. THIS MAN WHO RESCUED ME. I OWE EVERYTHING TO HIM.
ARIC AND HIS PEOPLE ARE A CONSTANT THREAT. THEIR INSISTENCE--THEIR BULL-HEADEDNESS--WAS GOING TO INEVITABLY PUSH US TO A NUCLEAR EVENT.
AND I WON'T... I WON'T ALLOW THAT...
I'M BRINGING YOUR JET AROUND. RUSSIANS, AMERICANS, AND THE CHINESE ARE ALL CONVERGING ON OUR LOCATION. I'LL LEAVE IT TO YOU TO BROKER A PEACE.
WHERE ARE YOU GOING?

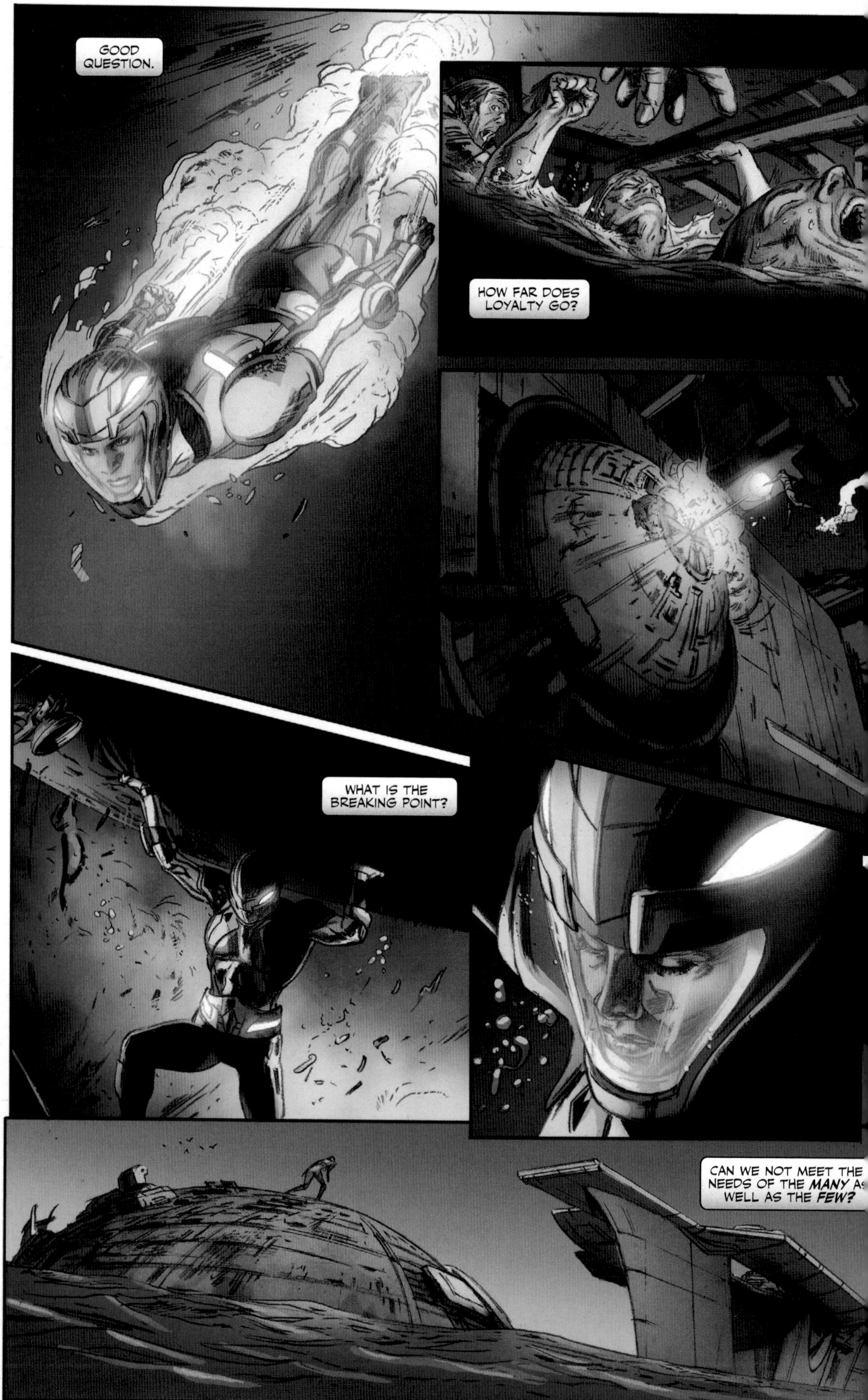
GOOD QUESTION.
HOW FAR DOES LOYALTY GO?
WHAT IS THE BREAKING POINT?
CAN WE NOT MEET THE NEEDS OF THE MANY AS WELL AS THE FEW?

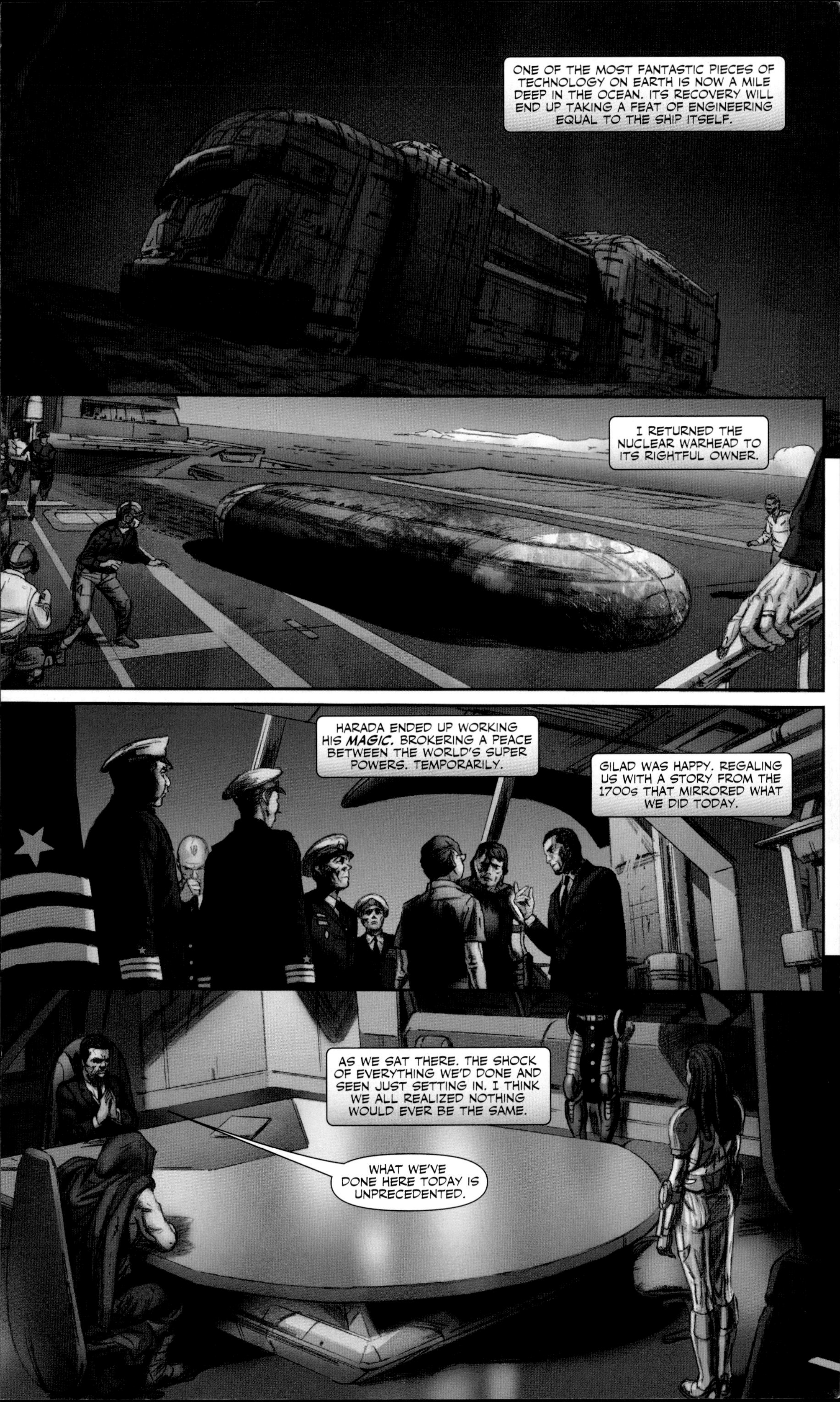

ONE OF THE MOST FANTASTIC PIECES OF TECHNOLOGY ON EARTH IS NOW A MILE DEEP IN THE OCEAN. ITS RECOVERY WILL END UP TAKING A FEAT OF ENGINEERING EQUAL TO THE SHIP ITSELF.
I RETURNED THE NUCLEAR WARHEAD TO ITS RIGHTFUL OWNER.
HARADA ENDED UP WORKING HIS *MAGIC.* BROKERING A PEACE BETWEEN THE WORLD'S SUPER POWERS. TEMPORARILY.
GILAD WAS HAPPY. REGALING US WITH A STORY FROM THE 1700s THAT MIRRORED WHAT WE DID TODAY.
AS WE SAT THERE. THE SHOCK OF EVERYTHING WE'D DONE AND SEEN JUST SETTING IN. I THINK WE ALL REALIZED NOTHING WOULD EVER BE THE SAME.
WHAT WE'VE DONE HERE TODAY IS UNPRECEDENTED.

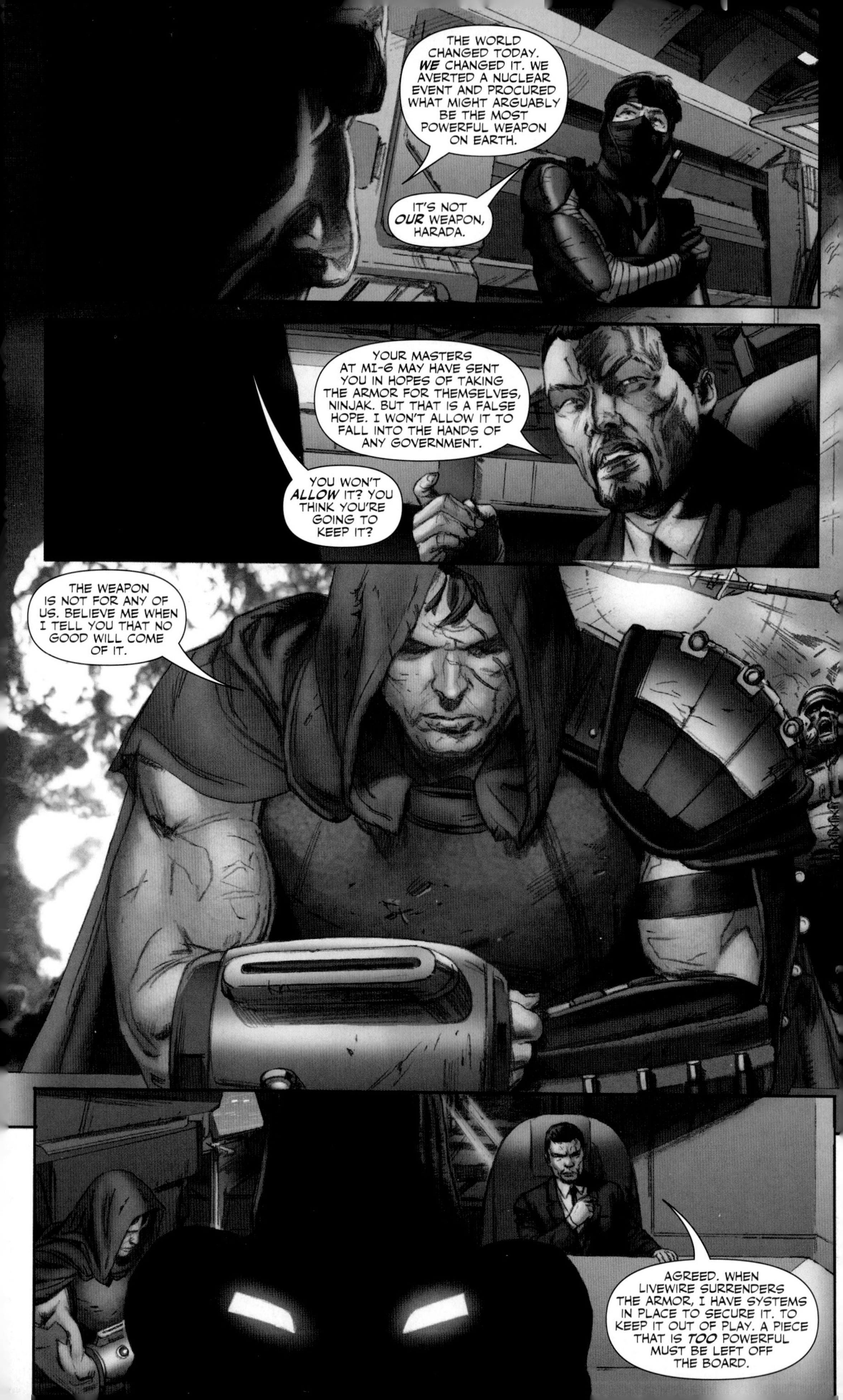
THE WORLD CHANGED TODAY. WE CHANGED IT. WE AVERTED A NUCLEAR EVENT AND PROCURED WHAT MIGHT ARGUABLY BE THE MOST POWERFUL WEAPON ON EARTH.
IT'S NOT OUR WEAPON, HARADA.
YOUR MASTERS AT MI-6 MAY HAVE SENT YOU IN HOPES OF TAKING THE ARMOR FOR THEMSELVES, NINJAK. BUT THAT IS A FALSE HOPE. I WON'T ALLOW IT TO FALL INTO THE HANDS OF ANY GOVERNMENT.
YOU WON'T ALLOW IT? YOU THINK YOU'RE GOING TO KEEP IT?
THE WEAPON IS NOT FOR ANY OF US. BELIEVE ME WHEN I TELL YOU THAT NO GOOD WILL COME OF IT.
AGREED. WHEN LIVEWIRE SURRENDERS THE ARMOR, I HAVE SYSTEMS IN PLACE TO SECURE IT. TO KEEP IT OUT OF PLAY. A PIECE THAT IS TOO POWERFUL MUST BE LEFT OFF THE BOARD.

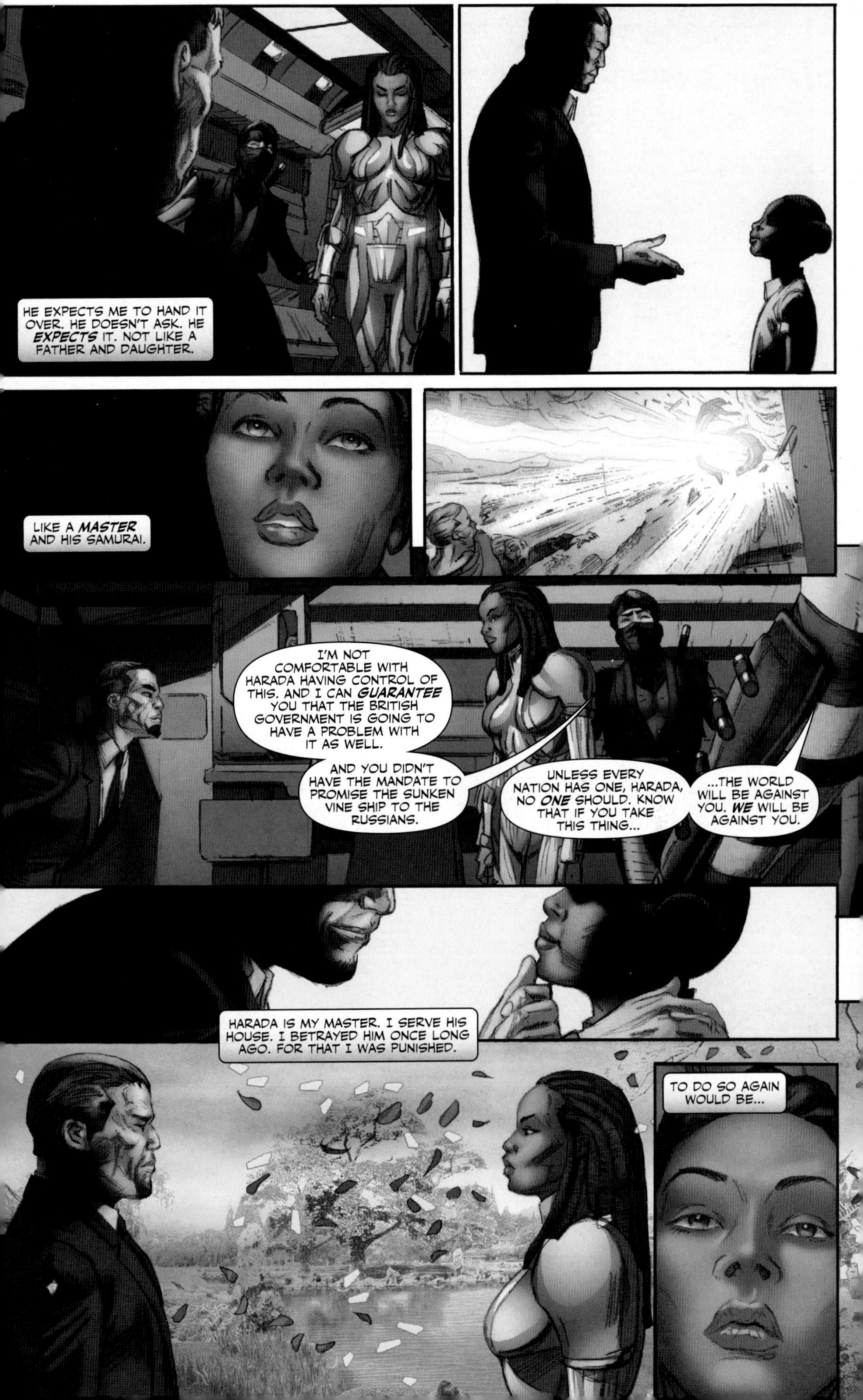
HE EXPECTS ME TO HAND IT OVER. HE DOESN'T ASK. HE *EXPECTS* IT. NOT LIKE A FATHER AND DAUGHTER.
LIKE A *MASTER* AND HIS SAMURAI.
I'M NOT COMFORTABLE WITH HARADA HAVING CONTROL OF THIS. AND I CAN *GUARANTEE* YOU THAT THE BRITISH GOVERNMENT IS GOING TO HAVE A PROBLEM WITH IT AS WELL.
AND YOU DIDN'T HAVE THE MANDATE TO PROMISE THE SUNKEN VINE SHIP TO THE RUSSIANS.
UNLESS EVERY NATION HAS ONE, HARADA, NO *ONE* SHOULD. KNOW THAT IF YOU TAKE THIS THING...
...THE WORLD WILL BE AGAINST YOU. *WE* WILL BE AGAINST YOU.
HARADA IS MY MASTER. I SERVE HIS HOUSE. I BETRAYED HIM ONCE LONG AGO. FOR THAT I WAS PUNISHED.
TO DO SO AGAIN WOULD BE...

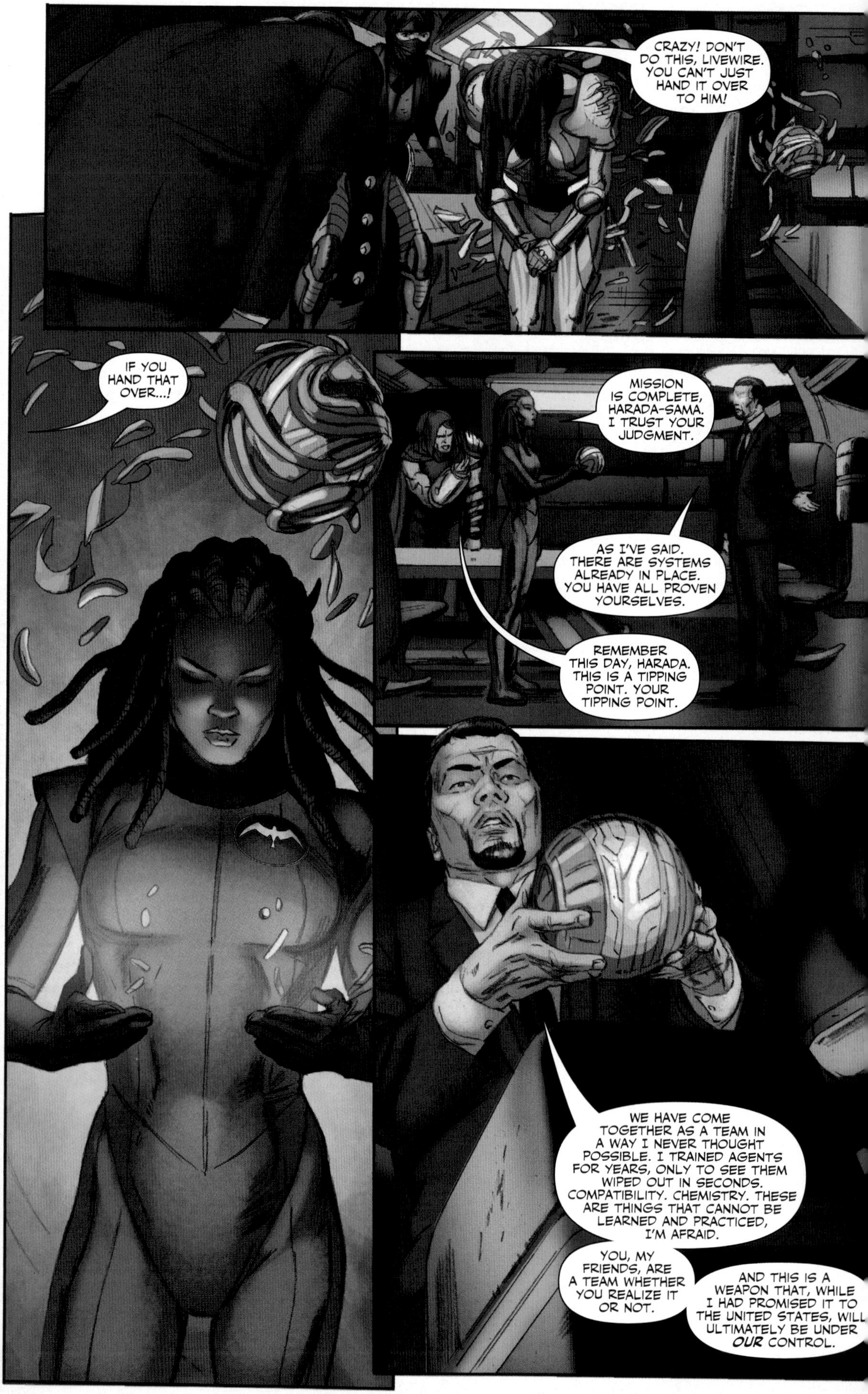
CRAZY! DON'T DO THIS, LIVEWIRE. YOU CAN'T JUST HAND IT OVER TO HIM!
IF YOU HAND THAT OVER...!
MISSION IS COMPLETE, HARADA-SAMA. I TRUST YOUR JUDGMENT.
AS I'VE SAID. THERE ARE SYSTEMS ALREADY IN PLACE. YOU HAVE ALL PROVEN YOURSELVES.
REMEMBER THIS DAY, HARADA. THIS IS A TIPPING POINT. YOUR TIPPING POINT.
WE HAVE COME TOGETHER AS A TEAM IN A WAY I NEVER THOUGHT POSSIBLE. I TRAINED AGENTS FOR YEARS, ONLY TO SEE THEM WIPED OUT IN SECONDS. COMPATIBILITY. CHEMISTRY. THESE ARE THINGS THAT CANNOT BE LEARNED AND PRACTICED, I'M AFRAID.
YOU, MY FRIENDS, ARE A TEAM WHETHER YOU REALIZE IT OR NOT.
AND THIS IS A WEAPON THAT, WHILE I HAD PROMISED IT TO THE UNITED STATES, WILL ULTIMATELY BE UNDER *OUR* CONTROL.

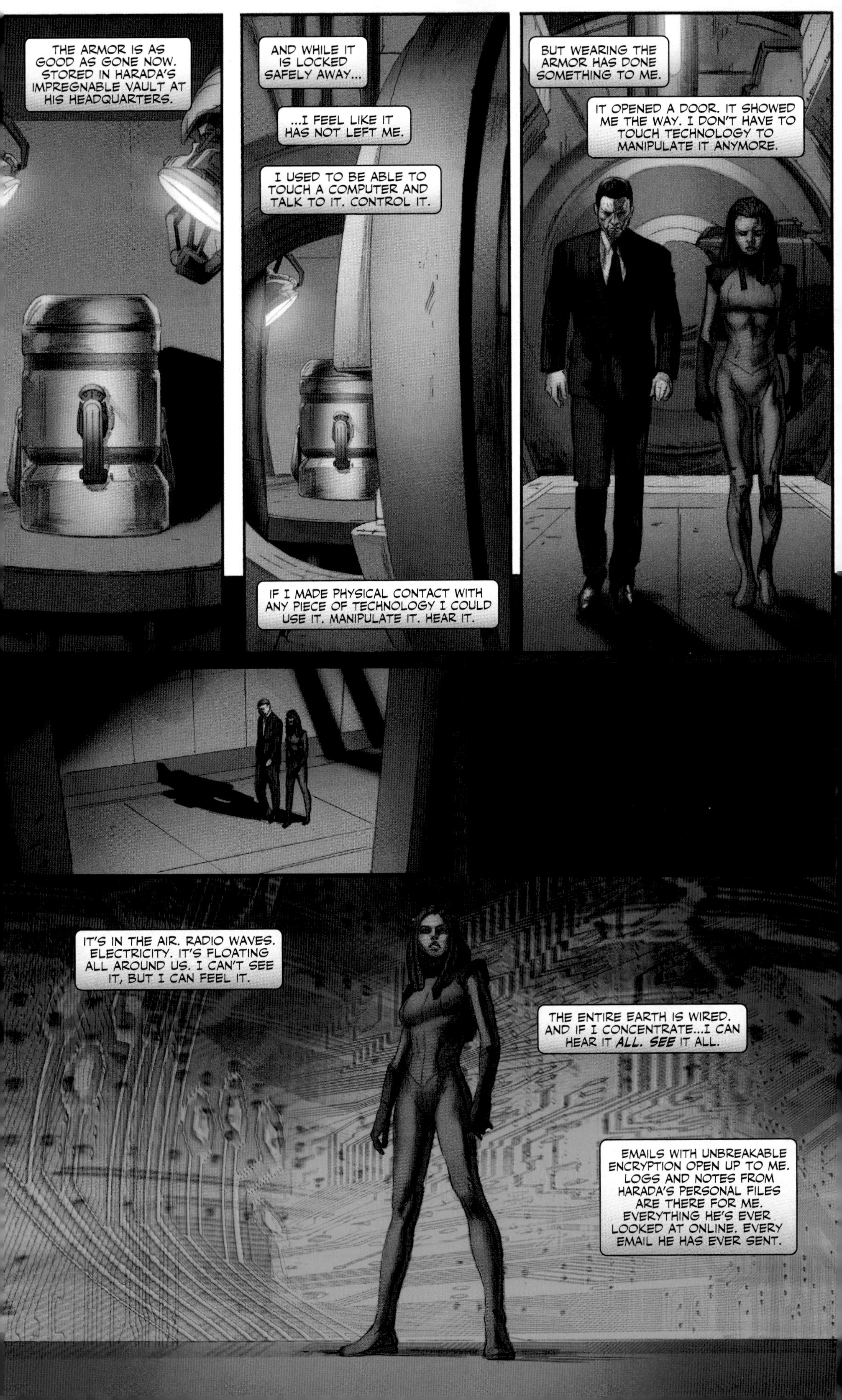

THE ARMOR IS AS GOOD AS GONE NOW. STORED IN HARADA'S IMPREGNABLE VAULT AT HIS HEADQUARTERS.
AND WHILE IT IS LOCKED SAFELY AWAY...
...I FEEL LIKE IT HAS NOT LEFT ME.
I USED TO BE ABLE TO TOUCH A COMPUTER AND TALK TO IT. CONTROL IT.
IF I MADE PHYSICAL CONTACT WITH ANY PIECE OF TECHNOLOGY I COULD USE IT. MANIPULATE IT. HEAR IT.
BUT WEARING THE ARMOR HAS DONE SOMETHING TO ME.
IT OPENED A DOOR. IT SHOWED ME THE WAY. I DON'T HAVE TO TOUCH TECHNOLOGY TO MANIPULATE IT ANYMORE.
IT'S IN THE AIR. RADIO WAVES. ELECTRICITY. IT'S FLOATING ALL AROUND US. I CAN'T SEE IT, BUT I CAN FEEL IT.
THE ENTIRE EARTH IS WIRED. AND IF I CONCENTRATE...I CAN HEAR IT *ALL*. *SEE* IT ALL.
EMAILS WITH UNBREAKABLE ENCRYPTION OPEN UP TO ME. LOGS AND NOTES FROM HARADA'S PERSONAL FILES ARE THERE FOR ME. EVERYTHING HE'S EVER LOOKED AT ONLINE. EVERY EMAIL HE HAS EVER SENT.

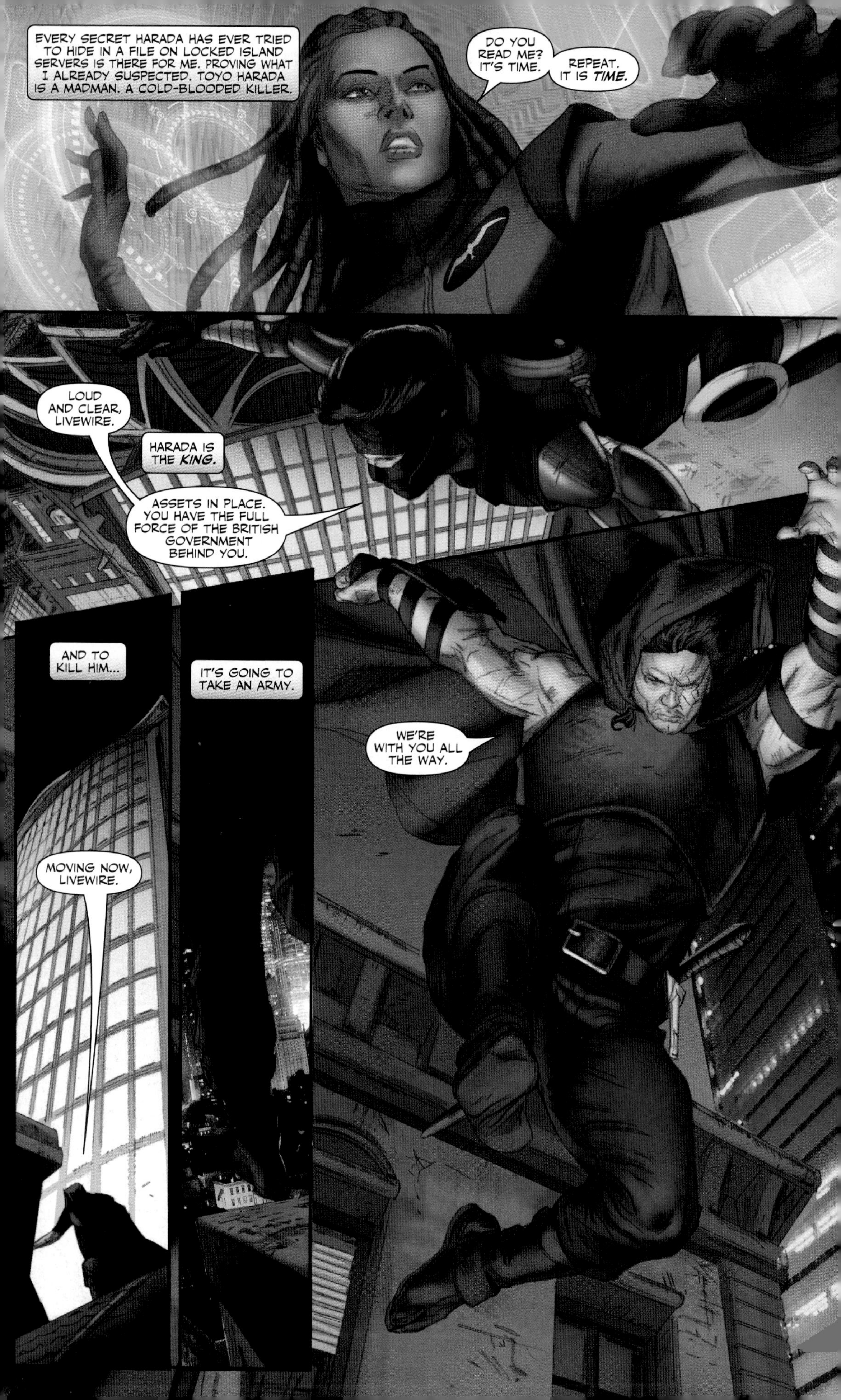
EVERY SECRET HARADA HAS EVER TRIED TO HIDE IN A FILE ON LOCKED ISLAND SERVERS IS THERE FOR ME. PROVING WHAT I ALREADY SUSPECTED. TOYO HARADA IS A MADMAN. A COLD-BLOODED KILLER.
DO YOU READ ME? IT'S TIME.
REPEAT. IT IS *TIME.*
LOUD AND CLEAR, LIVEWIRE.
HARADA IS THE *KING.*
ASSETS IN PLACE. YOU HAVE THE FULL FORCE OF THE BRITISH GOVERNMENT BEHIND YOU.
AND TO KILL HIM...
IT'S GOING TO TAKE AN ARMY.
WE'RE WITH YOU ALL THE WAY.
MOVING NOW, LIVEWIRE.

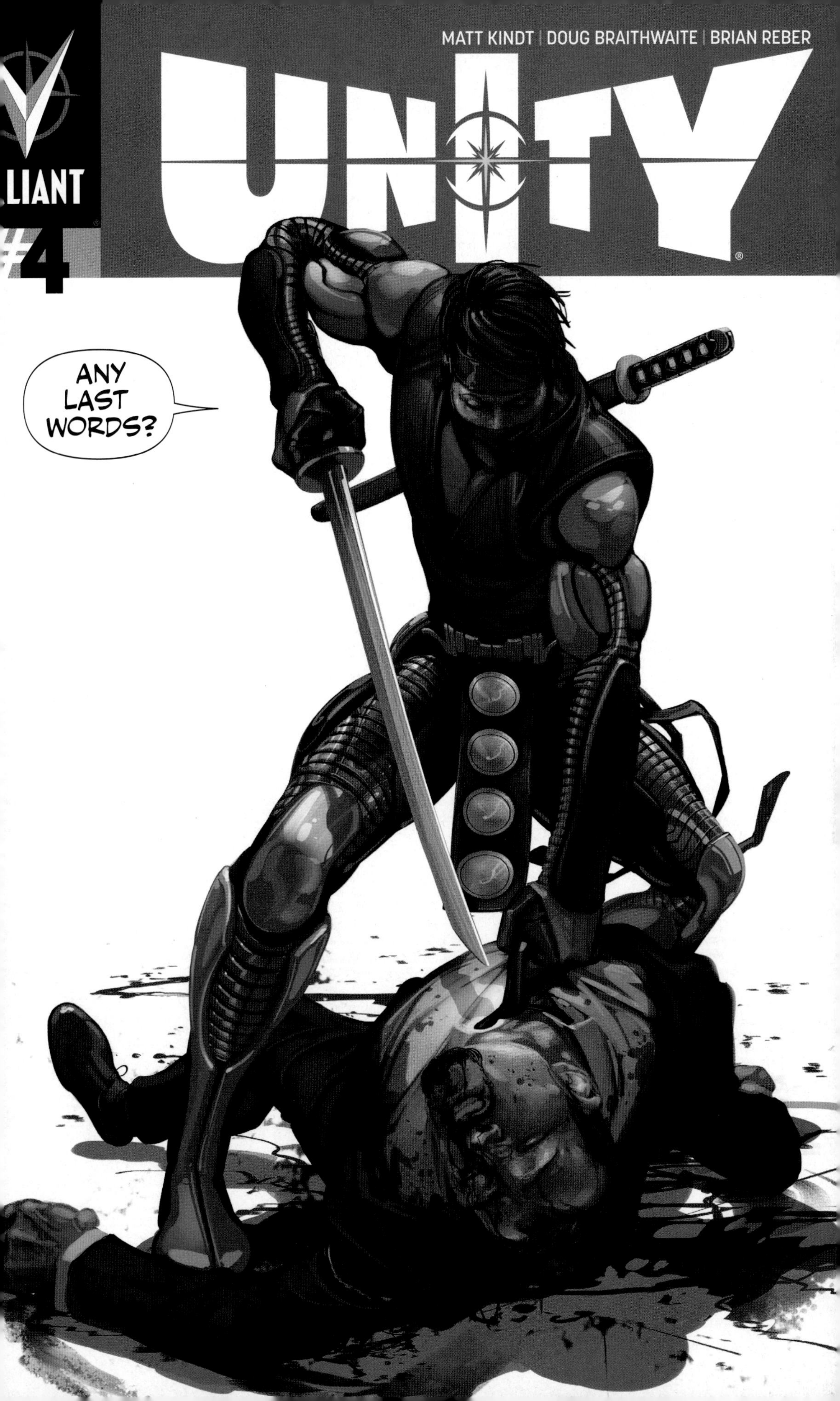
MATT KINDT | DOUG BRAITHWAITE | BRIAN REBER
UNITY
LIANT
#4
ANY LAST WORDS?

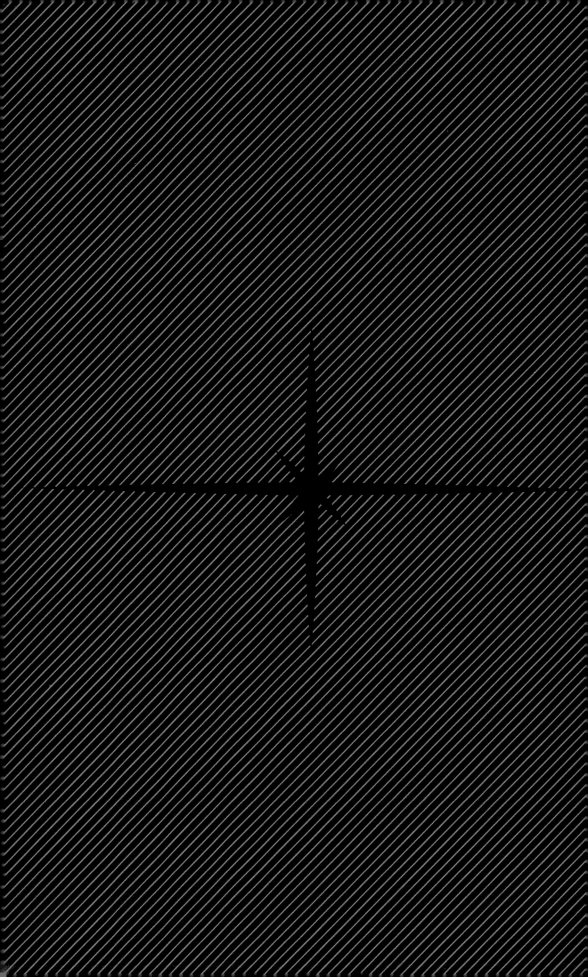

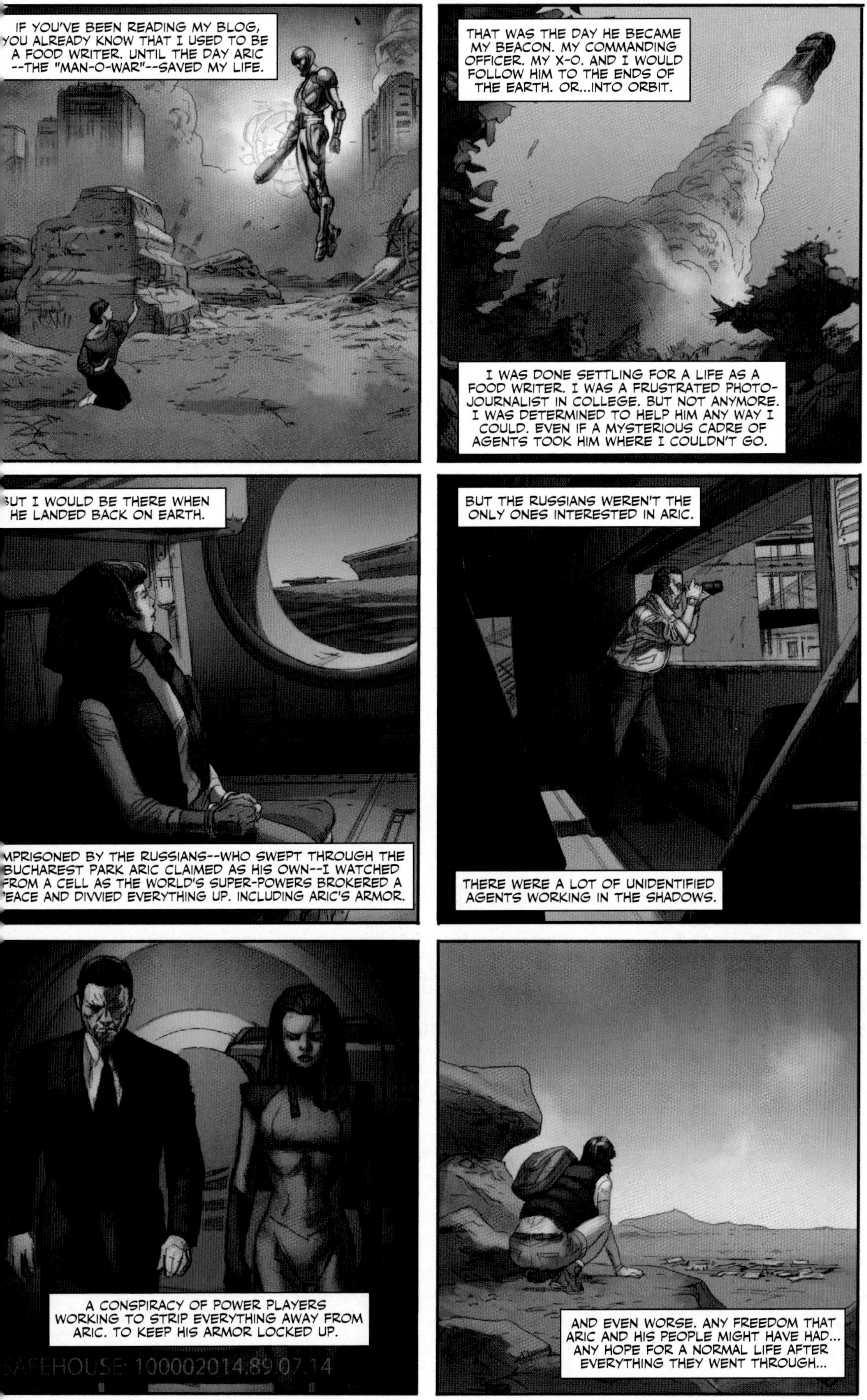
IF YOU'VE BEEN READING MY BLOG, YOU ALREADY KNOW THAT I USED TO BE A FOOD WRITER. UNTIL THE DAY ARIC --THE "MAN-O-WAR"--SAVED MY LIFE.
THAT WAS THE DAY HE BECAME MY BEACON. MY COMMANDING OFFICER. MY X-O. AND I WOULD FOLLOW HIM TO THE ENDS OF THE EARTH. OR...INTO ORBIT.
I WAS DONE SETTLING FOR A LIFE AS A FOOD WRITER. I WAS A FRUSTRATED PHOTO-JOURNALIST IN COLLEGE. BUT NOT ANYMORE. I WAS DETERMINED TO HELP HIM ANY WAY I COULD. EVEN IF A MYSTERIOUS CADRE OF AGENTS TOOK HIM WHERE I COULDN'T GO.
UT I WOULD BE THERE WHEN HE LANDED BACK ON EARTH.
MPRISONED BY THE RUSSIANS--WHO SWEPT THROUGH THE BUCHAREST PARK ARIC CLAIMED AS HIS OWN--I WATCHED FROM A CELL AS THE WORLD'S SUPER-POWERS BROKERED A EACE AND DIVVIED EVERYTHING UP. INCLUDING ARIC'S ARMOR.
BUT THE RUSSIANS WEREN'T THE ONLY ONES INTERESTED IN ARIC.
THERE WERE A LOT OF UNIDENTIFIED AGENTS WORKING IN THE SHADOWS.
A CONSPIRACY OF POWER PLAYERS WORKING TO STRIP EVERYTHING AWAY FROM ARIC. TO KEEP HIS ARMOR LOCKED UP.
AFEHOUSE: 100002014.89.07.14
AND EVEN WORSE. ANY FREEDOM THAT ARIC AND HIS PEOPLE MIGHT HAVE HAD... ANY HOPE FOR A NORMAL LIFE AFTER EVERYTHING THEY WENT THROUGH...

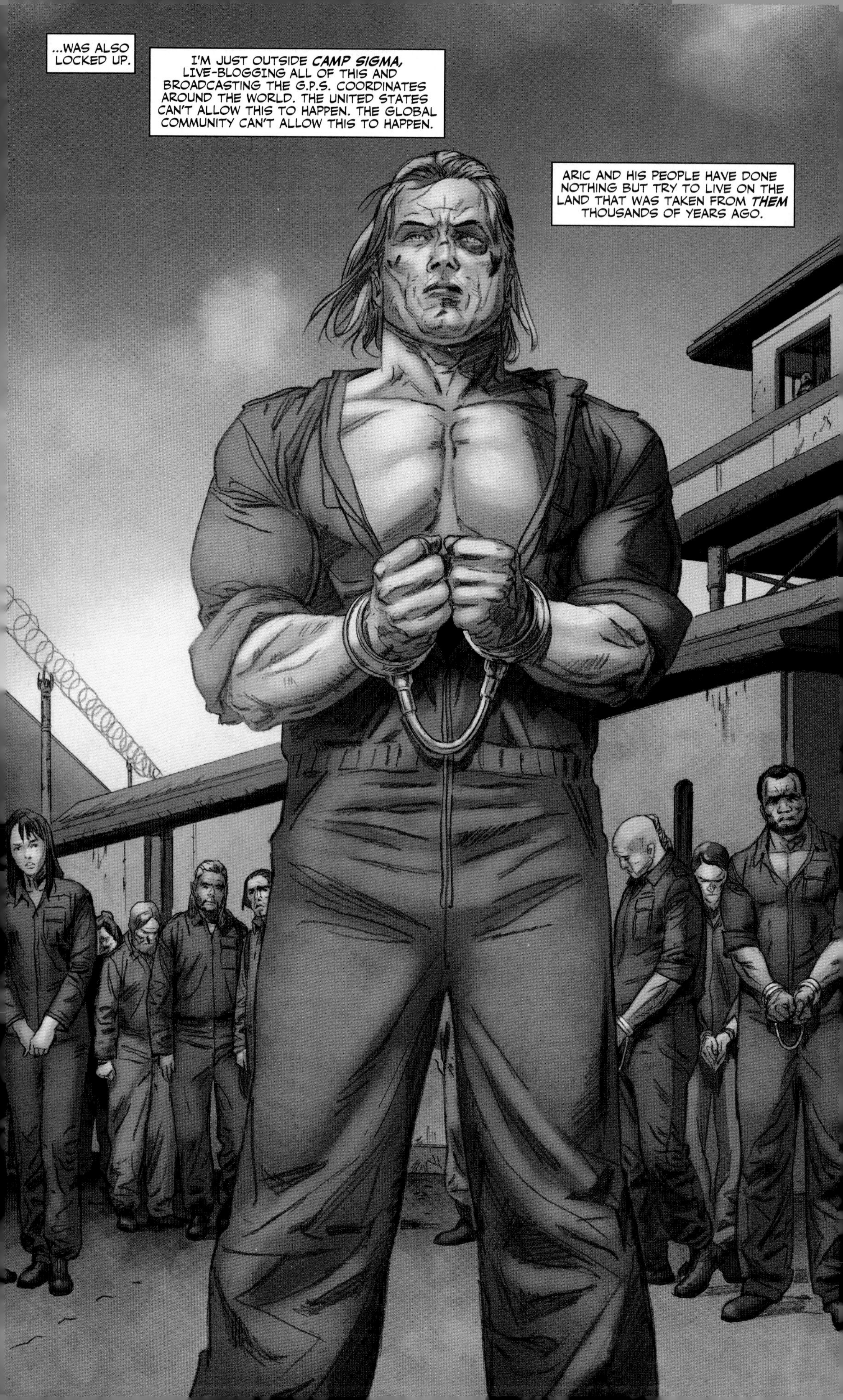
...WAS ALSO LOCKED UP.
I'M JUST OUTSIDE CAMP SIGMA, LIVE-BLOGGING ALL OF THIS AND BROADCASTING THE G.P.S. COORDINATES AROUND THE WORLD. THE UNITED STATES CAN'T ALLOW THIS TO HAPPEN. THE GLOBAL COMMUNITY CAN'T ALLOW THIS TO HAPPEN.
ARIC AND HIS PEOPLE HAVE DONE NOTHING BUT TRY TO LIVE ON THE LAND THAT WAS TAKEN FROM THEM THOUSANDS OF YEARS AGO.

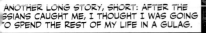
ANOTHER LONG STORY, SHORT: AFTER THE RUSSIANS CAUGHT ME, I THOUGHT I WAS GOING TO SPEND THE REST OF MY LIFE IN A GULAG.

THIS STORY IS TOO IMPORTANT TO IGNORE. TOO BIG TO JUST GO AWAY LIKE THIS.

CRAP. THEY SPOTTED ME.

BUT THE RUSSIANS ARE USING ME TO HARASS THE U.S. I'M USING THE RUSSIANS TO PUT ME INTO POSITION TO DO THE WORK I REALLY WANT TO DO.

ONCE I GET THESE PHOTOS UPLOADED AND ONLINE THERE'S NOTHING THEY CAN DO TO ME. IT'LL BE TOO LATE.

COME ON... COME ON... HURRY UP...!

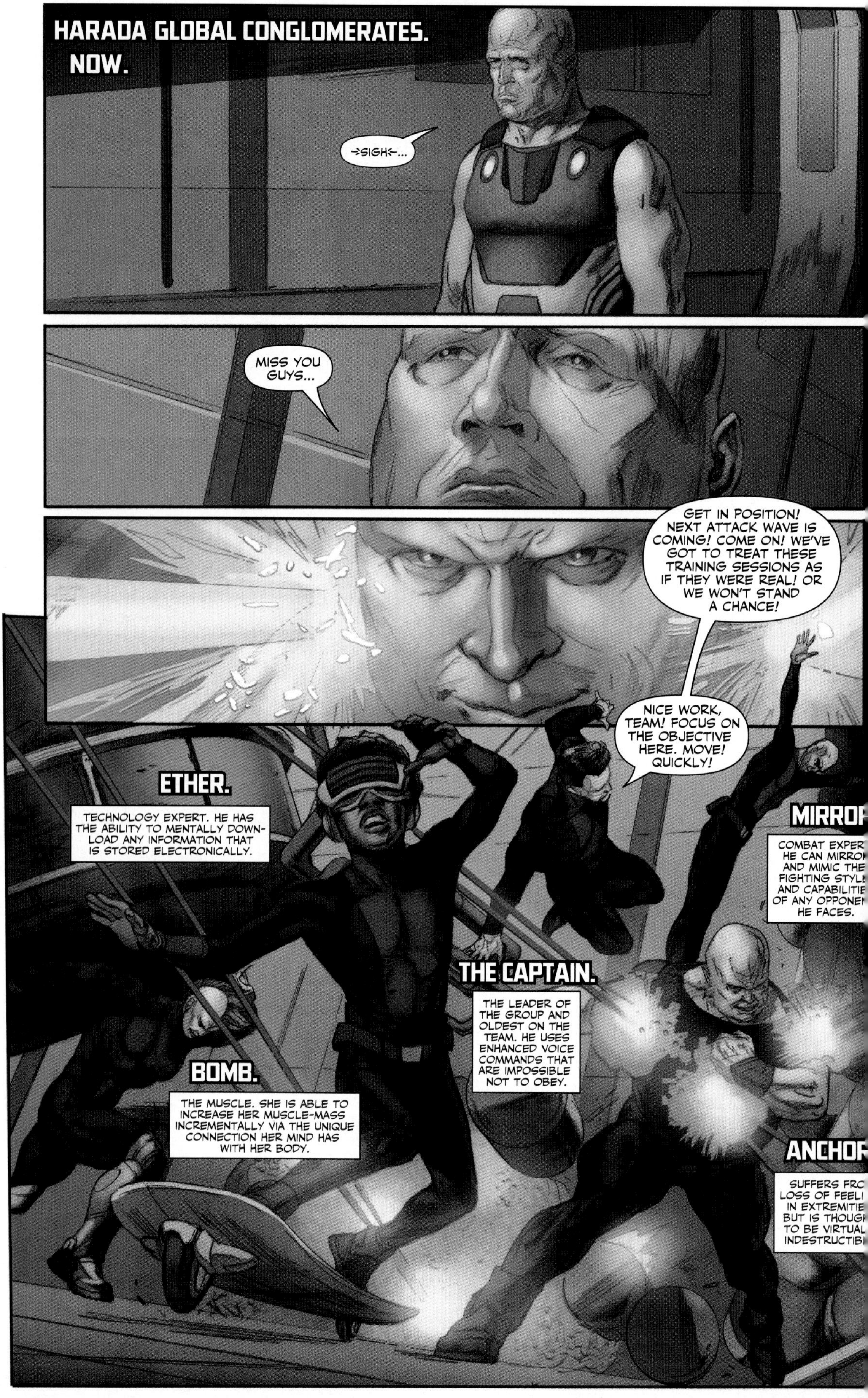

HARADA GLOBAL CONGLOMERATES. NOW.
>SIGH<...
MISS YOU GUYS...
GET IN POSITION! NEXT ATTACK WAVE IS COMING! COME ON! WE'VE GOT TO TREAT THESE TRAINING SESSIONS AS IF THEY WERE REAL! OR WE WON'T STAND A CHANCE!
NICE WORK, TEAM! FOCUS ON THE OBJECTIVE HERE. MOVE! QUICKLY!
ETHER.
TECHNOLOGY EXPERT. HE HAS THE ABILITY TO MENTALLY DOWN-LOAD ANY INFORMATION THAT IS STORED ELECTRONICALLY.
MIRRO
COMBAT EXPER HE CAN MIRRO AND MIMIC THE FIGHTING STYL AND CAPABILITI OF ANY OPPONE HE FACES.
THE CAPTAIN.
THE LEADER OF THE GROUP AND OLDEST ON THE TEAM. HE USES ENHANCED VOICE COMMANDS THAT ARE IMPOSSIBLE NOT TO OBEY.
BOMB.
THE MUSCLE. SHE IS ABLE TO INCREASE HER MUSCLE-MASS INCREMENTALLY VIA THE UNIQUE CONNECTION HER MIND HAS WITH HER BODY.
ANCHO
SUFFERS FR LOSS OF FEELI IN EXTREMITI BUT IS THOUG TO BE VIRTUAL INDESTRUCTI

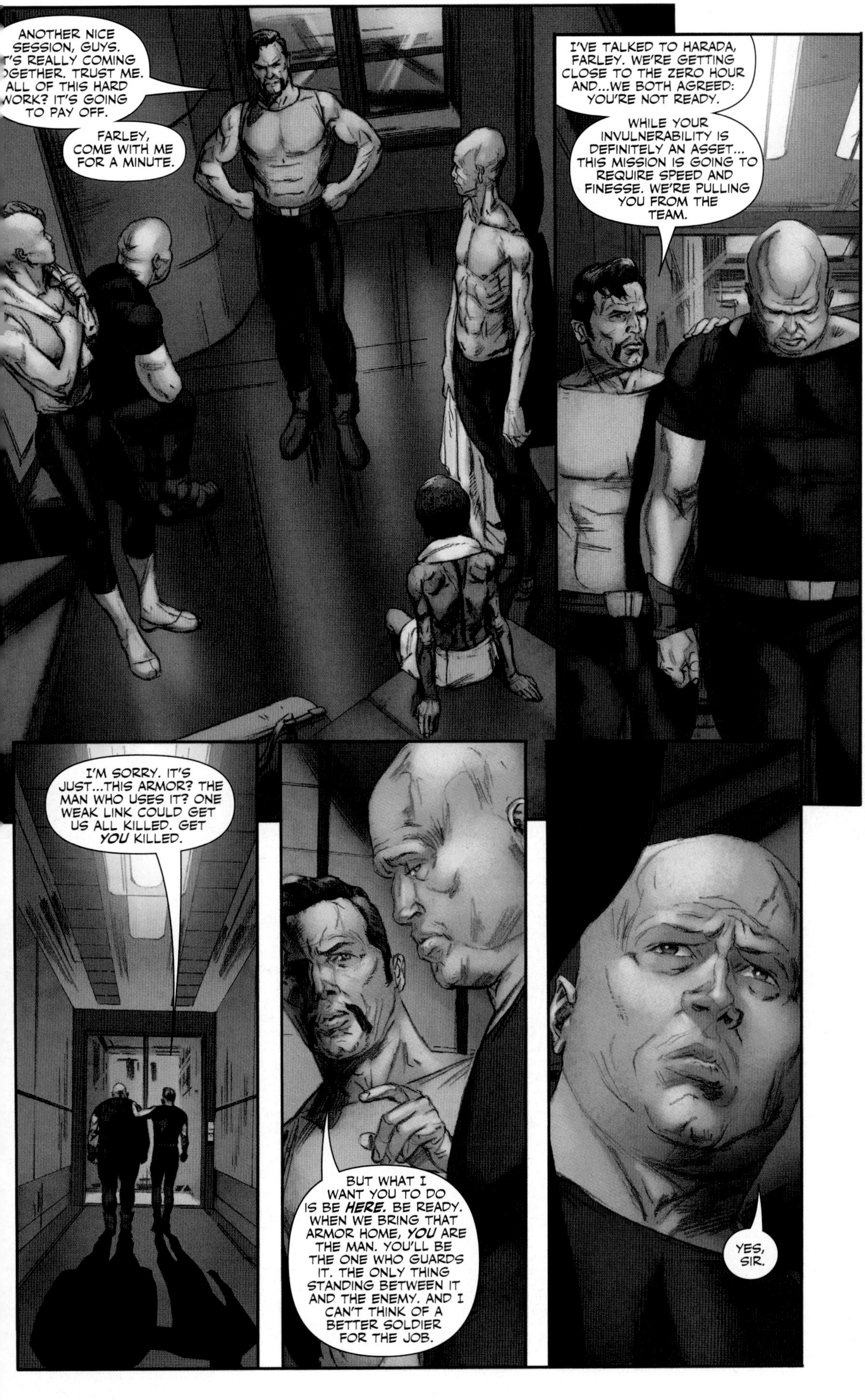

ANOTHER NICE SESSION, GUYS. T'S REALLY COMING OGETHER. TRUST ME. ALL OF THIS HARD WORK? IT'S GOING TO PAY OFF.
FARLEY, COME WITH ME FOR A MINUTE.
I'VE TALKED TO HARADA, FARLEY. WE'RE GETTING CLOSE TO THE ZERO HOUR AND...WE BOTH AGREED: YOU'RE NOT READY.
WHILE YOUR INVULNERABILITY IS DEFINITELY AN ASSET... THIS MISSION IS GOING TO REQUIRE SPEED AND FINESSE. WE'RE PULLING YOU FROM THE TEAM.
I'M SORRY. IT'S JUST...THIS ARMOR? THE MAN WHO USES IT? ONE WEAK LINK COULD GET US ALL KILLED. GET *YOU* KILLED.
BUT WHAT I WANT YOU TO DO IS BE ***HERE.*** BE READY. WHEN WE BRING THAT ARMOR HOME, *YOU* ARE THE MAN. YOU'LL BE THE ONE WHO GUARDS IT. THE ONLY THING STANDING BETWEEN IT AND THE ENEMY. AND I CAN'T THINK OF A BETTER SOLDIER FOR THE JOB.
YES, SIR.

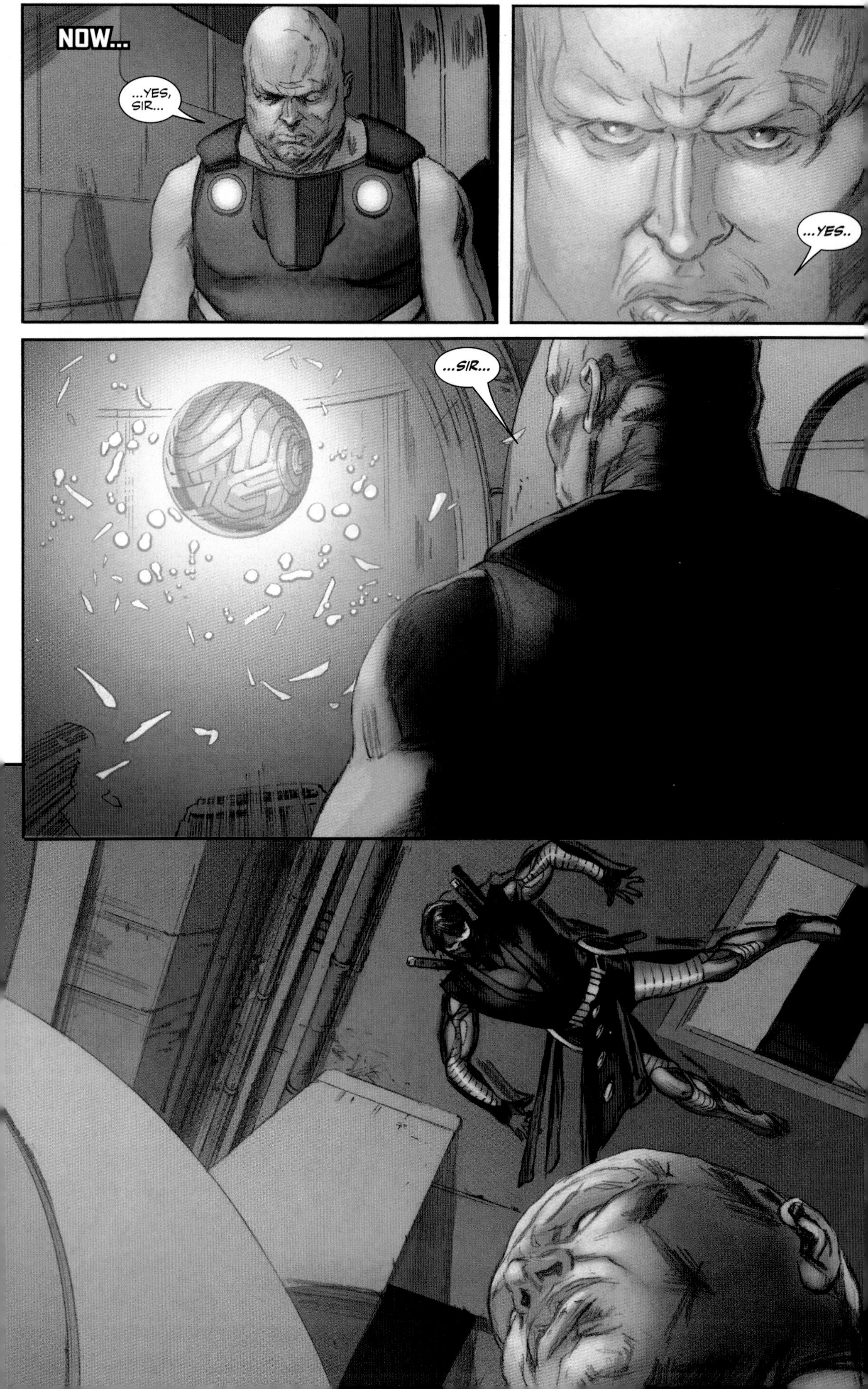
NOW...
...YES, SIR...
...YES..
...SIR...

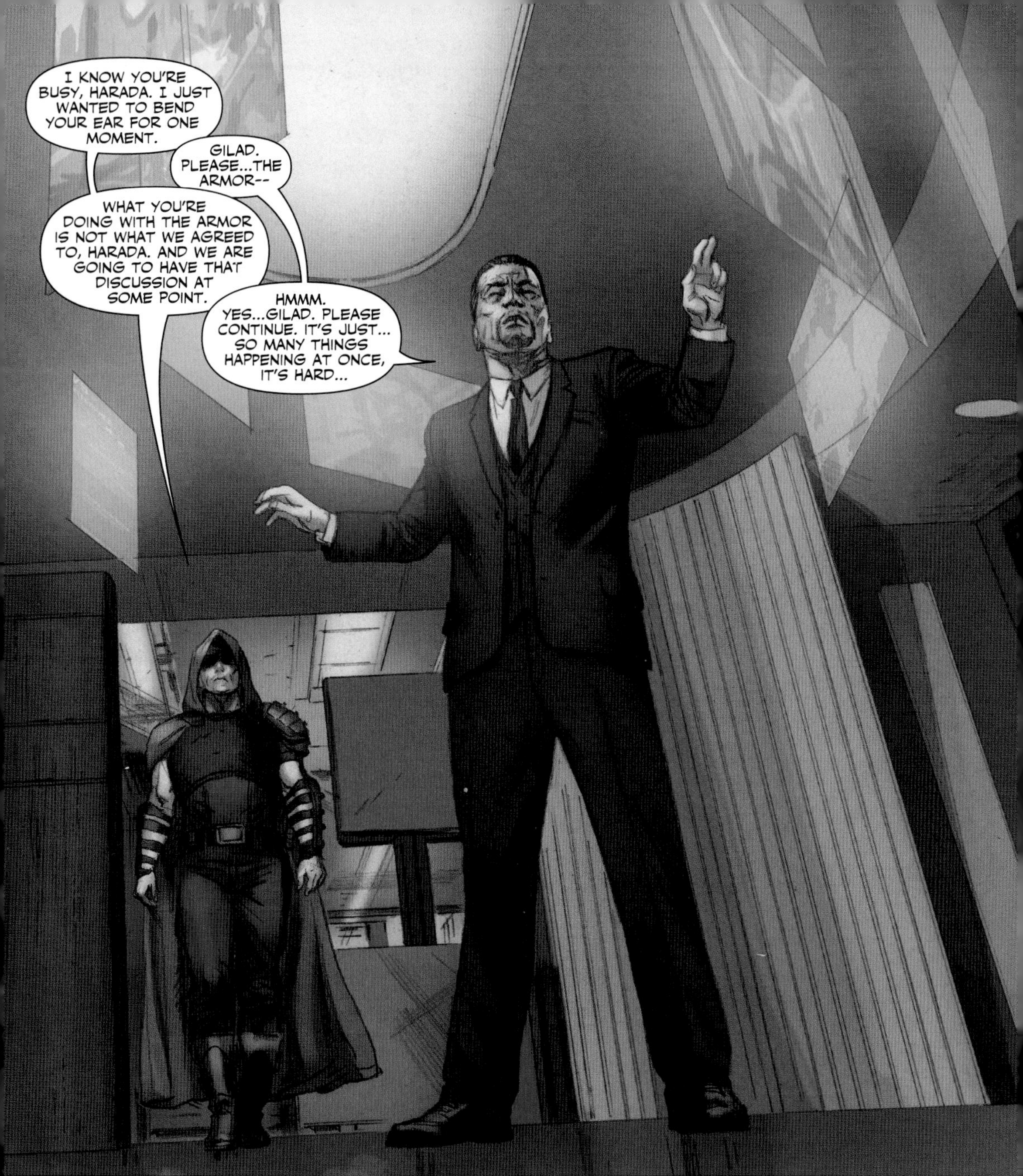
I KNOW YOU'RE BUSY, HARADA. I JUST WANTED TO BEND YOUR EAR FOR ONE MOMENT.
GILAD. PLEASE...THE ARMOR--
WHAT YOU'RE DOING WITH THE ARMOR IS NOT WHAT WE AGREED TO, HARADA. AND WE ARE GOING TO HAVE THAT DISCUSSION AT SOME POINT.
HMMM. YES...GILAD. PLEASE CONTINUE. IT'S JUST... SO MANY THINGS HAPPENING AT ONCE, IT'S HARD...

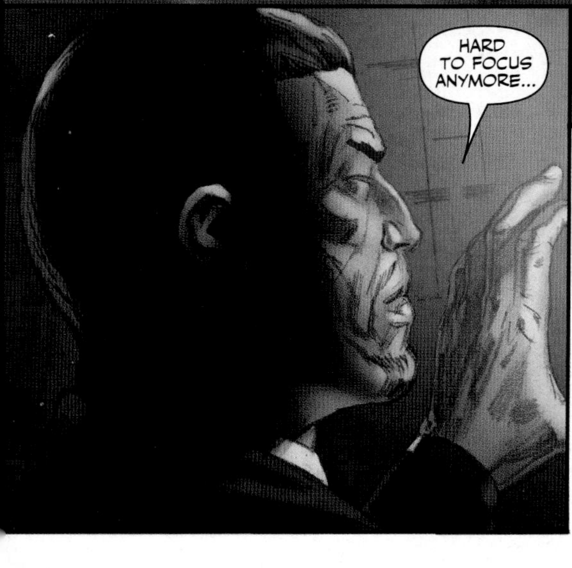
HARD TO FOCUS ANYMORE...

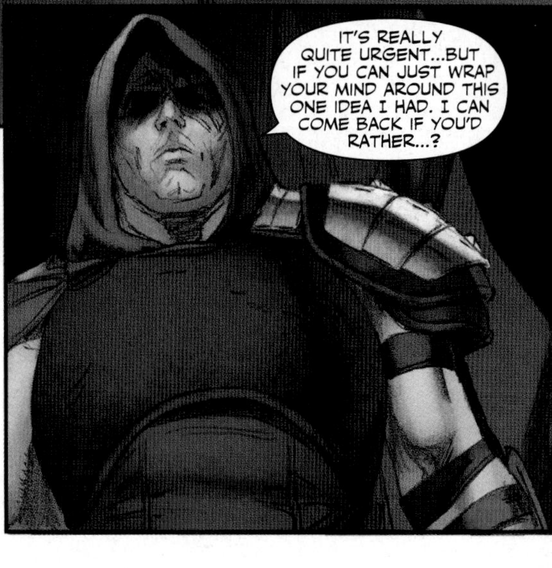
IT'S REALLY QUITE URGENT...BUT IF YOU CAN JUST WRAP YOUR MIND AROUND THIS ONE IDEA I HAD. I CAN COME BACK IF YOU'D RATHER...?

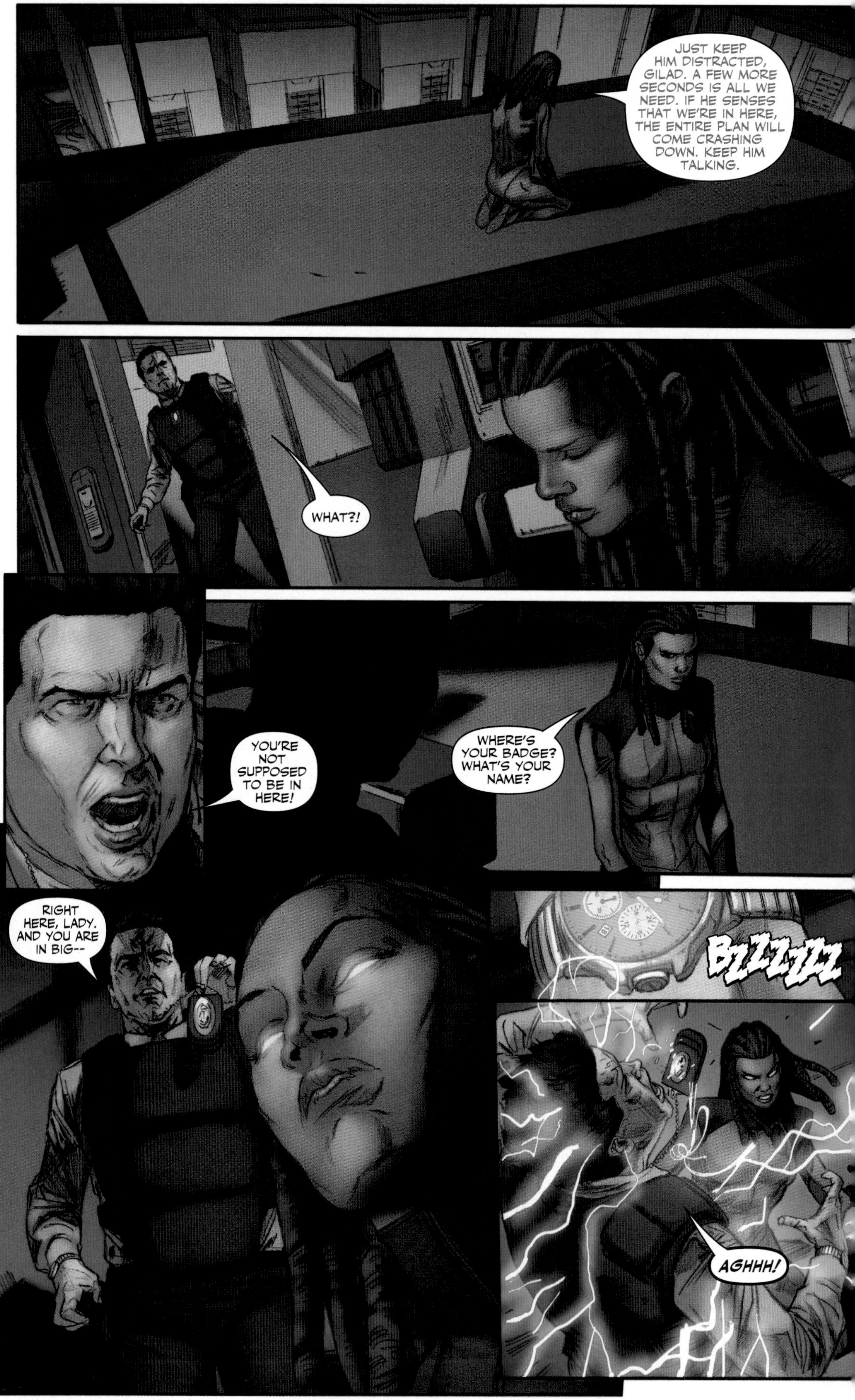
JUST KEEP HIM DISTRACTED, GILAD. A FEW MORE SECONDS IS ALL WE NEED. IF HE SENSES THAT WE'RE IN HERE, THE ENTIRE PLAN WILL COME CRASHING DOWN. KEEP HIM TALKING.
WHAT?!
YOU'RE NOT SUPPOSED TO BE IN HERE!
WHERE'S YOUR BADGE? WHAT'S YOUR NAME?
RIGHT HERE, LADY. AND YOU ARE IN BIG--
BZZZZZZ
AGHHH!

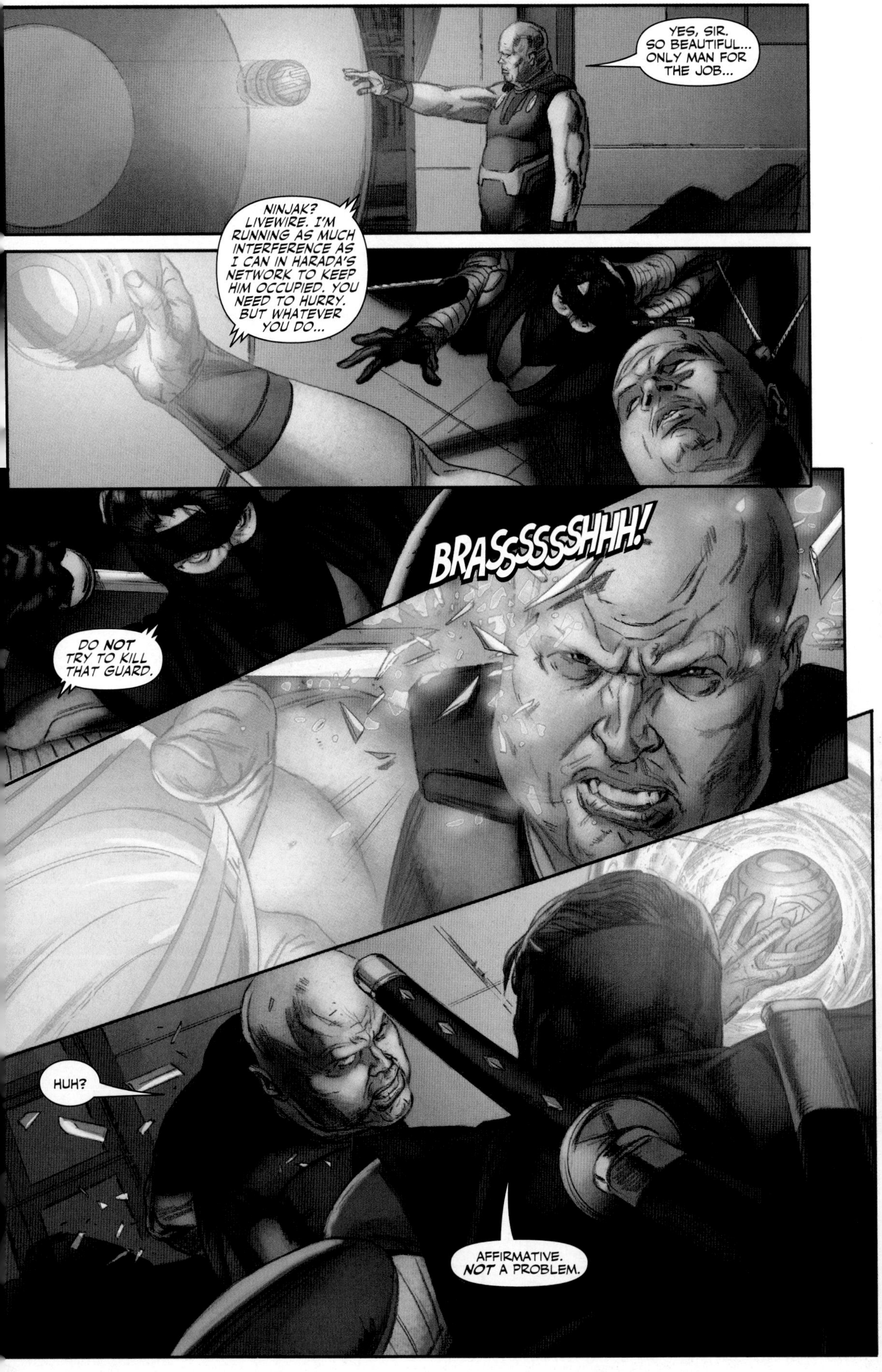
YES, SIR. SO BEAUTIFUL... ONLY MAN FOR THE JOB...
NINJAK? LIVEWIRE. I'M RUNNING AS MUCH INTERFERENCE AS I CAN IN HARADA'S NETWORK TO KEEP HIM OCCUPIED. YOU NEED TO HURRY. BUT WHATEVER YOU DO...
BRASSSSSSHHH!
DO NOT TRY TO KILL THAT GUARD.
HUH?
AFFIRMATIVE. NOT A PROBLEM.

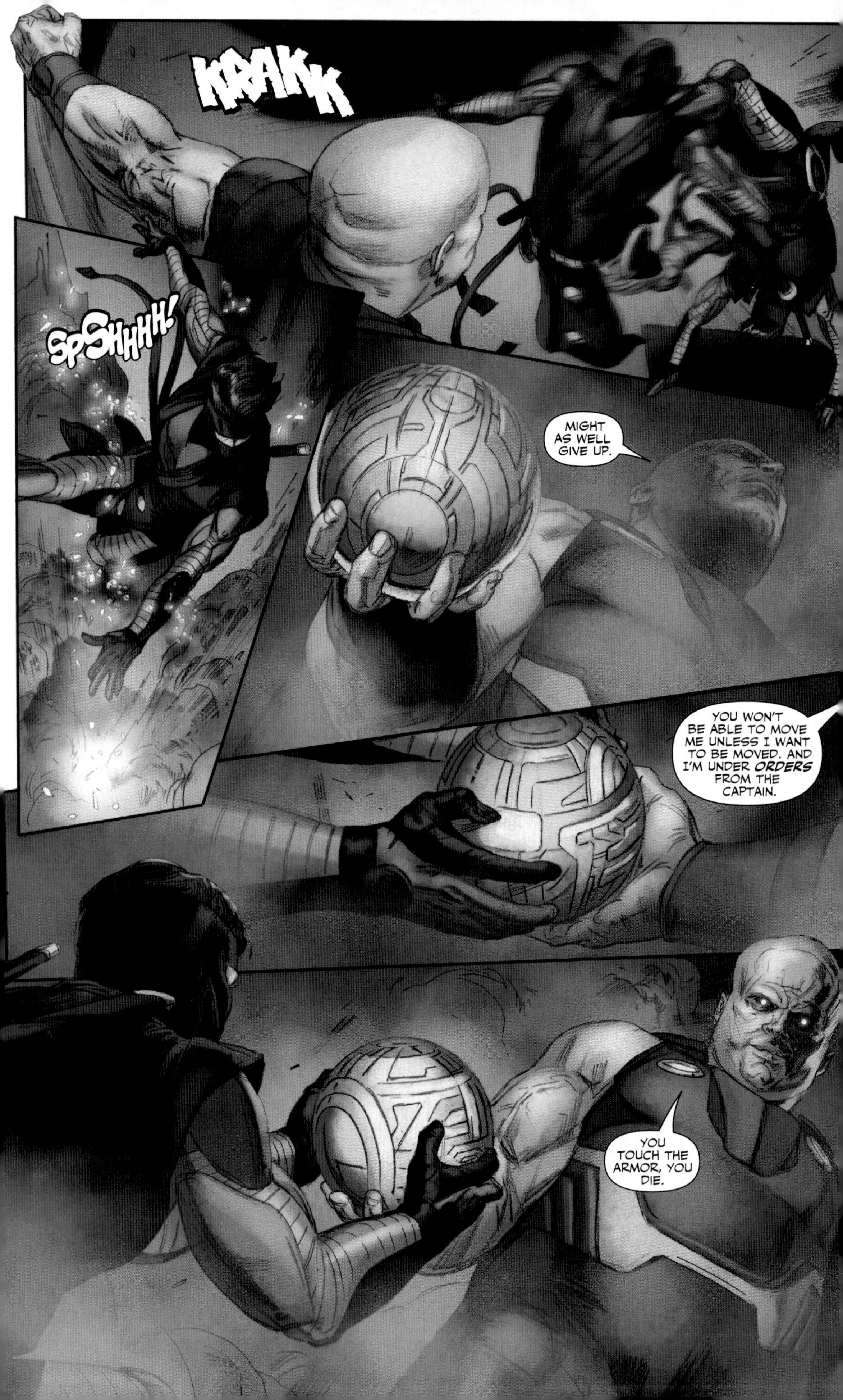
KRAKK
SPSHHHH!
MIGHT AS WELL GIVE UP.
YOU WON'T BE ABLE TO MOVE ME UNLESS I WANT TO BE MOVED. AND I'M UNDER *ORDERS* FROM THE CAPTAIN.
YOU TOUCH THE ARMOR, YOU DIE.

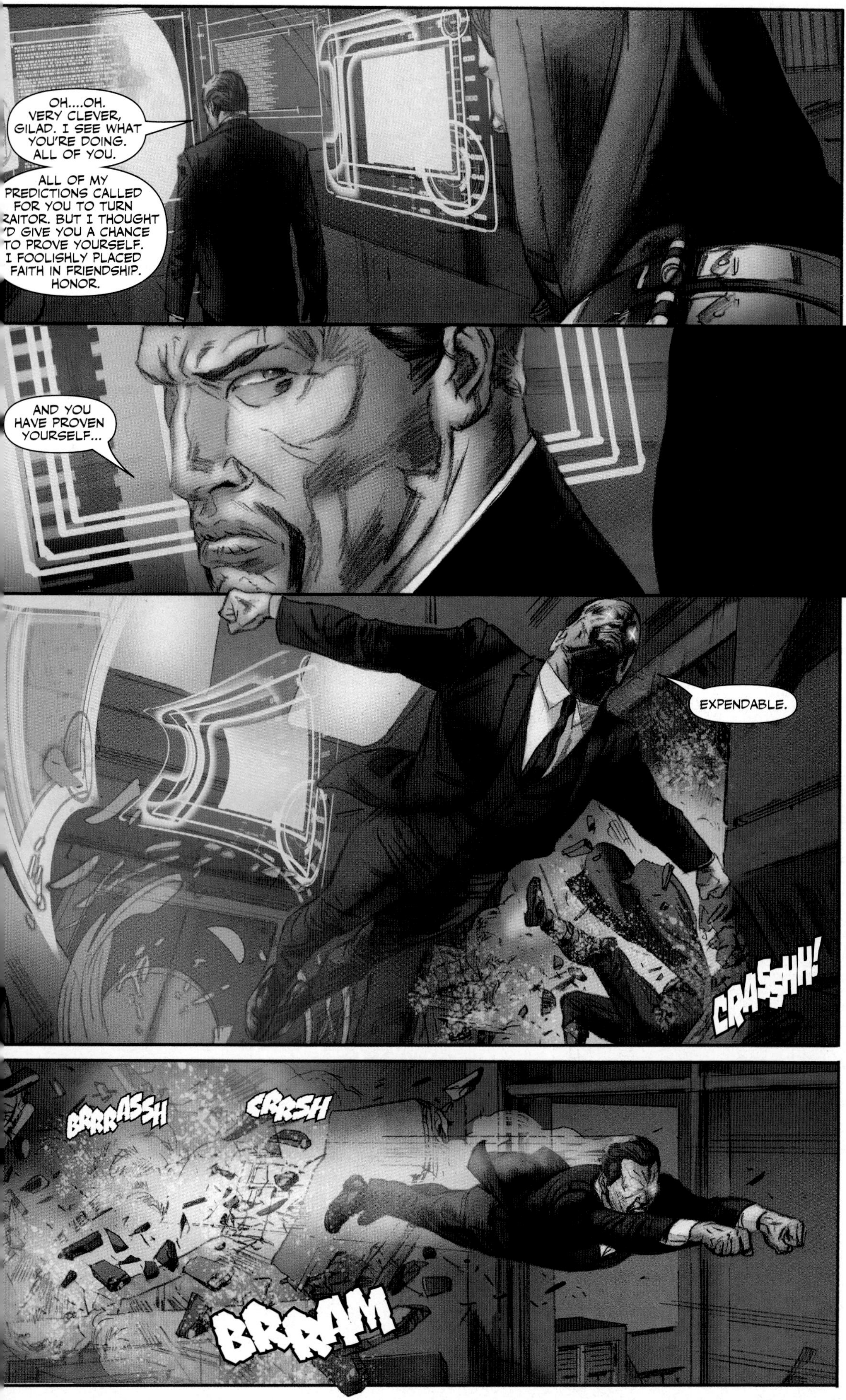
OH....OH. VERY CLEVER, GILAD. I SEE WHAT YOU'RE DOING. ALL OF YOU.
ALL OF MY PREDICTIONS CALLED FOR YOU TO TURN TRAITOR. BUT I THOUGHT I'D GIVE YOU A CHANCE TO PROVE YOURSELF. I FOOLISHLY PLACED FAITH IN FRIENDSHIP. HONOR.
AND YOU HAVE PROVEN YOURSELF...
EXPENDABLE.
CRASSHH!
BRRRASSH
CRRSH
BRRAM

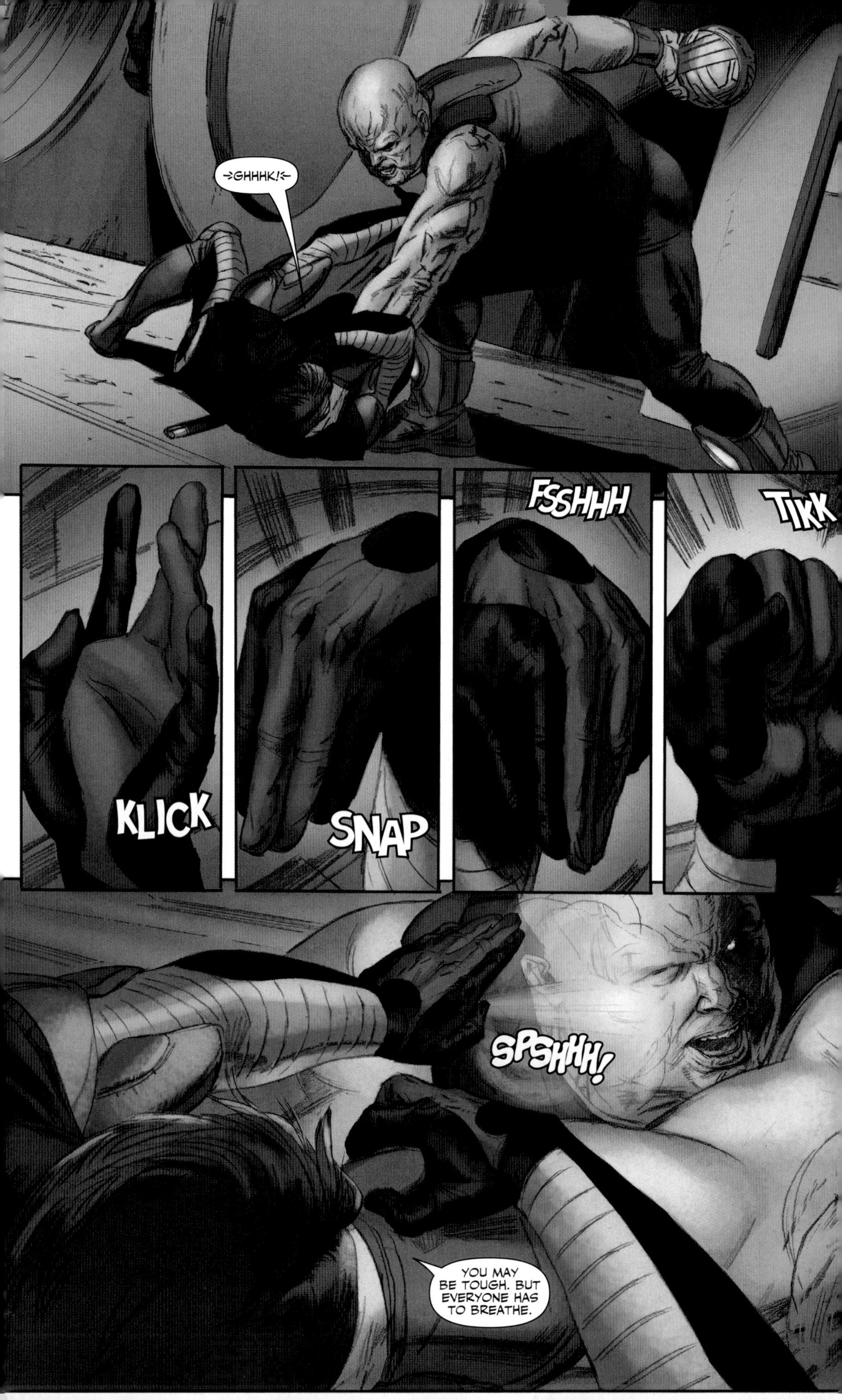
-GHHHK!-
KLICK
SNAP
FSSHHH
TIKK
SPSHHH!
YOU MAY BE TOUGH. BUT EVERYONE HAS TO BREATHE.

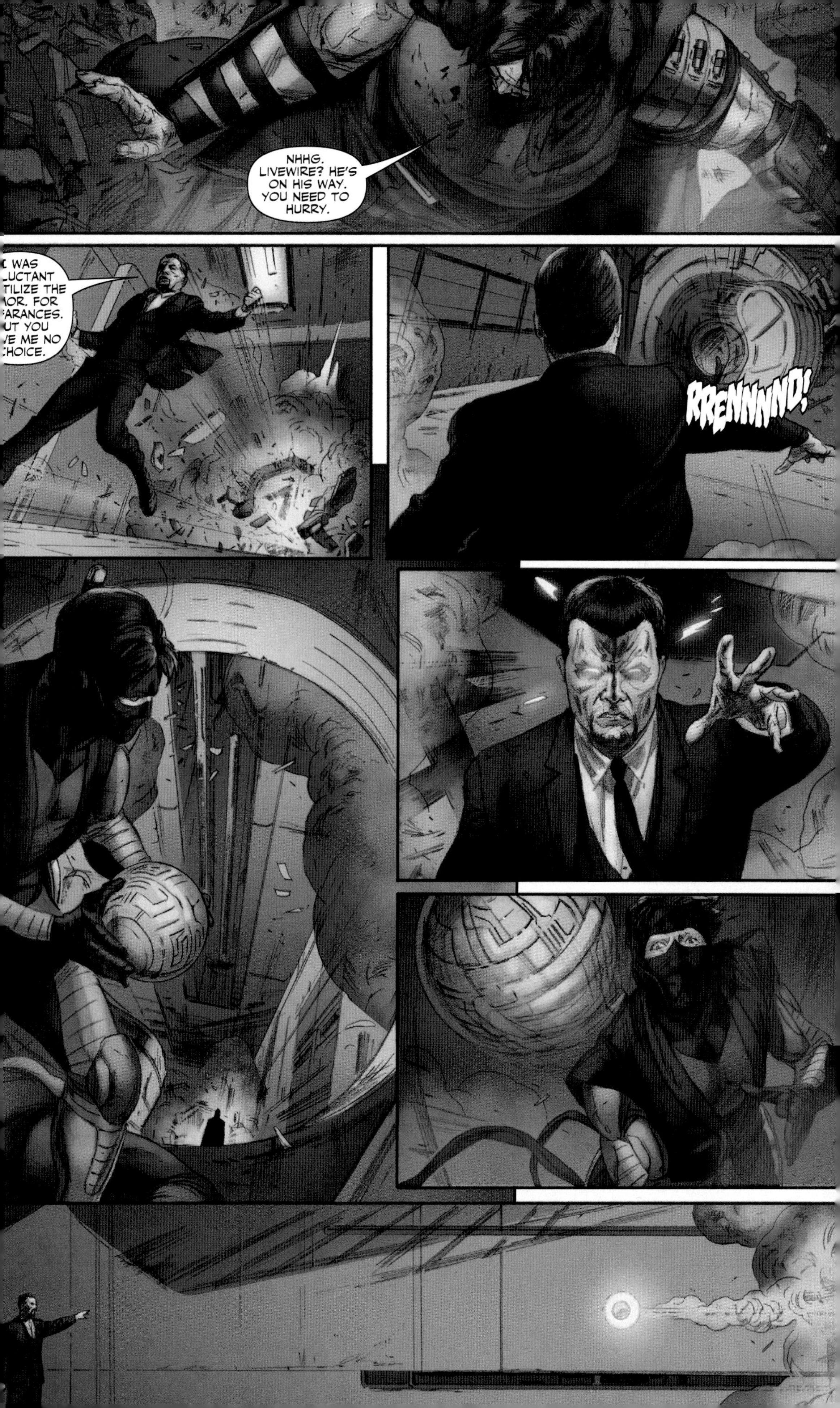
NHHG. LIVEWIRE? HE'S ON HIS WAY. YOU NEED TO HURRY.
I WAS LUCTANT TILIZE THE MOR. FOR FARANCES. UT YOU VE ME NO CHOICE.
RRENNNND!

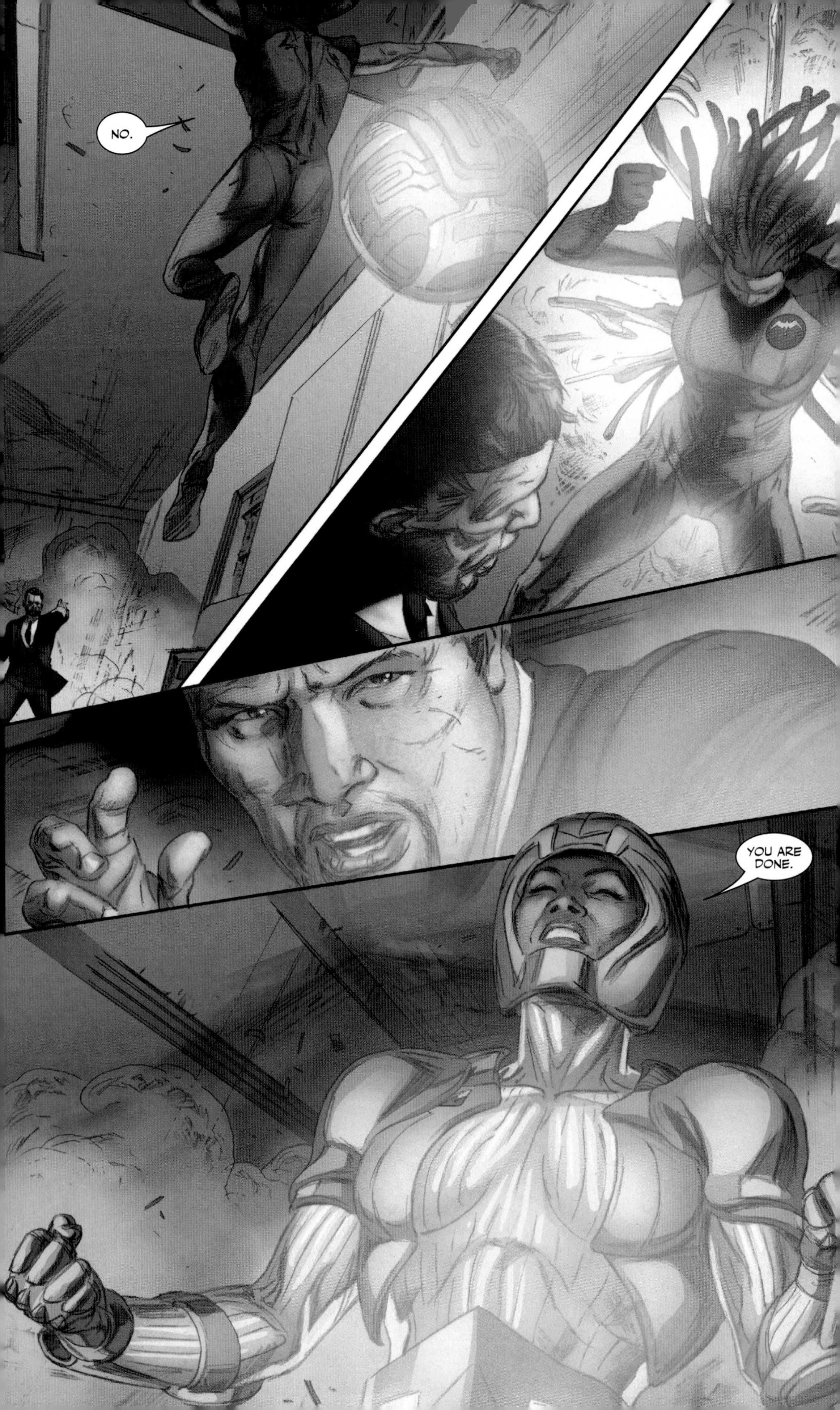
NO.
YOU ARE DONE.

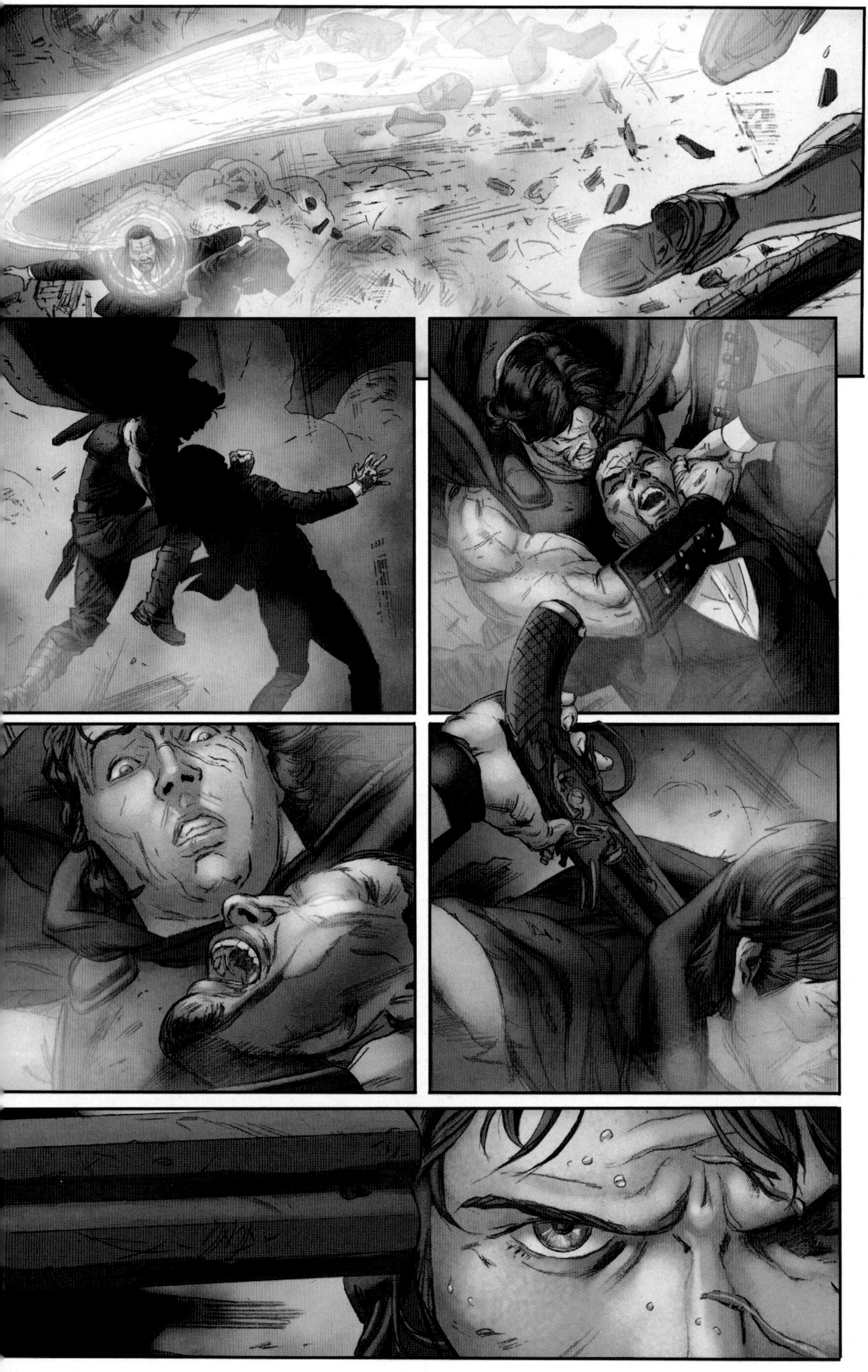

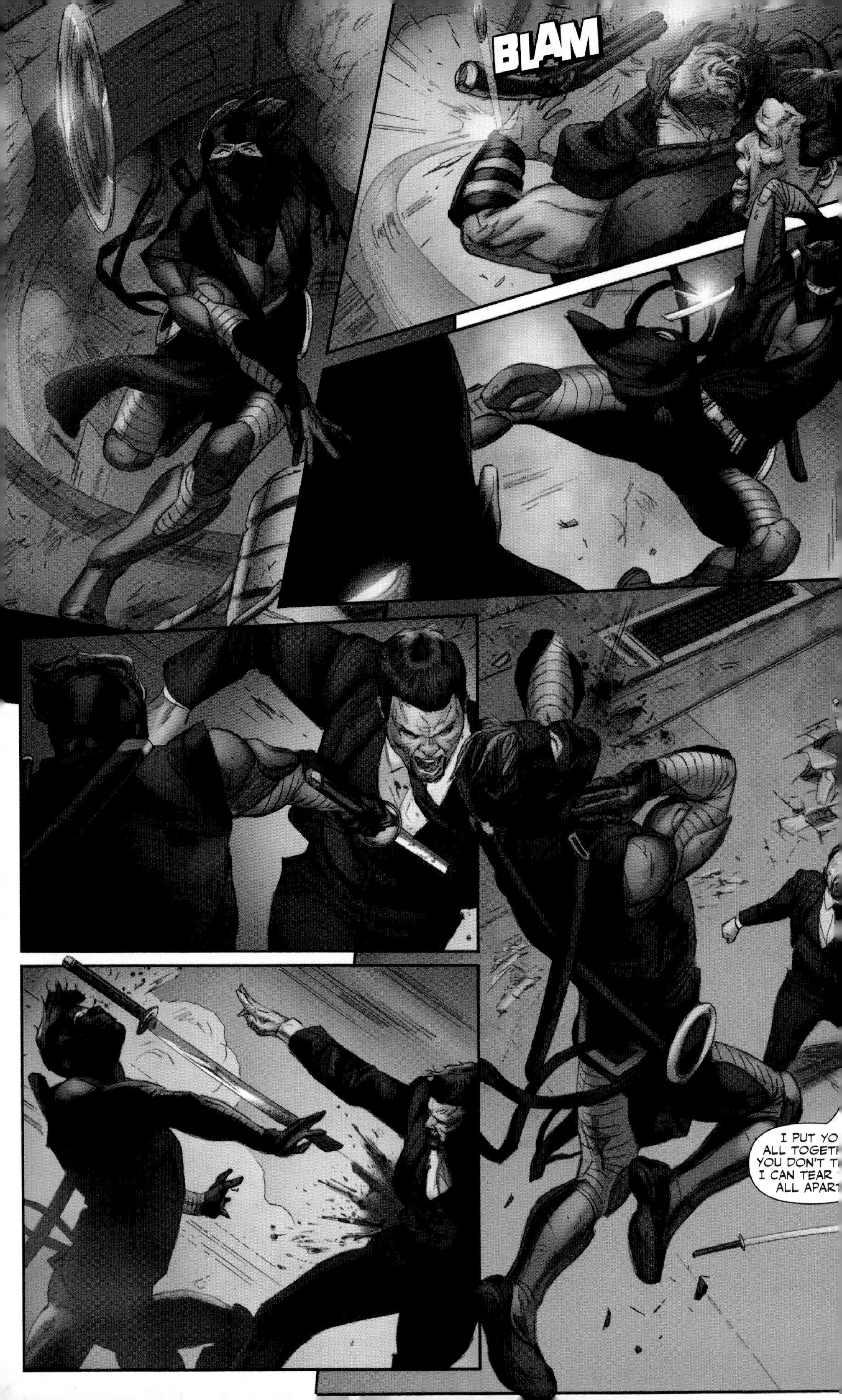
BLAM
I PUT YO ALL TOGET YOU DON'T T I CAN TEAR ALL APAR

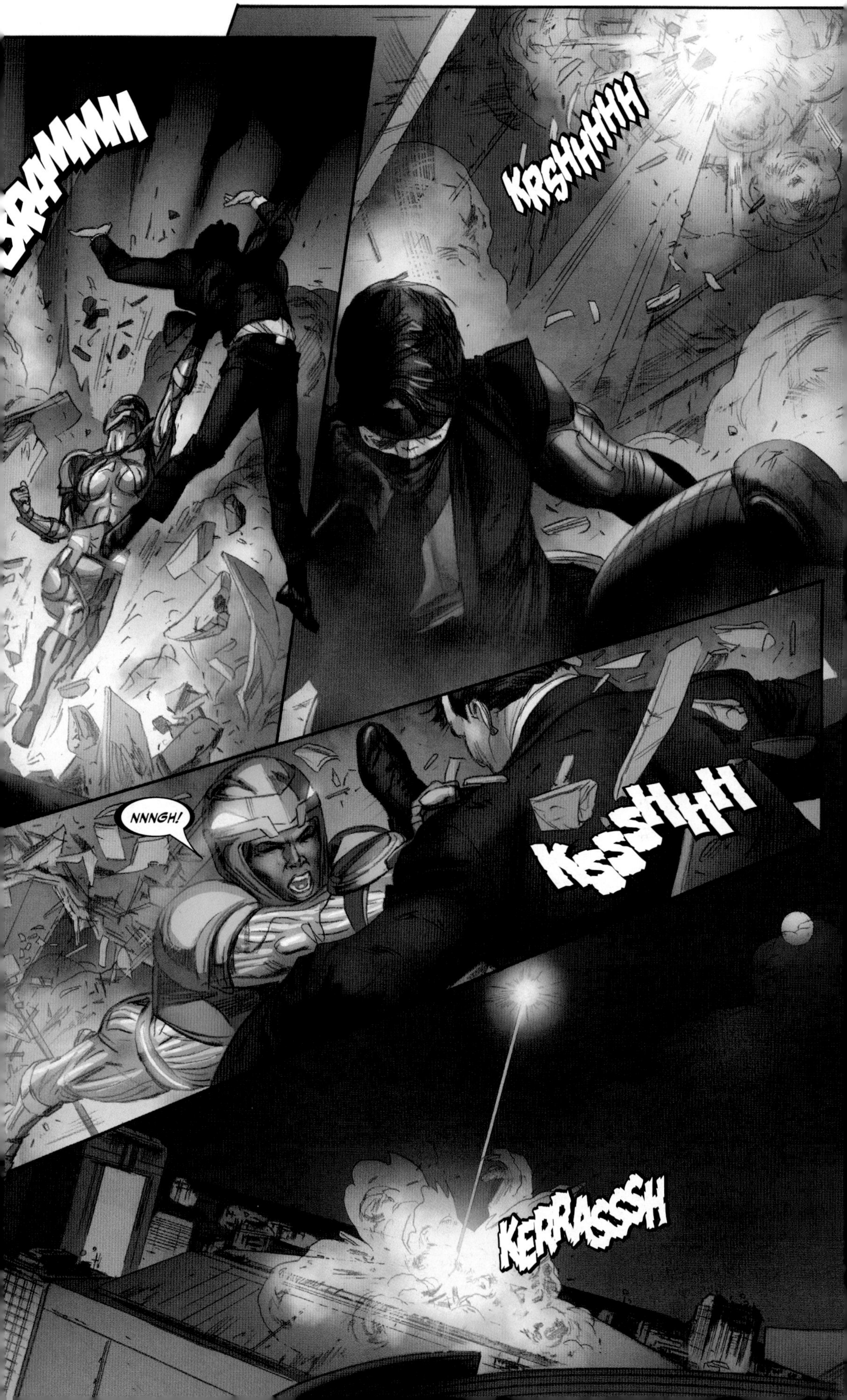
BRAMMMM
KRSHHHH
NNNGH!
KSSSHHH
KERRASSSH

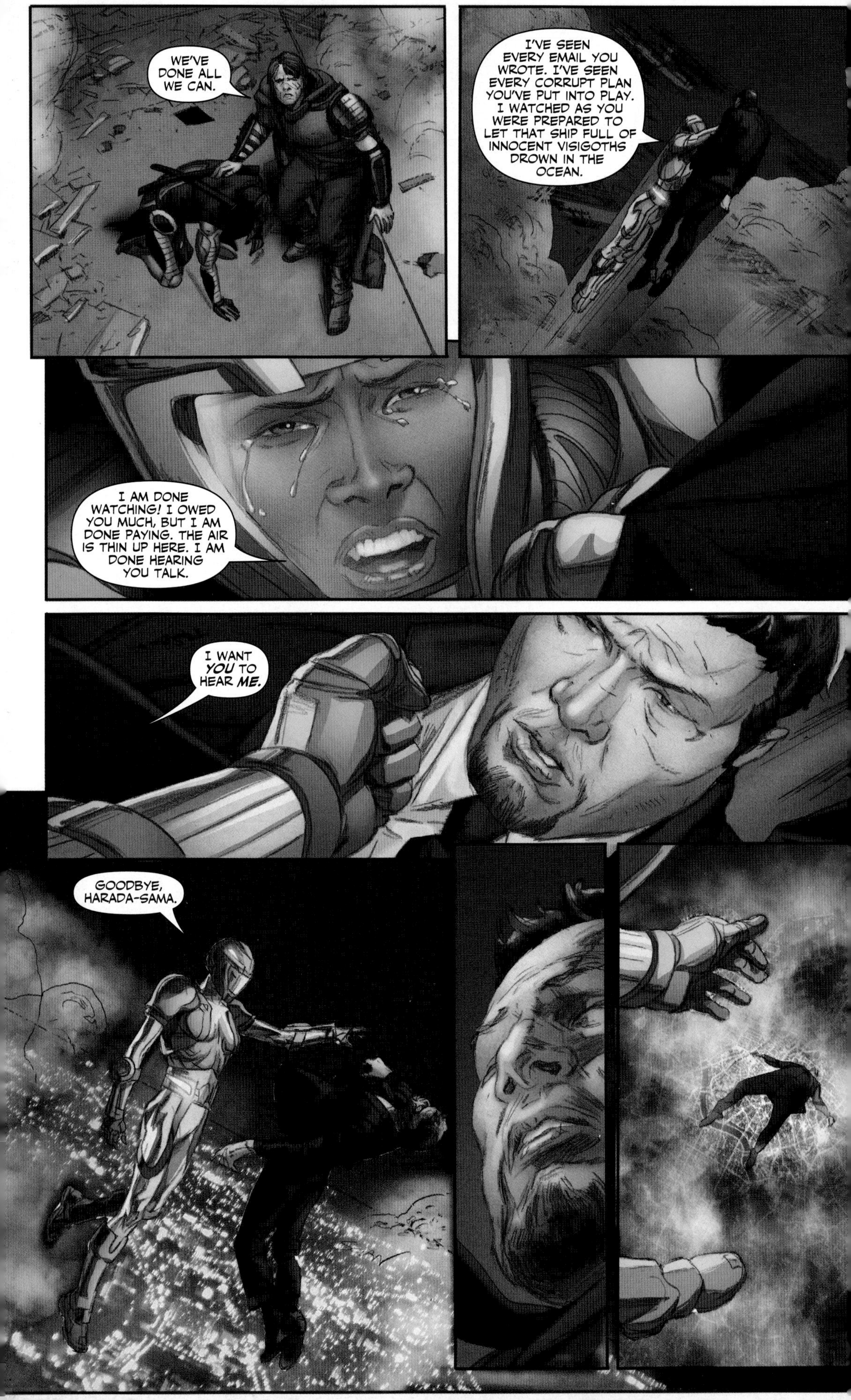
WE'VE DONE ALL WE CAN.
I'VE SEEN EVERY EMAIL YOU WROTE. I'VE SEEN EVERY CORRUPT PLAN YOU'VE PUT INTO PLAY. I WATCHED AS YOU WERE PREPARED TO LET THAT SHIP FULL OF INNOCENT VISIGOTHS DROWN IN THE OCEAN.
I AM DONE WATCHING! I OWED YOU MUCH, BUT I AM DONE PAYING. THE AIR IS THIN UP HERE. I AM DONE HEARING YOU TALK.
I WANT *YOU* TO HEAR *ME*.
GOODBYE, HARADA-SAMA.

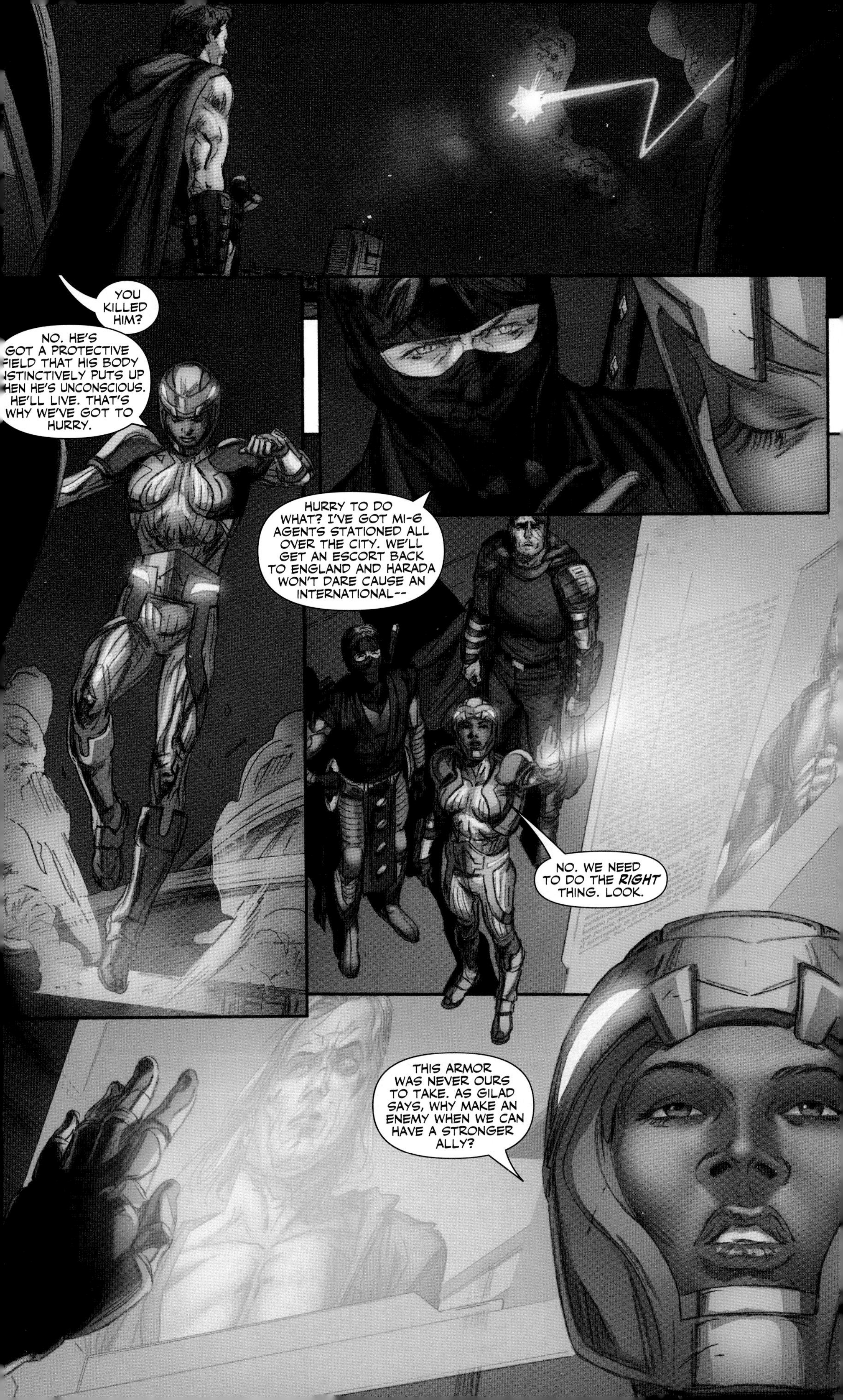
YOU KILLED HIM?
NO. HE'S GOT A PROTECTIVE FIELD THAT HIS BODY INSTINCTIVELY PUTS UP WHEN HE'S UNCONSCIOUS. HE'LL LIVE. THAT'S WHY WE'VE GOT TO HURRY.
HURRY TO DO WHAT? I'VE GOT MI-6 AGENTS STATIONED ALL OVER THE CITY. WE'LL GET AN ESCORT BACK TO ENGLAND AND HARADA WON'T DARE CAUSE AN INTERNATIONAL--
NO. WE NEED TO DO THE *RIGHT* THING. LOOK.
THIS ARMOR WAS NEVER OURS TO TAKE. AS GILAD SAYS, WHY MAKE AN ENEMY WHEN WE CAN HAVE A STRONGER ALLY?

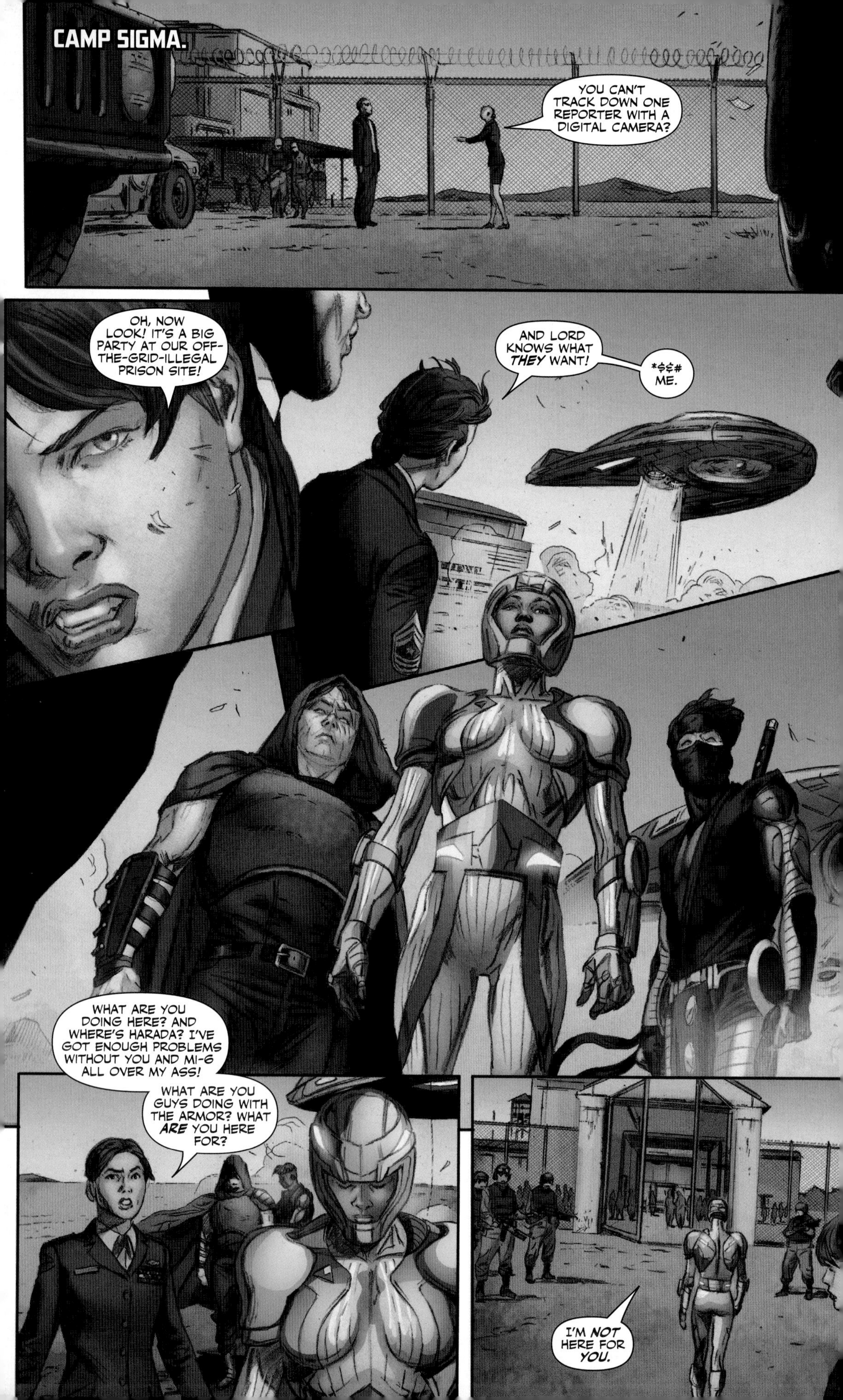
CAMP SIGMA.
YOU CAN'T TRACK DOWN ONE REPORTER WITH A DIGITAL CAMERA?
OH, NOW LOOK! IT'S A BIG PARTY AT OUR OFF-THE-GRID-ILLEGAL PRISON SITE!
AND LORD KNOWS WHAT THEY WANT!
*$¢# ME.
WHAT ARE YOU DOING HERE? AND WHERE'S HARADA? I'VE GOT ENOUGH PROBLEMS WITHOUT YOU AND MI-6 ALL OVER MY ASS!
WHAT ARE YOU GUYS DOING WITH THE ARMOR? WHAT ARE YOU HERE FOR?
I'M NOT HERE FOR YOU.

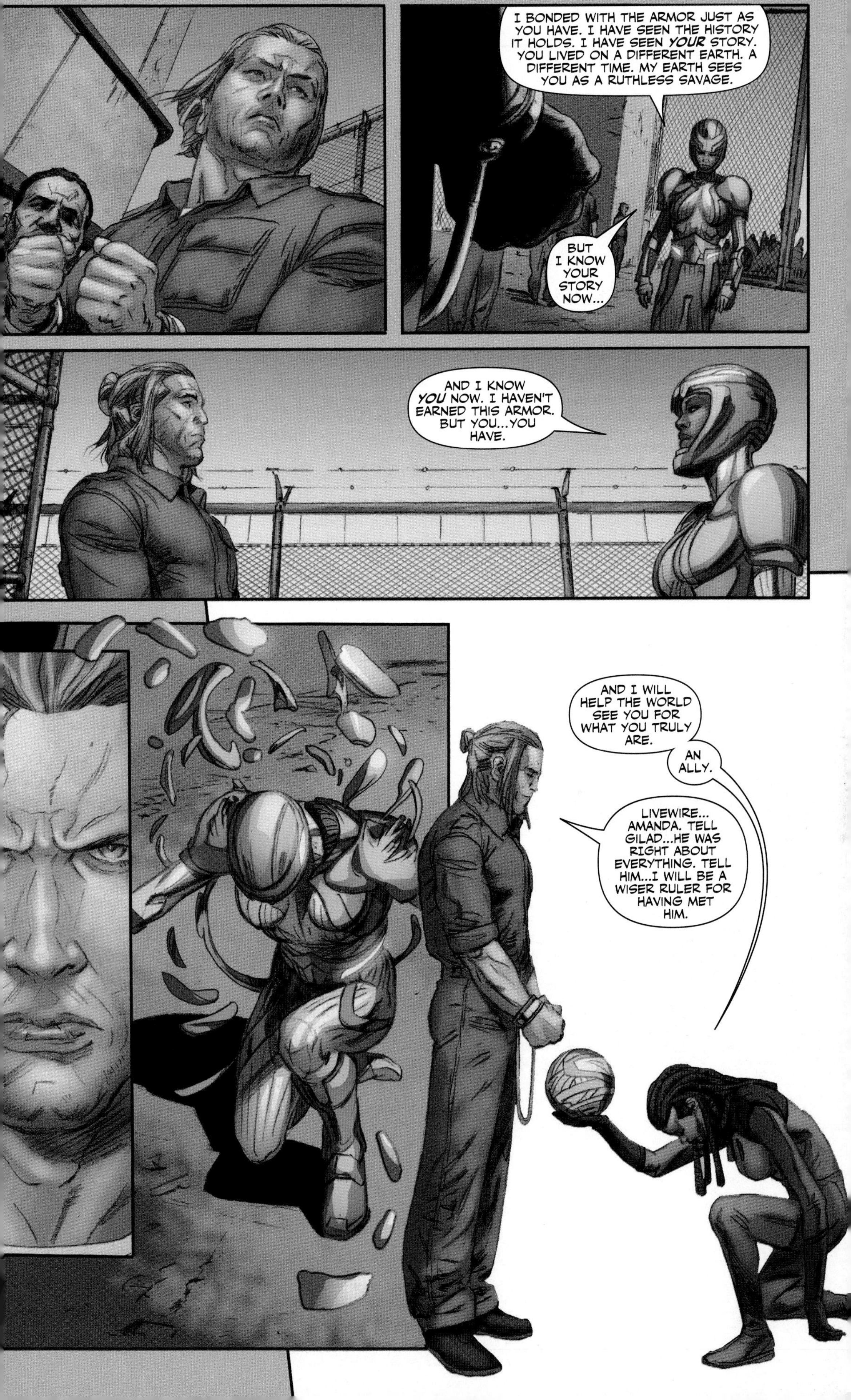
I BONDED WITH THE ARMOR JUST AS YOU HAVE. I HAVE SEEN THE HISTORY IT HOLDS. I HAVE SEEN YOUR STORY. YOU LIVED ON A DIFFERENT EARTH. A DIFFERENT TIME. MY EARTH SEES YOU AS A RUTHLESS SAVAGE.
BUT I KNOW YOUR STORY NOW...
AND I KNOW YOU NOW. I HAVEN'T EARNED THIS ARMOR. BUT YOU...YOU HAVE.
AND I WILL HELP THE WORLD SEE YOU FOR WHAT YOU TRULY ARE.
AN ALLY.
LIVEWIRE... AMANDA. TELL GILAD...HE WAS RIGHT ABOUT EVERYTHING. TELL HIM...I WILL BE A WISER RULER FOR HAVING MET HIM.

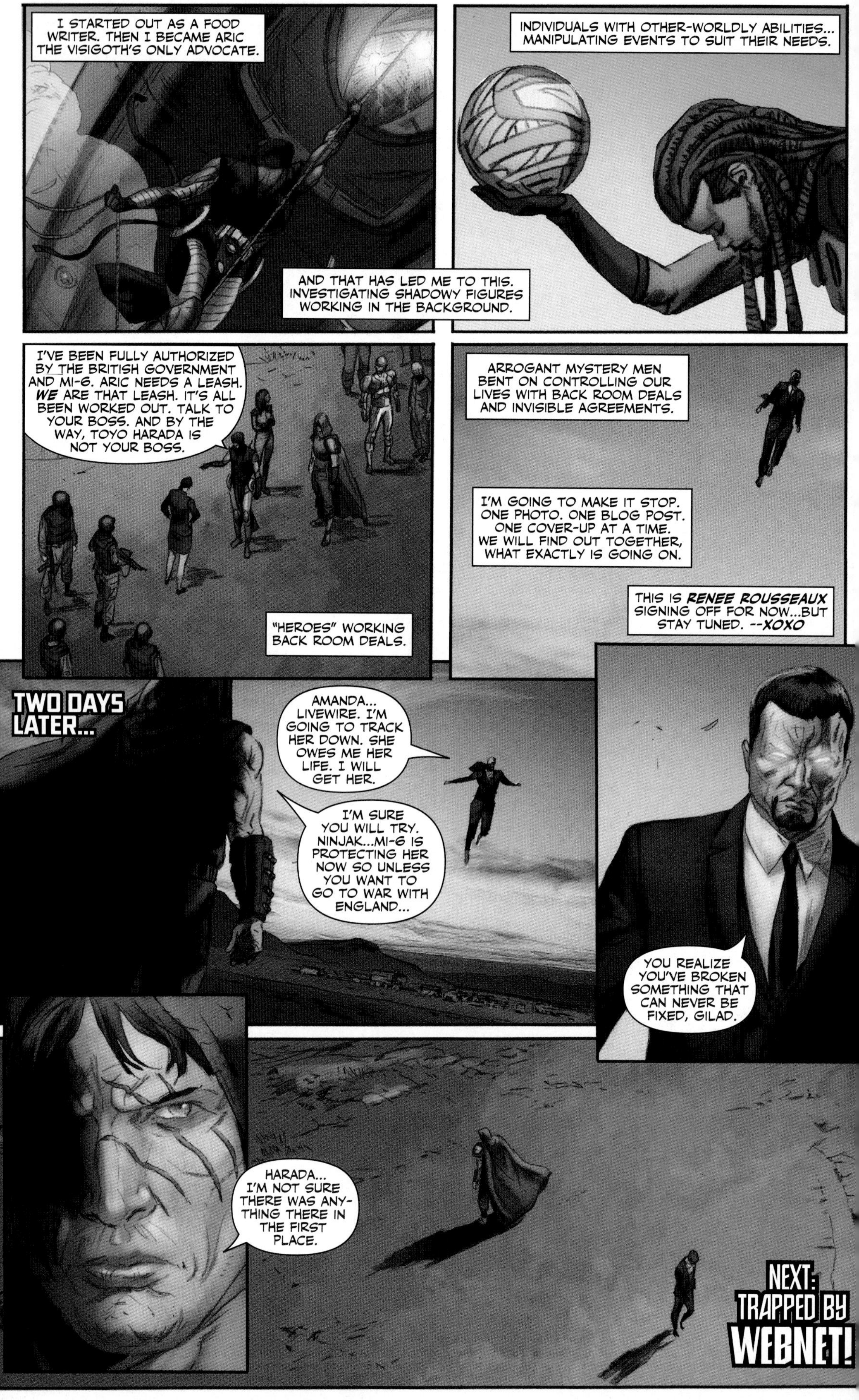
I STARTED OUT AS A FOOD WRITER. THEN I BECAME ARIC THE VISIGOTH'S ONLY ADVOCATE.
AND THAT HAS LED ME TO THIS. INVESTIGATING SHADOWY FIGURES WORKING IN THE BACKGROUND.
INDIVIDUALS WITH OTHER-WORLDLY ABILITIES... MANIPULATING EVENTS TO SUIT THEIR NEEDS.
I'VE BEEN FULLY AUTHORIZED BY THE BRITISH GOVERNMENT AND MI-6. ARIC NEEDS A LEASH. *WE* ARE THAT LEASH. IT'S ALL BEEN WORKED OUT. TALK TO YOUR BOSS. AND BY THE WAY, TOYO HARADA IS NOT YOUR BOSS.
"HEROES" WORKING BACK ROOM DEALS.
ARROGANT MYSTERY MEN BENT ON CONTROLLING OUR LIVES WITH BACK ROOM DEALS AND INVISIBLE AGREEMENTS.
I'M GOING TO MAKE IT STOP. ONE PHOTO. ONE BLOG POST. ONE COVER-UP AT A TIME. WE WILL FIND OUT TOGETHER, WHAT EXACTLY IS GOING ON.
THIS IS ***RENEE ROUSSEAUX*** SIGNING OFF FOR NOW...BUT STAY TUNED. --***XOXO***
TWO DAYS LATER...
AMANDA... LIVEWIRE. I'M GOING TO TRACK HER DOWN. SHE OWES ME HER LIFE. I WILL GET HER.
I'M SURE YOU WILL TRY. NINJAK...MI-6 IS PROTECTING HER NOW SO UNLESS YOU WANT TO GO TO WAR WITH ENGLAND...
YOU REALIZE YOU'VE BROKEN SOMETHING THAT CAN NEVER BE FIXED, GILAD.
HARADA... I'M NOT SURE THERE WAS ANY-THING THERE IN THE FIRST PLACE.
NEXT: TRAPPED BY WEBNET!

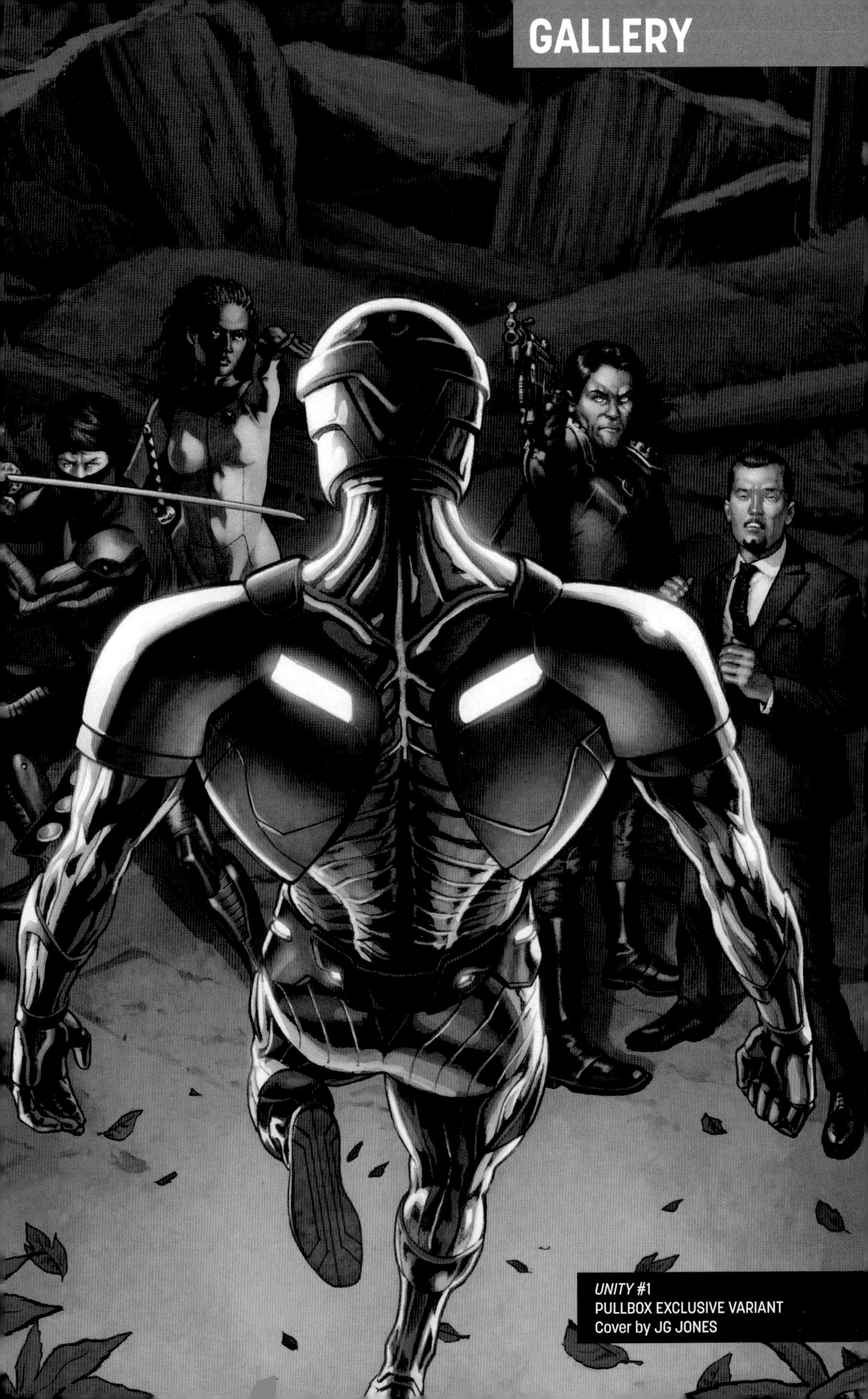

UNITY #1
PULLBOX EXCLUSIVE VARIANT
Cover by JG JONES

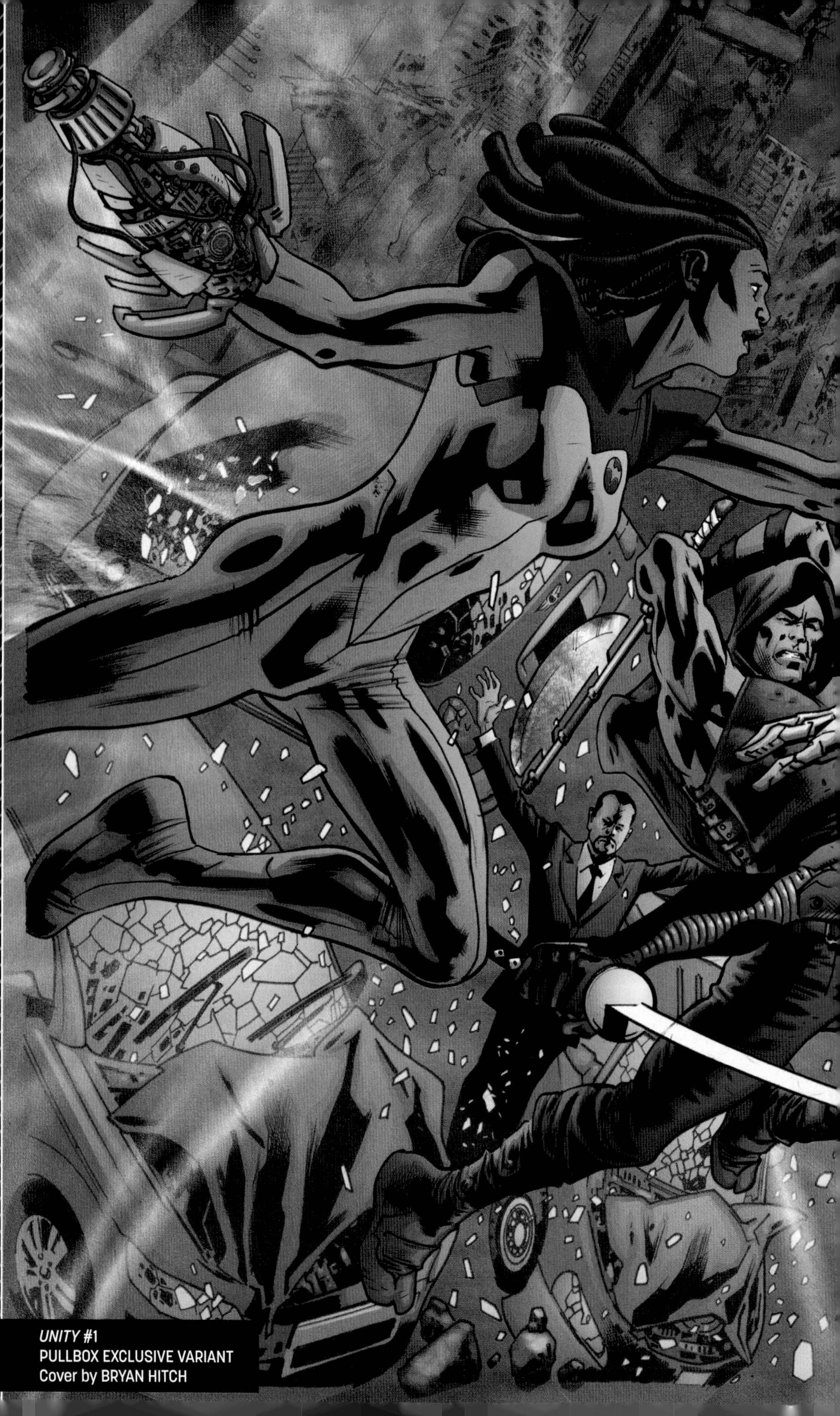

UNITY #1
PULLBOX EXCLUSIVE VARIANT
Cover by BRYAN HITCH

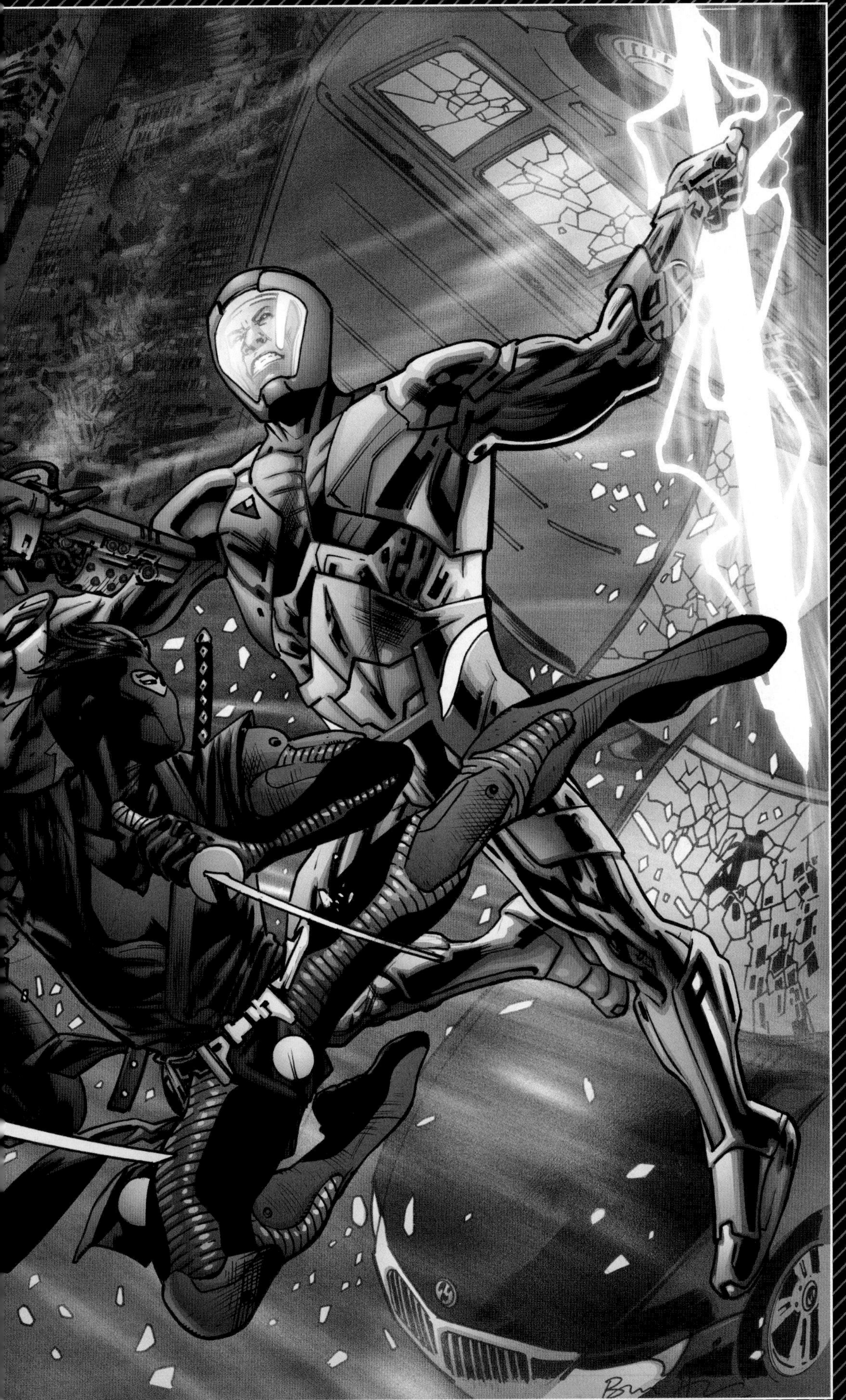

UNITY #1 VALIANT
8-BIT EVOLUTION VARIANT
Cover by DONOVAN SANTIAGO

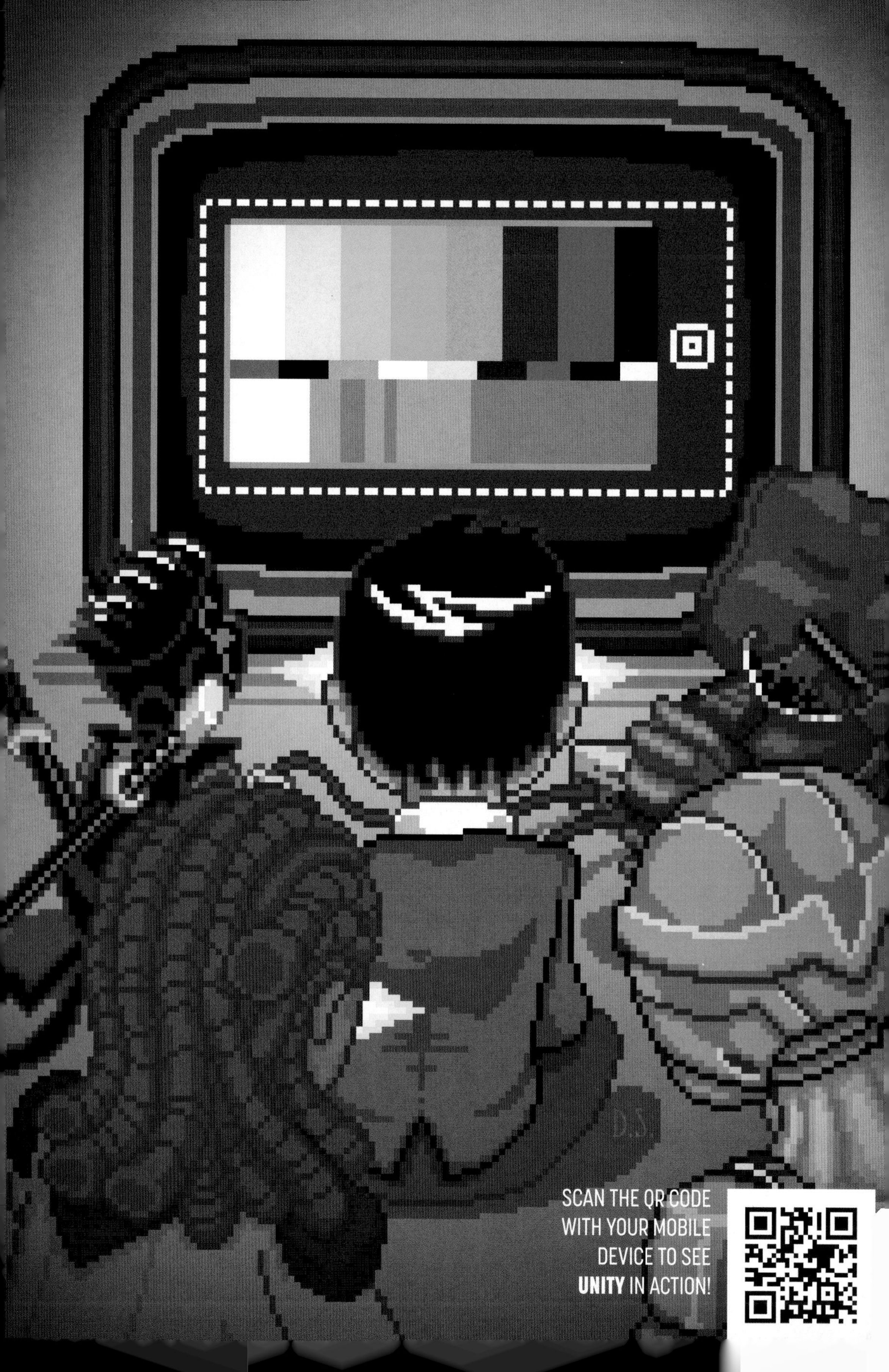
D.S.

SCAN THE QR CODE
WITH YOUR MOBILE
DEVICE TO SEE
UNITY IN ACTION!

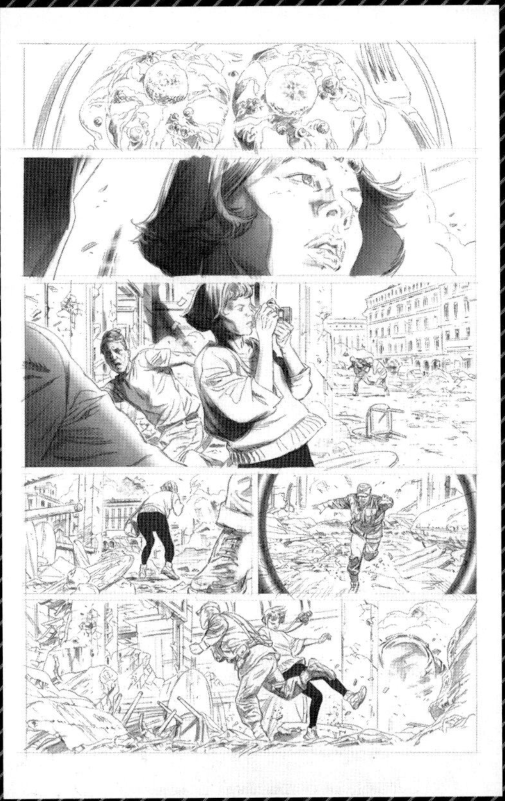

UNITY #1, p. 1
Art by DOUG BRAITHWAITE

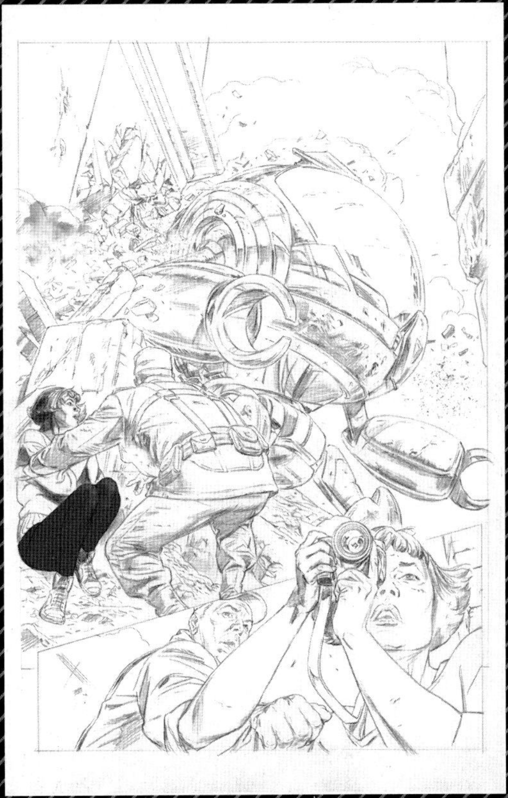

UNITY #1, p. 2
Art by DOUG BRAITHWAITE

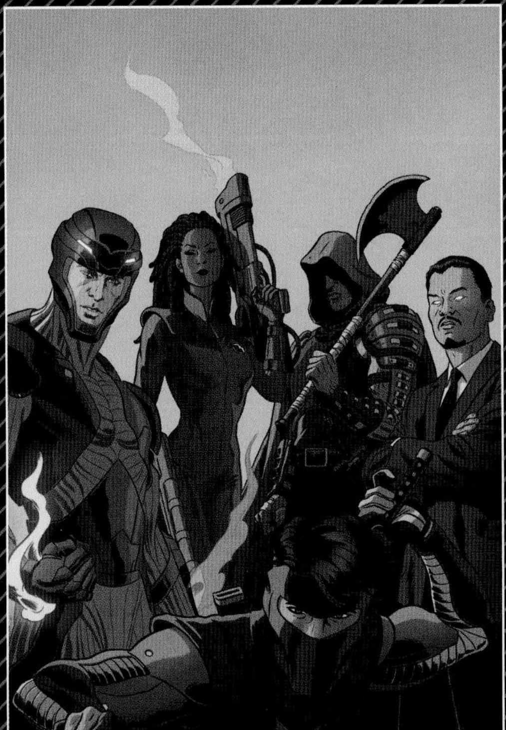

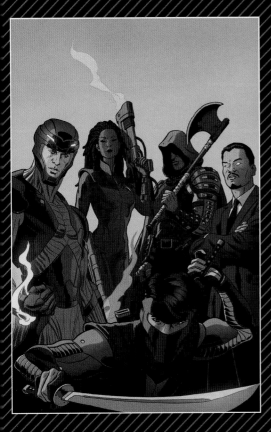

UNITY #1
PULLBOX EXCLUSIVE VARIANT
Cover by PAOLO RIVERA

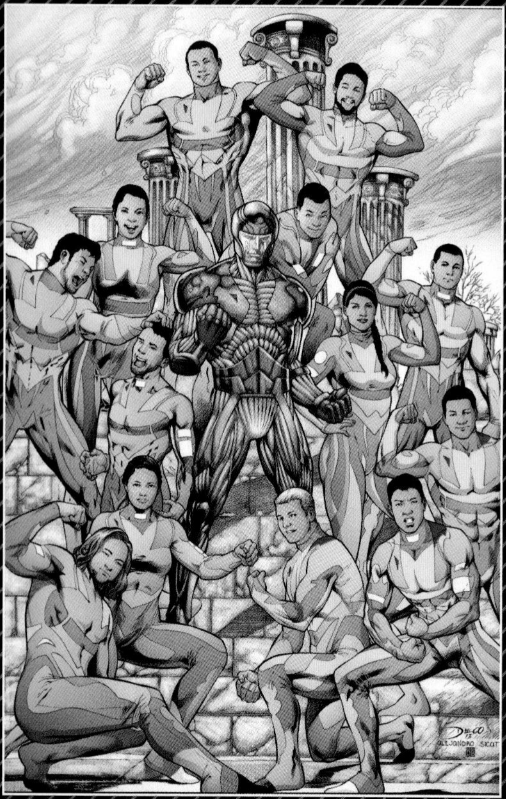

UNITY #1
TEAM USA LUGE VARIANT
Cover by DIEGO BERNARD

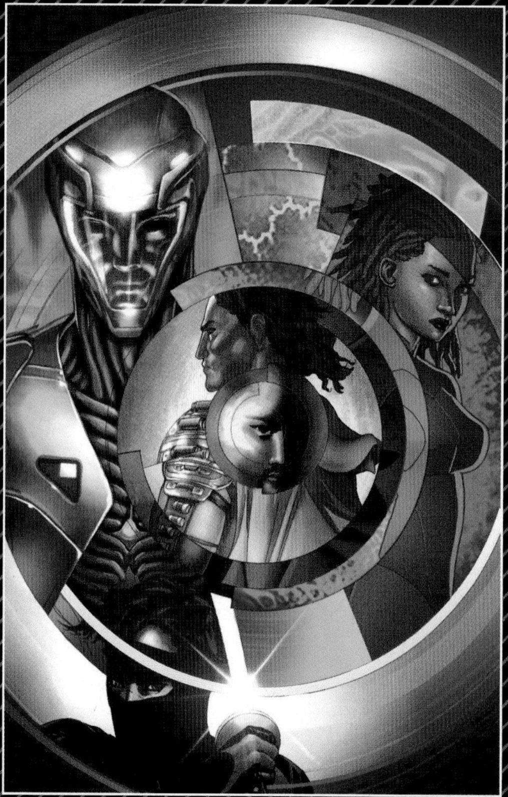

UNITY #1 PULLBOX EXCLUSIVE VARIANT
Cover by TRAVEL FOREMAN

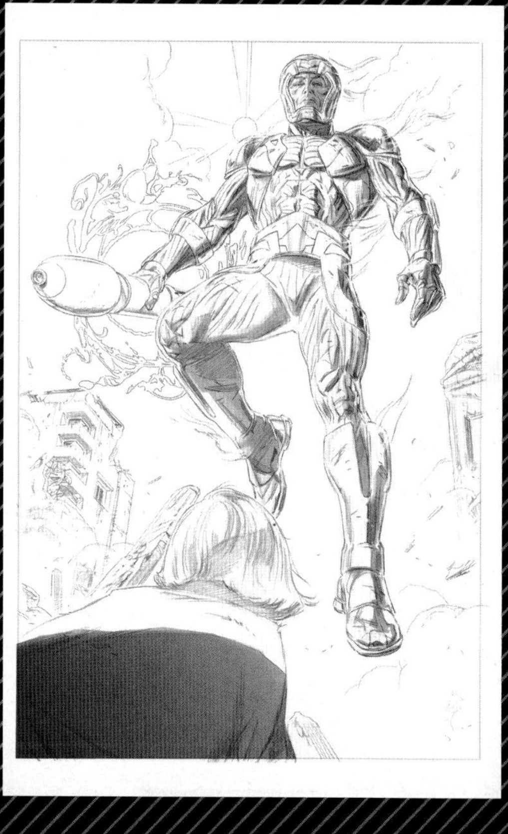

UNITY #1, p. 4
Art by DOUG BRAITHWAITE

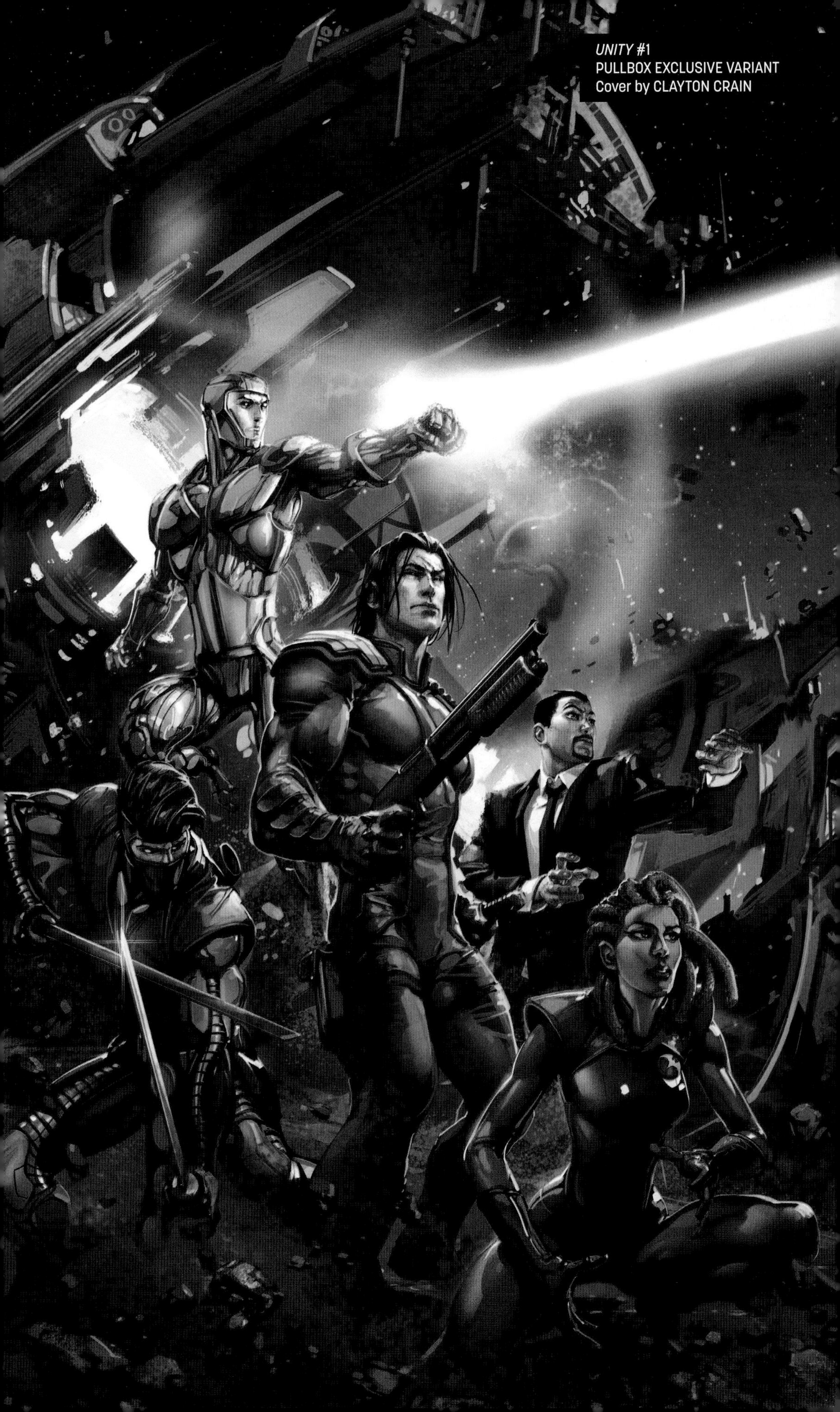

UNITY #1
PULLBOX EXCLUSIVE VARIANT
Cover by CLAYTON CRAIN

UNITY #1 VARIANT
Cover by NEAL ADAMS

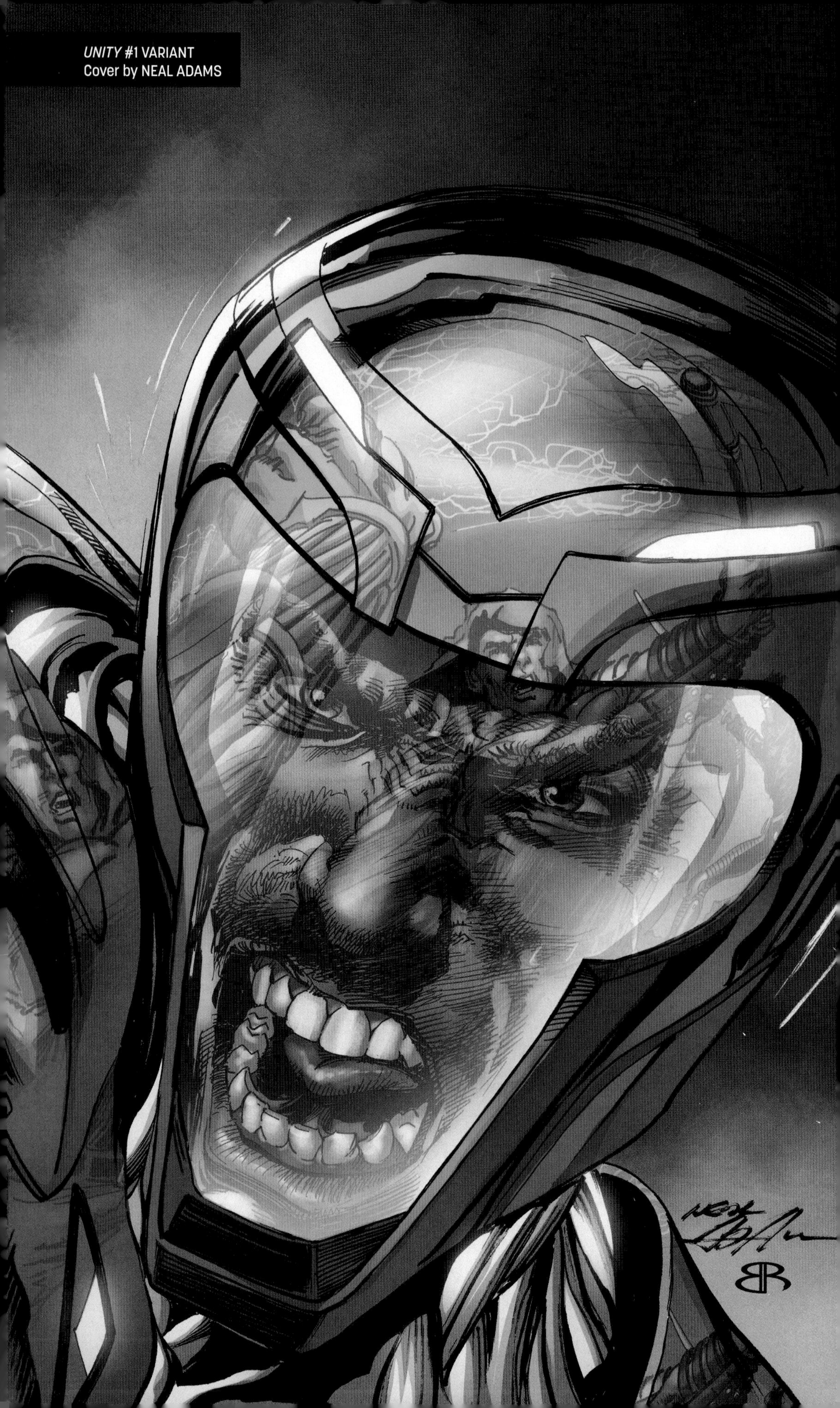

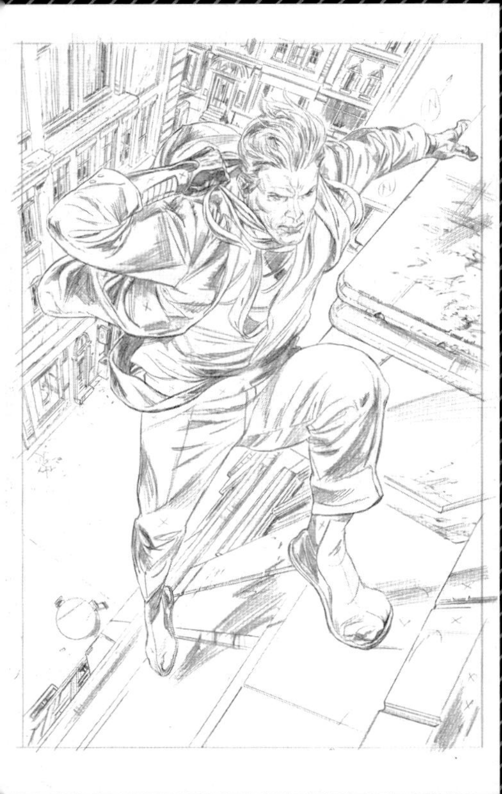

UNITY #1, p. 16
Art by DOUG BRAITHWAITE

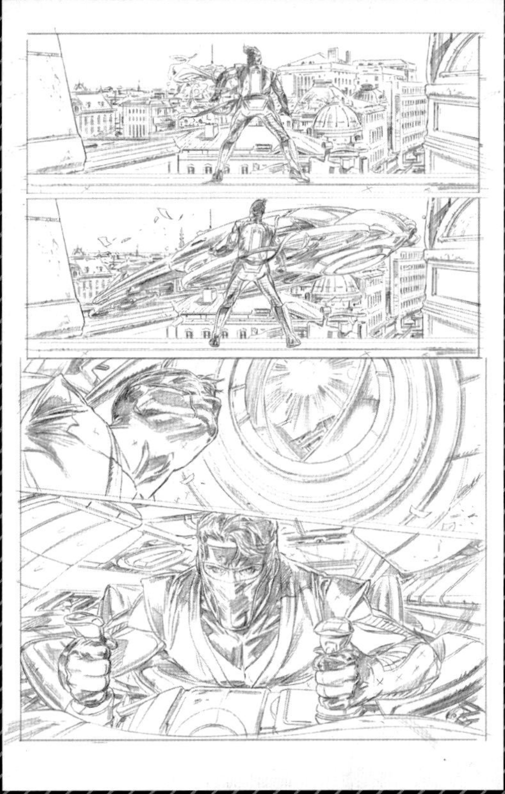

UNITY #1, p. 17
Art by DOUG BRAITHWAITE

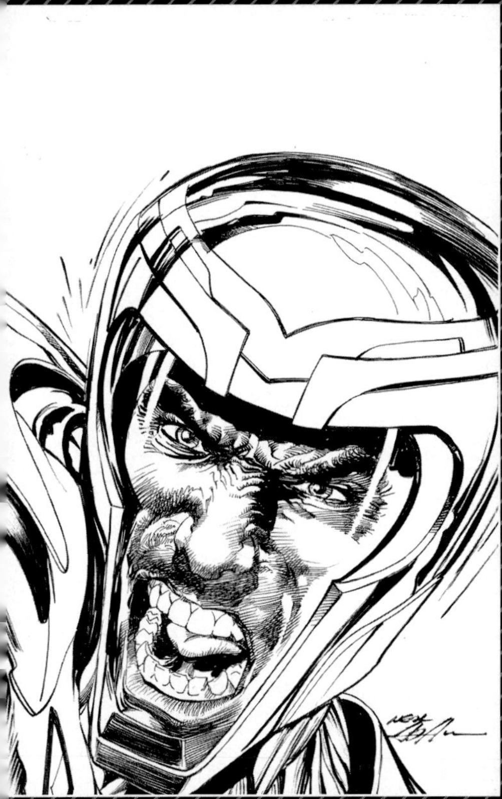

UNITY #1 SKETCH VARIANT
Cover by NEAL ADAMS

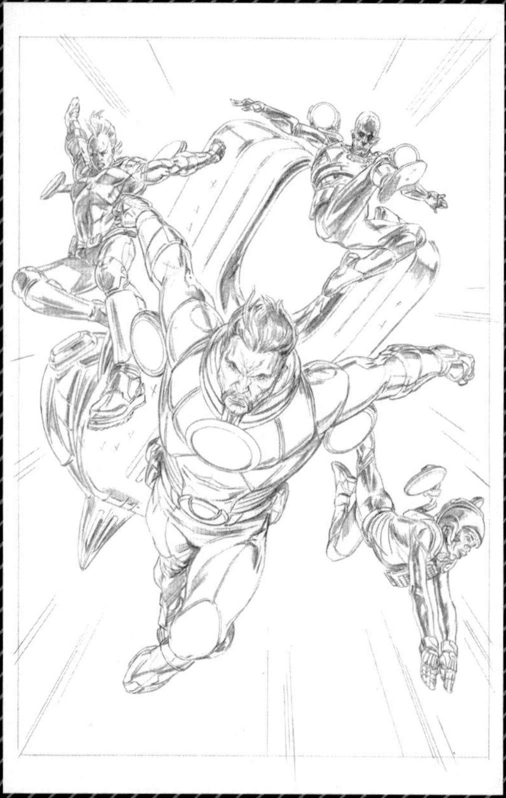

UNITY #1, p. 22
Art by DOUG BRAITHWAITE

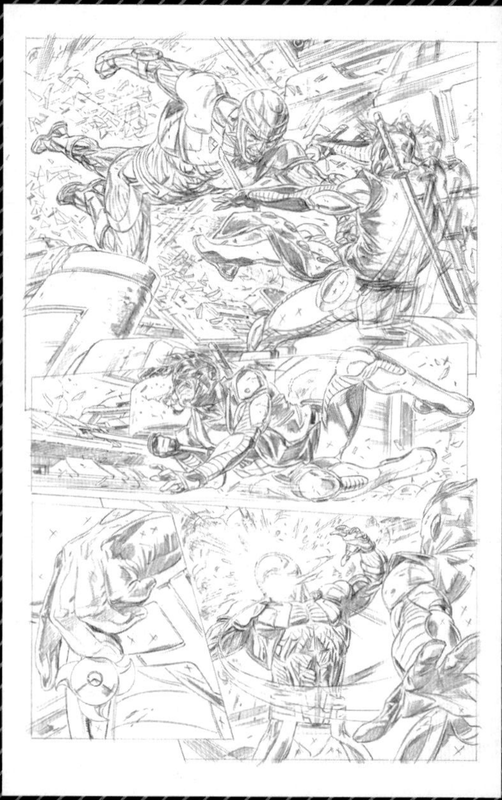

UNITY #1, p. 27
Art by DOUG BRAITHWAITE

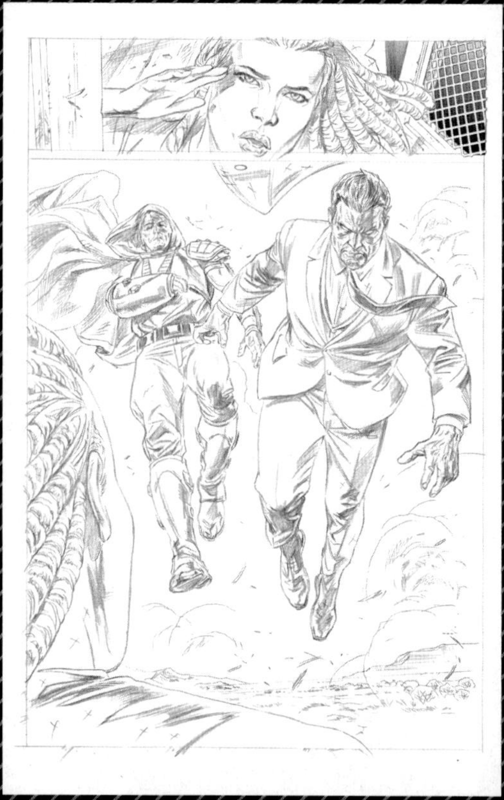

UNITY #1, p. 30
Art by DOUG BRAITHWAITE

UNITY #1
VALIANT SIGNATURE SERIES VARIANT
Cover by BART SEARS

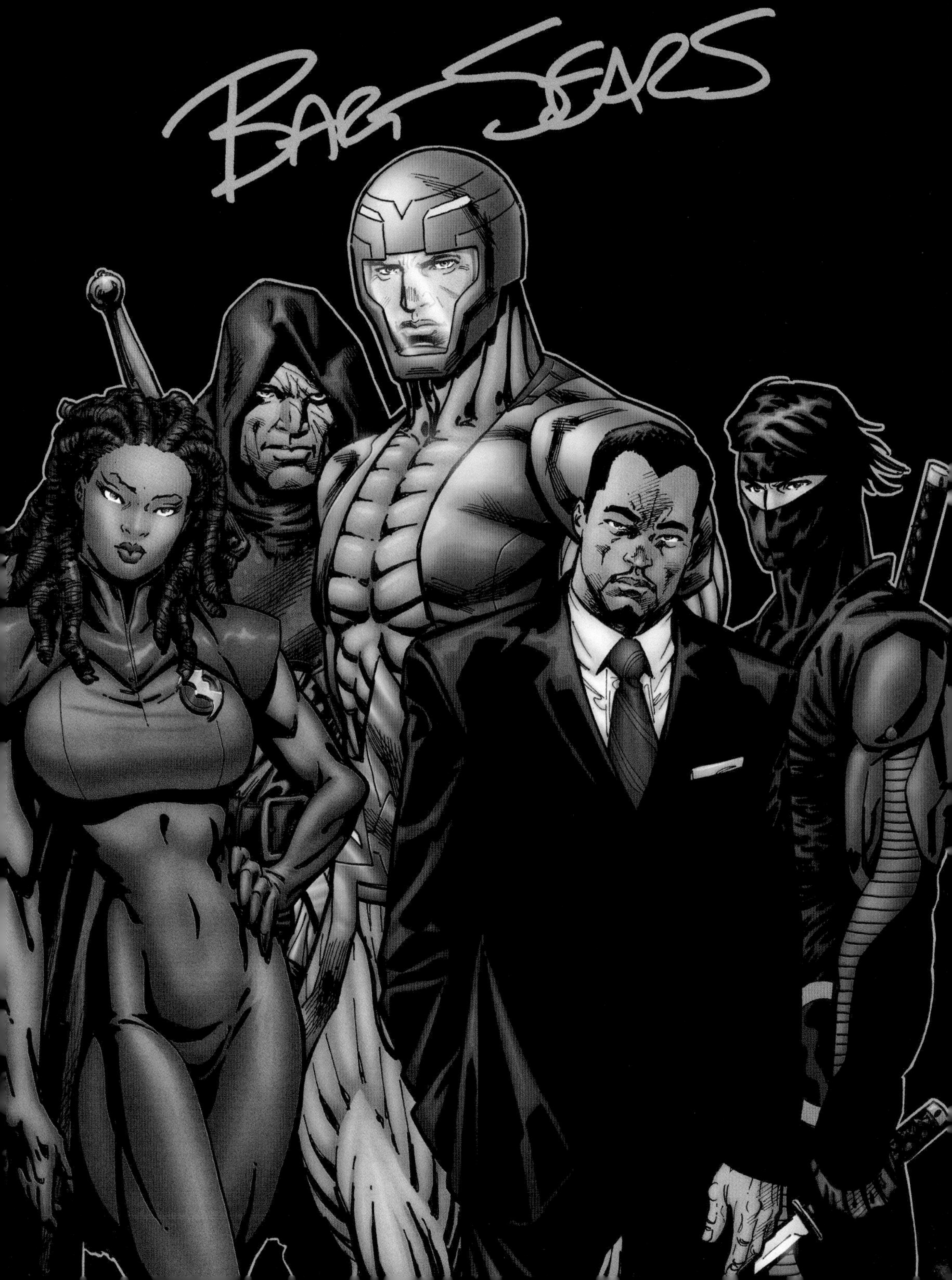
BART SEARS

UNITY #2 VARIANT
Cover by CARY NORD

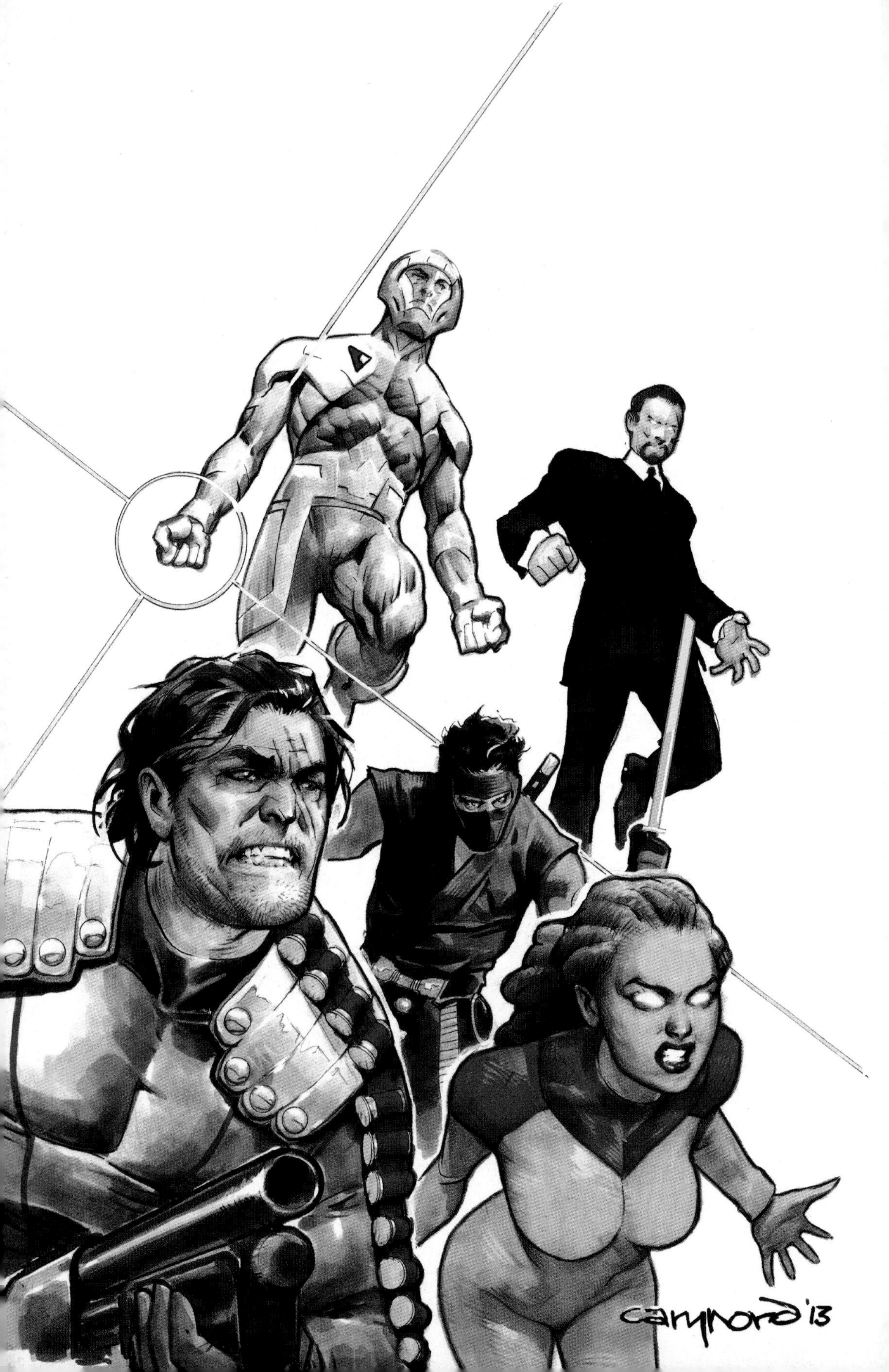
carynord '13

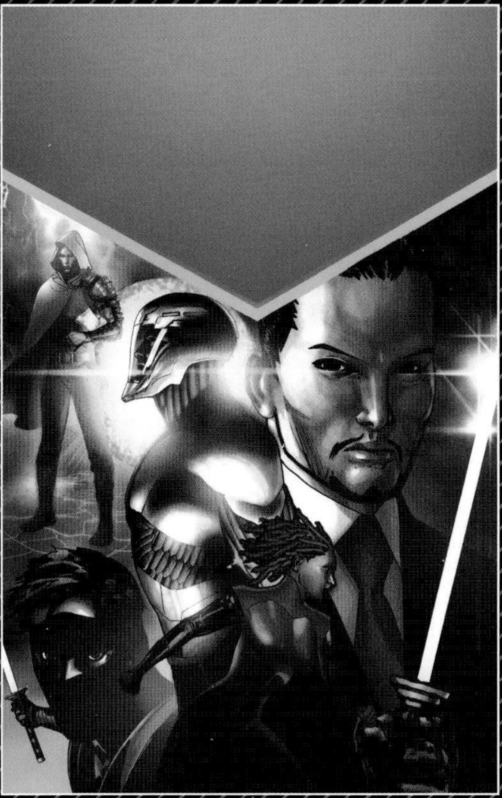

UNITY #2 VARIANT
Cover by TRAVEL FOREMAN with LEN O'GRADY

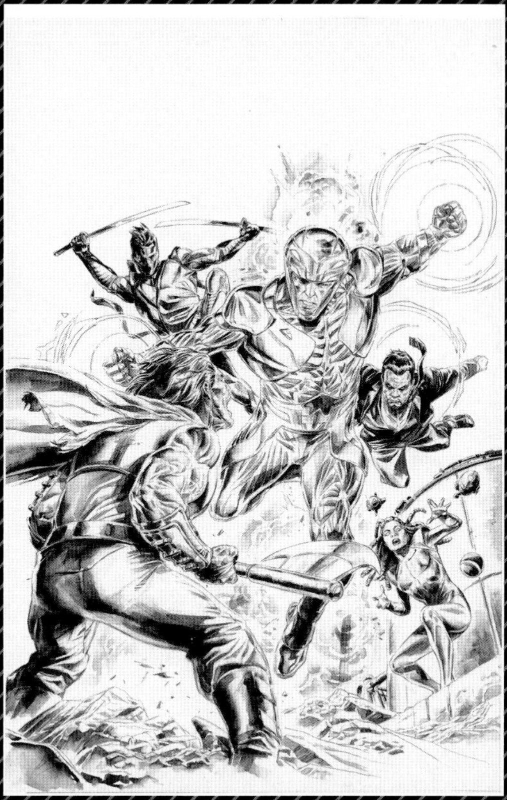

UNITY #2 SKETCH VARIANT
Cover by DOUG BRAITHWAITE

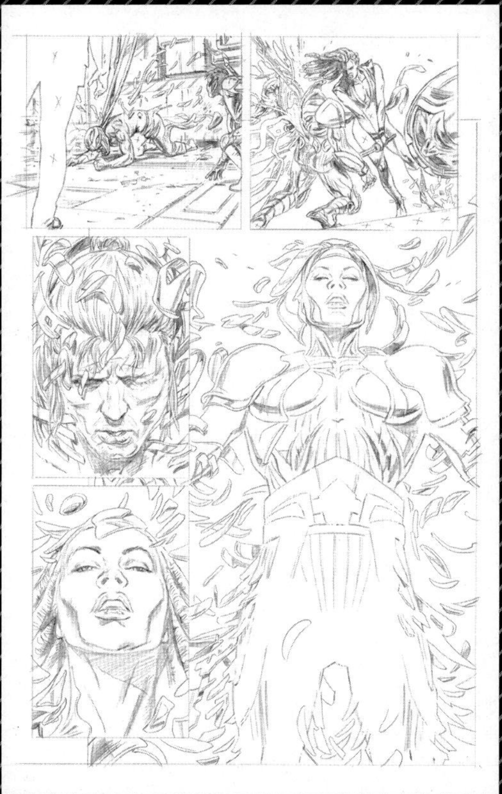

UNITY #2, p. 21
Art by DOUG BRAITHWAITE

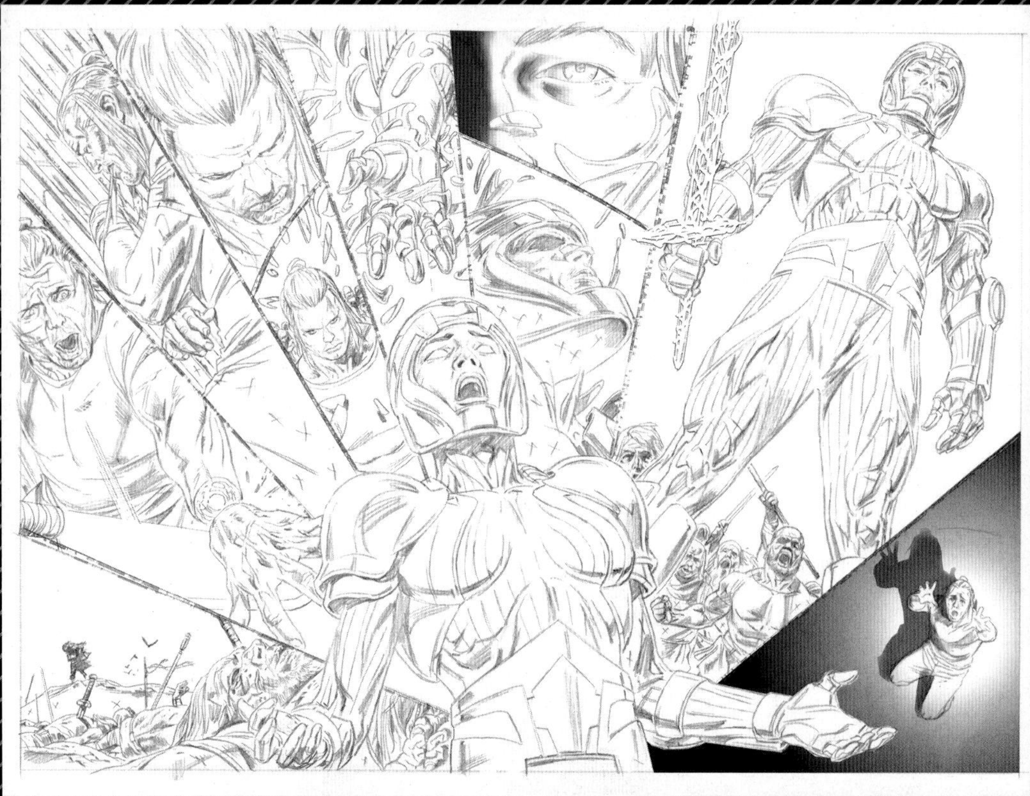

UNITY #3, pp. 6-7
Art by DOUG BRAITHWAITE

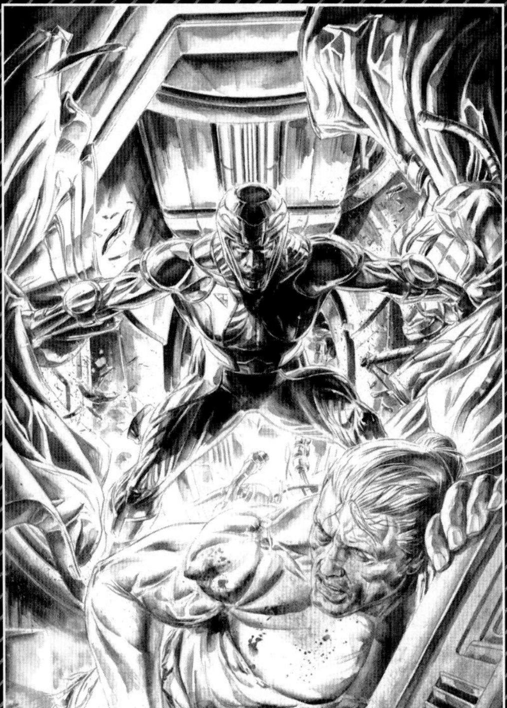

UNITY #3 SKETCH VARIANT
Cover by DOUG BRAITHWAITE

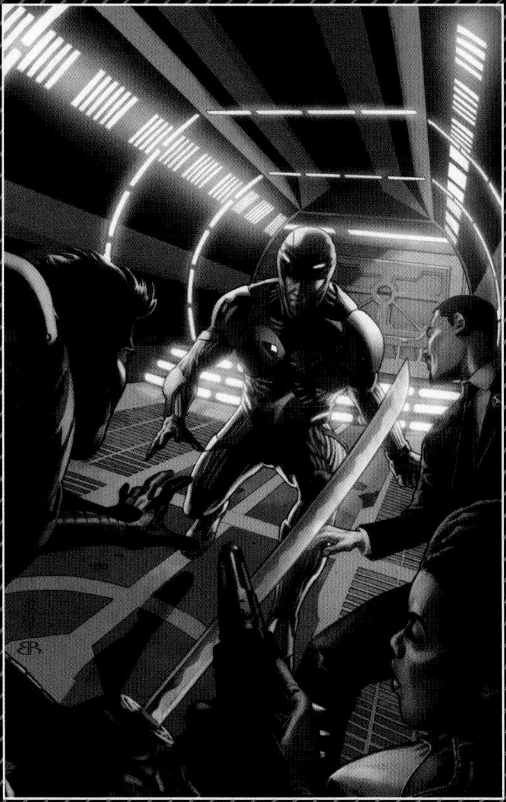

UNITY #3 VARIANT
Cover by JG JONES

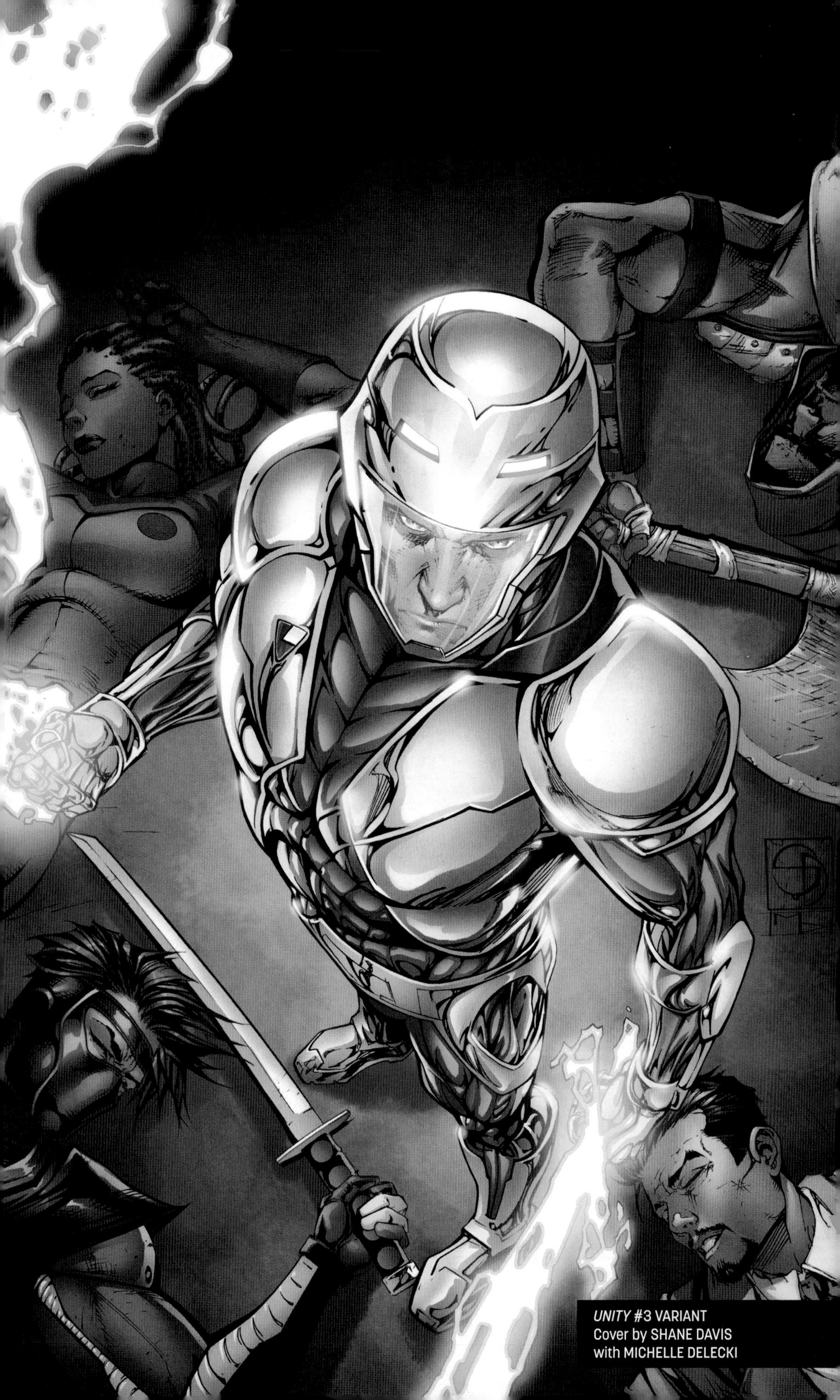

UNITY #3 VARIANT
Cover by SHANE DAVIS
with MICHELLE DELECKI

UNITY #4 VARIANT
Cover by RILEY ROSSMO

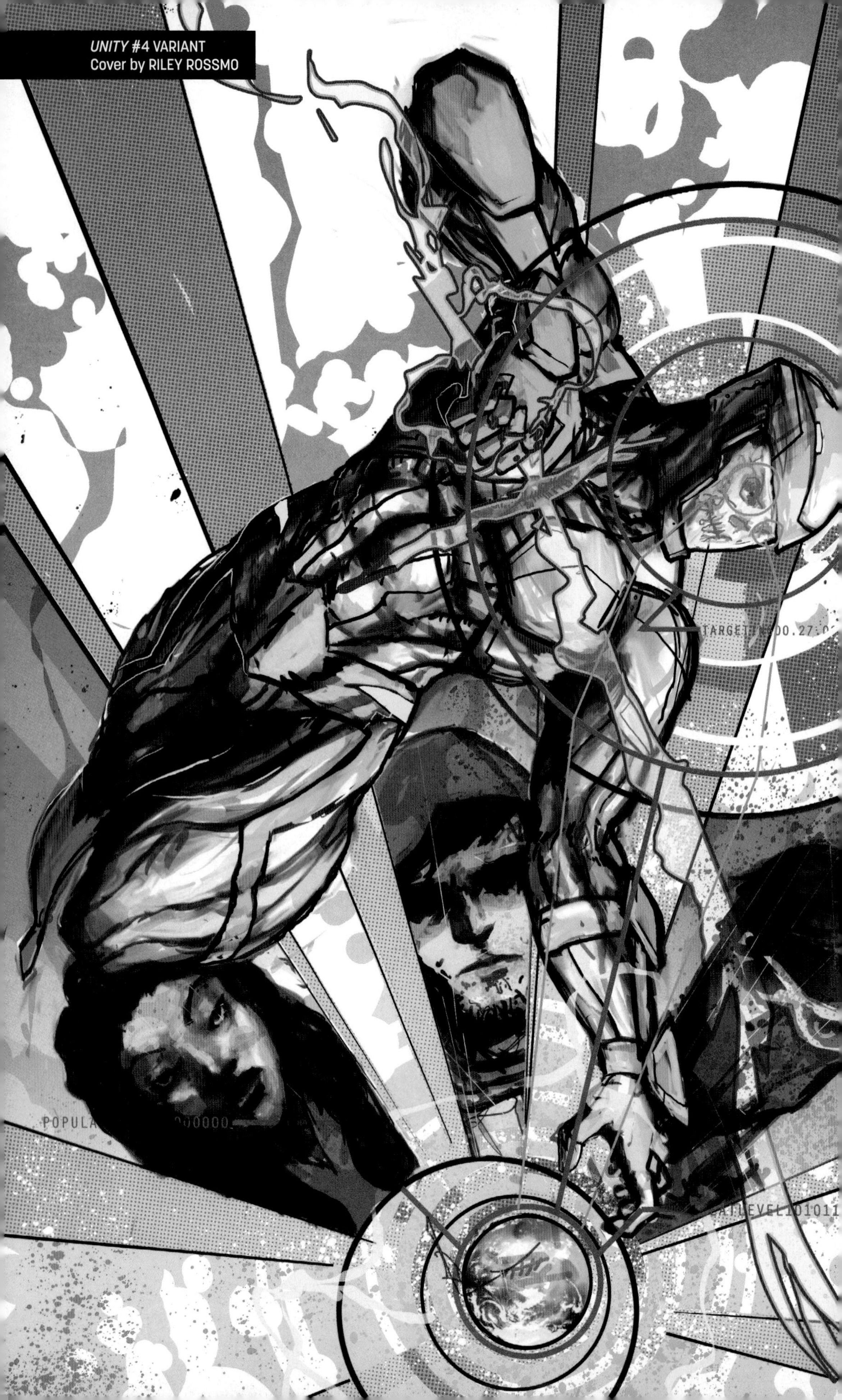

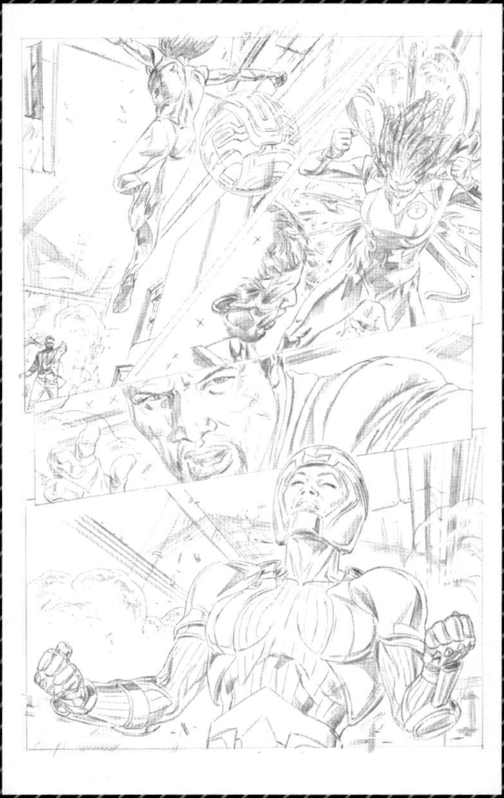

UNITY #4, p. 14
Art by DOUG BRAITHWAITE

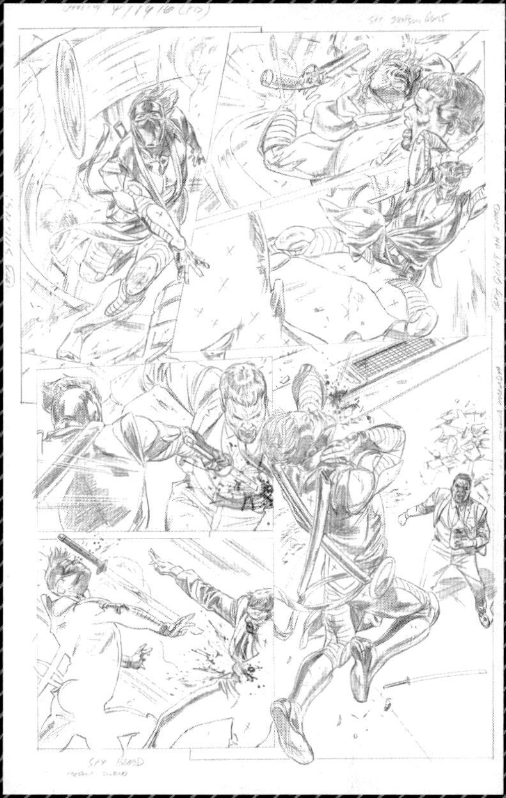

UNITY #4, p. 16
Art by DOUG BRAITHWAITE

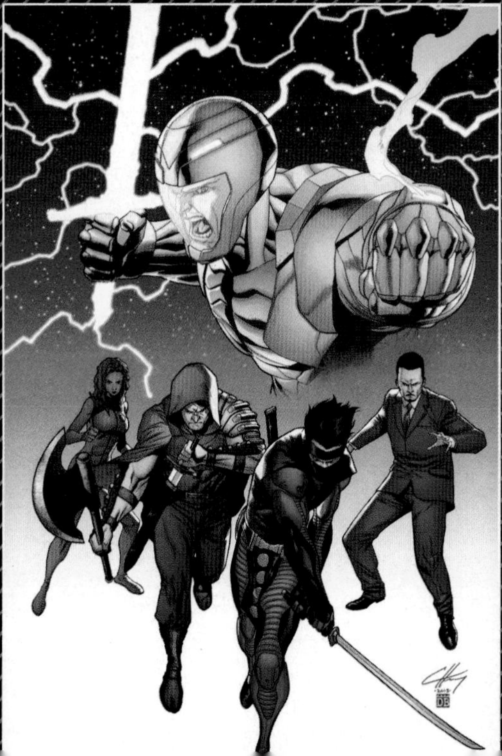

VALIANT COLLECTIONS

TRADE PAPERBACKS

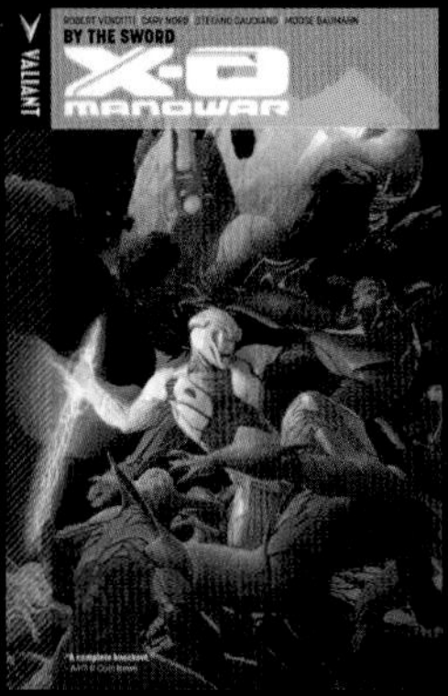

VALIANT
BY THE SWORD
X-O MANOWAR

X-O MANOWAR VOL. 1:
BY THE SWORD

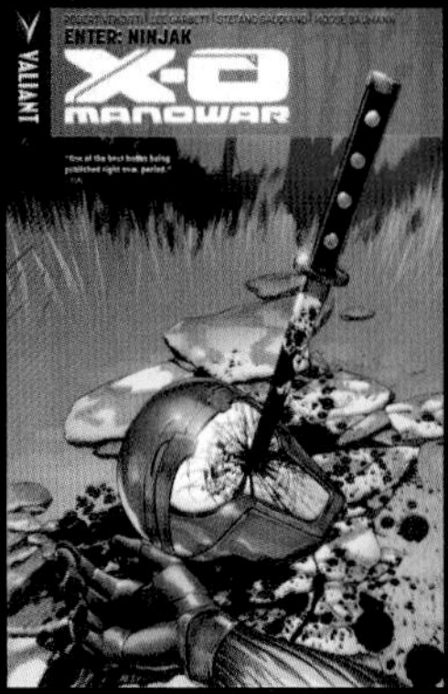

VALIANT
ENTER: NINJAK
X-O MANOWAR

X-O MANOWAR VOL. 2:
ENTER NINJAK

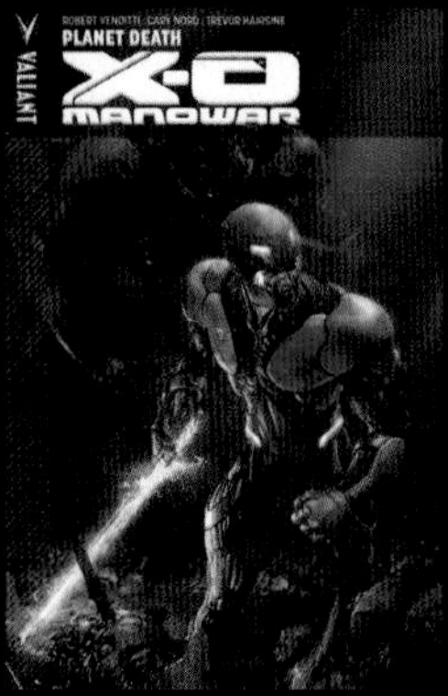

VALIANT
PLANET DEATH
X-O MANOWAR

X-O MANOWAR VOL. 3:
PLANET DEATH

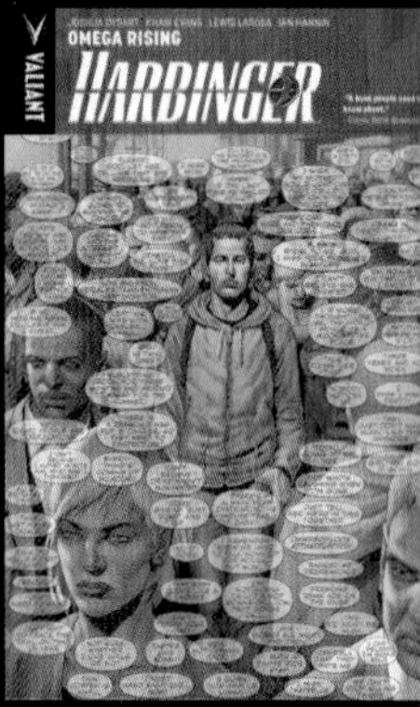

VALIANT
OMEGA RISING
HARBINGER

HARBINGER VOL. 1:
OMEGA RISING

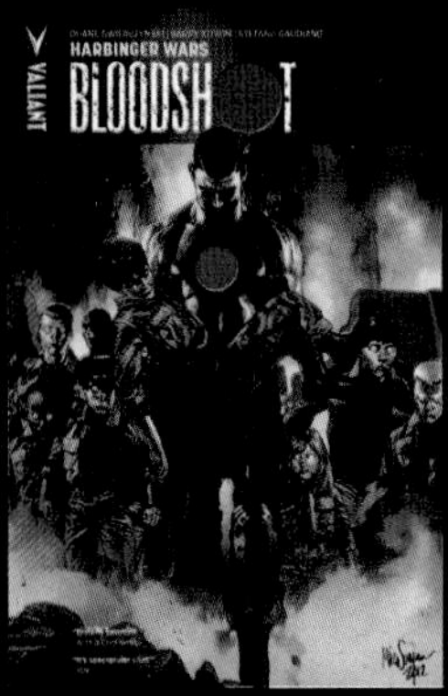

VALIANT
HARBINGER WARS
BLOODSHOT

BLOODSHOT VOL. 3:
HARBINGER WARS

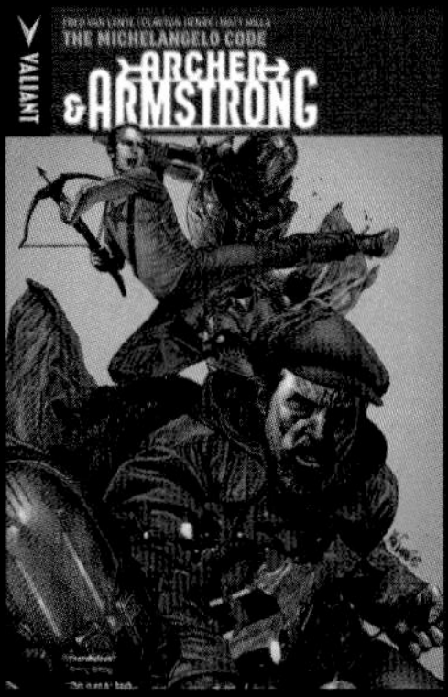

VALIANT
THE MICHELANGELO CODE
ARCHER & ARMSTRONG

ARCHER & ARMSTRONG VOL. 1:
THE MICHELANGELO CODE

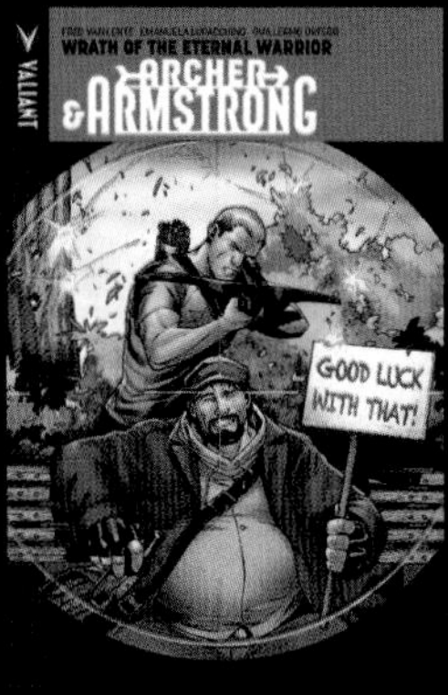

VALIANT
WRATH OF THE ETERNAL WARRIOR
ARCHER & ARMSTRONG
GOOD LUCK WITH THAT!

ARCHER & ARMSTRONG VOL. 2:
WRATH OF THE ETERNAL WARRIOR

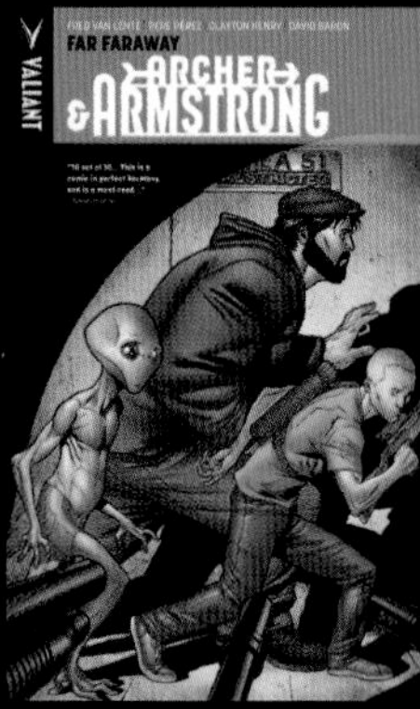

VALIANT
FAR FARAWAY
ARCHER & ARMSTRONG

ARCHER & ARMSTRONG VOL. 3:
FAR FARAWAY

DELUXE EDITIONS

X-O MANOWAR DELUXE EDITION BOOK 1

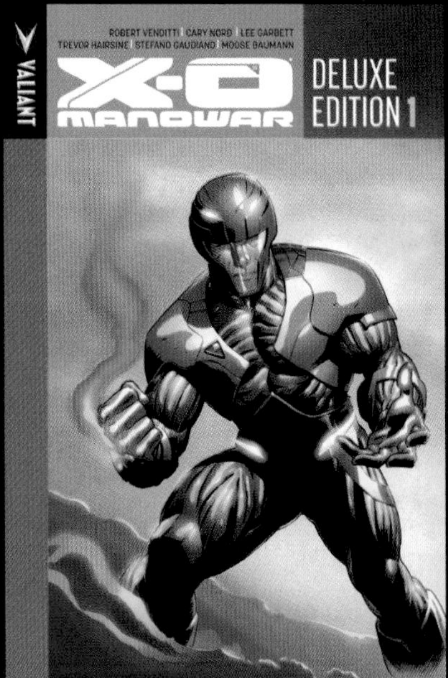

VALIANT
ROBERT VENDITTI | CARY NORD | LEE GARBETT
TREVOR HAIRSINE | STEFANO GAUDIANO | MOOSE BAUMANN
X-O MANOWAR
DELUXE EDITION 1

HARBINGER DELUXE EDITION BOOK 1

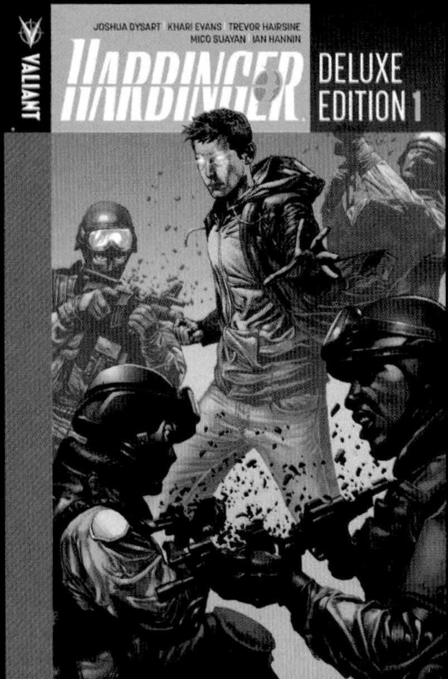

VALIANT
JOSHUA DYSART | KHARI EVANS | TREVOR HAIRSINE
MICO SUAYAN | IAN HANNIN
HARBINGER
DELUXE EDITION 1

THE STORY STARTS HERE.

HARBINGER VOL. 2:
RENEGADES

HARBINGER VOL. 3:
HARBINGER WARS

BLOODSHOT VOL. 1:
SETTING THE WORLD ON FIRE

BLOODSHOT VOL. 2:
THE RISE AND THE FALL

SHADOWMAN VOL. 1:
BIRTH RITES

SHADOWMAN VOL. 2:
DARQUE RECKONING

QUANTUM AND WOODY VOL. 1:
THE WORLD'S WORST
SUPERHERO TEAM

HARBINGER WARS

VALIANT MASTERS

VALIANT MASTERS: BLOODSHOT VOL. 1:
BLOOD OF THE MACHINE

VALIANT MASTERS: NINJAK VOL. 1:
BLACK WATER

VALIANT MASTERS: SHADOWMAN VOL. 1:
SPIRITS WITHIN

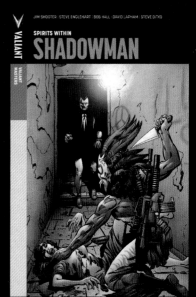